DIVINE PRESCRIPTIONS

Divine Prescriptions

Using Your Sixth Sense—
Spiritual Solutions for You
and Your Loved Ones

DOREEN VIRTUE, Ph.D.
Author of *Divine Guidance*

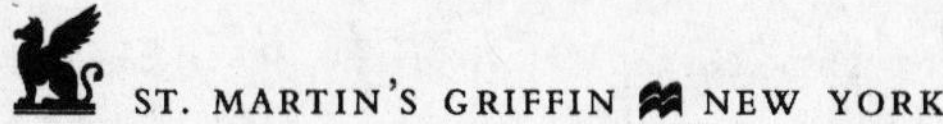

 For information, address St. Martin's Press, 175 Fifth Avenue, New York, N.Y. 10010.

www.stmartins.com

Designed by Lisa-Theresa Lenthall

ISBN 1-58063-216-5

First published in the United States by Renaissance Books

10 9 8

To God, Holy Spirit, Jesus, and the Angels,
who are my very best friends
and a major reason why I feel happy,
loved, safe, and peaceful.
Thank you for loving us unconditionally!

Contents

GRATITUDES

Over the past few years, my prayers for help, assistance, and support have been generously answered. I can't begin to name all of the individuals who have been instrumental in opening doors and opening my heart. However, I do want to publicly acknowledge my gratitude to Frederique, Winston, Michael, Pearl Reynolds, Emmet Fox, Michael Dietch, Steve Allen, Steve Prutting, Richard F. X. O'Connor, Jean Marie Stine, Bill Hartley, Mike Dougherty, Arthur Morey, Lisa Lenthall, Abigail Park, Kathryn Mills, Jill Whitesides, William Clark, Charles Schenk, Grant Schenk, Neale Donald Walsch, Justin Hilton, Gregory Roberts, Deb Evans, Bronwynn "Bronny" Daniels, William and Joan Hannan, Reid Tracy, Ariel Wolfe, Liz Dawn, Nick Bunick, Georgia Malki, Cathy Franklin, Wayne Dyer, Louise L. Hay, James and Salle Redfield, Gregg Braden, Jimmy Twyman, Marianne Williamson, John Edward, Rita Curtis, John Austin, Dannion Brinkley, Keilisi Gyan Freeman, Tiffany Lach, Lee Carroll, Jordan Weiss, Joe and Shanti Moriarty, and all the CSCs.

AUTHOR'S NOTE

This is a nondenominational spiritual self-help book. It is intended for people of all faiths, religions, and belief systems, as well as nonbelievers. *Divine Prescriptions* is not about religion, although much of the text may remind readers of religious terminology. Instead, this book is about spiritual principles that can help us in everyday circumstances.

All the stories in this book are true. Some names and identifying details have been changed to preserve anonymity. Stories in which a person's real name is given have been published with the individual's permission.

When discussing our Creator, I use the name God and the pronouns He, His, and Him. This in no way implies that I see God as a man. To me, our beloved Creator is an androgynous, loving force, not a male or female person. I simply use the masculine terms out of Western habit and to avoid the awkward he/she phrasing. If you feel more comfortable with a term for our Creator other than God, or if you prefer using feminine or neutral pronouns, I hope you will feel free to substitute the terminology that mirrors your beliefs.

Divine messages, primarily from the angelic realm, appear in italics throughout the book.

PREFACE

How I Began Receiving Divine Prescriptions

In the spring of 1999 I appeared on a radio program to discuss how the angels desire to help us in every facet of our lives. "Yes, everything except the trivial stuff," the radio show host commented matter-of-factly.

"Actually, they want to help us with everything," I emphasized, "and that definitely includes the so-called trivial stuff. The angels say that the size of the problem doesn't matter. It doesn't matter *what* you are asking for, whether it's a life-and-death miracle or a small favor, whether you're asking for a healing from addiction or for a convenient parking space. To the angels, all that's important is that you receive the support you need with all your difficulties, so that you can be freed of other concerns to work on fulfilling your life's mission."

In short, the angels' Divine messages aren't limited to revelations about the nature of the universe and life after death. Messages from heaven often are profound in their simplicity. Their topics are as infinite as the universe, and offer perceptions for solving personal, romantic, family, and career problems, both large and small.

When I say this, I'm not trying to convince people about the existence of angels or to convert others to a certain philosophy. I am simply a trained therapist with a scientific background who has had some remarkable experiences with angels both personally and professionally. My own life has dramatically improved as I've applied the prescriptions the angels have "written" for my clients to problems and challenges in my own family, health, and career, and in other areas of life. I am convinced anyone, believer or skeptic, can benefit from this heavenly advice, whether they are trying to get past the pain of infidelity, attract a soulmate, heal an addiction, find a meaningful career, have sufficient income, cope with childhood abuse, or address other universal human dilemmas.

This book is about Divine prescriptions for everyday problems, how you can benefit from the insights contained in the hundreds of prescriptions the angels have given my clients, and how you can learn to become a conduit for these heavenly messages yourself.

How I Lost—and Found—My Sixth Sense

Perhaps you are wondering how a doctor of psychology, a pragmatic healer, with traditional training and a clinical background came to work with angels and heavenly prescriptions. Maybe you'll understand if I say I am one of those people whose only concern when they hear about something new is, Does it work? I seek help from the angels simply because the Divine prescriptions they have given my clients produced effective and practical results far exceeding those of any method of psychology I have ever tried or studied.

The fact of the matter is that I never expected to be an advocate for the angelic realm. Years ago, when patients told me they saw visions or heard voices, I immediately diagnosed them as possible schizophrenics. How ironic that today I teach other people how to communicate with the Divine realm and "hear" angelic voices for themselves.

Like a lot of children, I had invisible friends when I was a young girl. In fact, the 1999 movie *The Sixth Sense* reminds me, in a way, of my childhood. Like the little boy,

Cole, portrayed in the film, I saw deceased people everywhere and always wondered why my mother and friends couldn't see them as well. Unlike the movie, the people I saw weren't bloodied or gory-looking; they just weren't anyone I recognized. This wasn't my aunt Betty or uncle Ned. I felt frightened whenever I saw these strangers staring wordlessly at me. I wish I'd known then that these people were coming to me for help. They knew I could see them, and they were seeking relief from their angst from someone, anyone who could possibly help. Even from a kid.

In the middle of the night, I'd also see sparkles of light that gave me comfort. I know now that I was seeing angel trails, light that the angels leave behind as they move across our field of vision. These were happy, peaceful visions that were accompanied by a huge, unearthly silence, as if I'd fallen into a blissful black hole devoid of worldly sounds. When the sparkles and noiselessness came around, I felt totally loved and at peace.

Still, my visions left me feeling lonely. I learned quickly not to mention them to the other kids at school, lest I suffer their rolling eyes and sharp taunts. To counter my rapidly growing reputation of being weird, I shut my mouth about my visions. I even tried to block them out so that I could be "normal." Eventually I lost much of my awareness of the spiritual world.

I'm not blaming anyone or anything for my choice to turn off my childhood clairvoyance. In the long run, it was a blessing that I experienced nonclairvoyant life as a young adult. That experience helps me to teach others how to turn on their clairvoyance, because I truly know what it's like to see and not to see.

I've always been a spiritually minded person, but I didn't always focus on angels or life after death. I was raised in a loving Christian home; however, we didn't discuss angels or the afterlife much at home or at church. Our focus was more centered around Jesus' healings and teachings on earth. So, after a while, I pushed the awareness of angels out of my mind.

My training in psychology, as an undergraduate and graduate student at Chapman University in Southern California and as a counselor at a psychiatric hospital specializing in addictions, largely influenced my view of the world. I had earned three degrees in counseling psychology and attended training sessions led by Carl Rogers, Irvin Yalom, William Glasser, Rollo May, and other famed authors in the field of psychology. My passion was psychological research, and I spent my free time in university libraries poring over journal articles on human behavior.

My first position in the field was as an intake counselor in the psychological admissions department. A person who was considering checking into the mental hospital would have an interview with me. My job involved assessing and diagnosing the person's mental health. I developed an eye and ear for detecting abnormalities in human behavior and thinking styles.

I dealt with hundreds of people who told me about things they saw or heard that I diagnosed as hallucinations. Many of these visions and voices most likely were hallucinations brought on by the person's intoxication. But I'm sure that I also diagnosed people who actually *were* seeing angels or hearing true Divine voices. I had convinced myself at the time that the real world consisted of whatever I experienced with my senses. If I couldn't see it with my eyes, hear it with my ears, or touch it with my fingers, it wasn't real. To me any patient who experienced things through nonphysical senses was hallucinating or intoxicated. Period.

Throughout my life, however I'd experienced some intensely mystical situations that my science and psychology books couldn't explain. Rather than focus on these experiences, I had consciously willed myself to overlook them.

One of my earlier mystical experiences that I'd tried to ignore occurred when I was seventeen. My grandmother Pearl and my stepgrandfather, "Pop-pop" Ben, had driven south from Bishop, California, to spend several days with us at our family's home in Escondido. I remember excitedly awaiting their arrival, intently listening for the sound of their station wagon pulling into our driveway. We had a wonderful visit. I felt especially close to both my grandparents as I watched them pull out of the driveway and head for home.

Several hours after they'd left, the phone rang. I watched as my dad tightenend his grip on the telephone receiver and his body shuddered and jerked. "Ben and my mom were in a car accident," he said with urgency. "A drunk driver crossed over and hit them head-on. Mom's in the hospital, and . . . Ben's dead."

We reacted with tears and cries of "No, no!" I ran into my darkened bedroom and grabbed my acoustic guitar, hugging it for comfort. I played some strums and the music helped me to feel peace in my heart. I could hear my parents and brother crying in the living room and I felt guilty that I was at peace and didn't share their grief. Yes, I loved my Pop-pop as much as anyone. Yes, I would greatly miss his presence. But in the depth of my soul, I didn't feel sadness at his death. My only despair was the fact that I didn't feel any grief.

Just then, a glowing light beyond the foot of my bed caught my attention. I looked over and there, clear as day, was my Pop-pop Ben. He looked exactly as he had when I'd last seen him, wearing a plaid shirt and comfortable pants, only he was smaller and slightly transparent. The colors of his clothes were muted from the bluish white light that seemed to emanate from within him. He clearly expressed to me through some sort of telepathic means, "You are right to feel this way, Doreen. I am fine and everything is OK." Then his image dissolved and he was gone. I was left with the certainty that my peacefulness was appropriate.

Some time later, when I told my parents about Ben's appearance, they shared with me that Ben's brother, who lived far from our home in Escondido, had also seen Ben shortly after his death. Had Ben visited all of us, unbeknownst to the other family members? Perhaps the intense grief of my parents and brother prevented them from noticing his presence, or maybe their strong feelings actually blocked his arrival. I don't know, but I *do* know that while grief is a perfectly normal emotion that can serve a useful healing function, it also can block our awareness of life after death.

Into adulthood, I was always aware of the presence of angels and many of my deceased relatives. The awareness was similar to the partial focus one has on a fly buzzing around a room when one is highly focused on a pressing project. But I tried to avoid thinking about the spirit world. After all, by this point I was a successful psychotherapist specializing in eating disorders. My second book, *The Yo-Yo Diet Syndrome*, was a best-seller and I was busy on the speaker and talk show circuit in addition to managing a psychiatric hospital unit. The last thing I wanted was to suffer the slings and arrows of my peers, if I admitted my mystical experiences publicly.

Besides, I didn't like the messages that my angels insistently gave to me. Their incessant nagging told me that I should make major changes in my life: quit drinking my nightly glasses of wine; start meditating and studying spirituality; and trade in my traditional psychotherapy practice and writing for spiritually based therapy. The angels reminded me that when I was a child, a male angel's voice had told me clearly that my life's purpose was to teach about spirituality. Not wanting to be controlled or upset the balance of success I'd achieved in my life, I turned a deaf ear on my angels.

I realize now that I had, on a soul level, "contracted" with my angels to have them push me to keep me on the path of my life's mission. Their prodding became increasingly loud and frequent. One day they pushed me to attend a workshop being given by author and psychotherapist Wayne Dyer. He discussed a struggle similar to the one I'd endured that had led him to finally abandon his traditional psychotherapy practice and quit his drinking habit.

That day, I stopped drinking and began meditating. With my sober and focused mind, my clairvoyance rapidly returned to the clarity I'd had in childhood. I found I knew all sorts of facts and information about total strangers before they would introduce themselves to me. In the morning I'd awaken knowing who I was going to run into that day and what they would say. The angels taught me how to alter my diet (as you'll read about in appendix B) to increase my intuitive gift even further. I experienced one long feeling of déjà vu that first year after I surrendered to my angels. I also felt a sense of peace that I'd long forgotten.

Still, I didn't have the courage to come out of the spiritual closet and discuss my psychic revelations with my clients, friends, readers, or family members. My mystical experiences were a closely guarded secret that I held close to my chest for fear of being ridiculed, abandoned, and criticized. My angels urged me to speak publicly about my spiritual beliefs, but I resisted.

I lost all my fears about what people might think, though, in 1995. That's when an angel saved my life by actually speaking out loud to warn me of an impending car-jacking, then advising me how to save myself when two armed men attempted to car-jack me only a half hour later. (I describe this incident in greater detail in my book *Divine Guidance*.)

After the car-jacking, my mind reeled with fear and wonder. Hearing voices was a sign of insanity according to my clinical training. Yet this voice had known my future and saved my life! I reasoned that my unconscious might produce imaginary voices, but it couldn't have known the future. As someone interested in psychological research, the latter characteristic fascinated me more than anything else about the event. What could produce a disembodied voice that knew my car was going to be stolen?

Memories of my experiences with my sixth sense in childhood washed over me. As a child, I had believed that heaven was watching over me. Now, after the attempted car-jacking, I had the same warm feeling. Instead of feeling like I was in a fishbowl, I was oddly comforted. However, the scientist in me prodded me to investigate what I'd experienced so I could somehow understand this inexplicable incident.

Over the next few months, I sought out and interviewed people I read about in newspapers and magazines who had heard warning voices that had saved their lives. As a psychologist, I could tell that these people weren't hallucinating. Their stories had a seamless flow and unshakable foundation not found in hallucinations. The hallucinations experienced by schizophrenics, for instance, usually involve feelings of persecution and/or grandiosity. For example, a schizophrenic will imagine seeing FBI agents spying on him, will hear voices directing him to inflict wounds upon himself, or will believe that UFOs have singled him out as a special and chosen person.

The voices heard by those who have experienced lifesaving interventions, however, gave them feelings of comfort and led them to become more thoughtful, loving, and compassionate. And because I had been trained to detect lies and exaggerations by reading body language and voice pitch, I knew these people were telling the truth.

As I continued my interviews, a clear pattern emerged that helped persuade me that these people's stories were true:

- They didn't care whether anyone believed them or not.
- They weren't on any campaign to convert people to their way of thinking.
- They were reluctant to publicly discuss their experiences. Most instances involved hearing a voice deliver lifesaving guidance while they were driving a car.

The more people I spoke with, the more any remaining doubts I'd had about Divine interventions fell away. I began to understand why a reported 75 to 85 percent of American adults say they believe in angels. At the same time that I was conducting these interviews, I was attempting to use whatever sixth sense I still had left from my childhood to contact the source of the voice who had warned and guided me during my ordeal.

My experience during the car-jacking incident made me curious about whether I could access the voice at other times, or if it was available only during a crisis. I wasn't sure exactly how to go about contacting whatever it was I was trying to contact, so I tried speaking to it aloud, sending mental messages, and writing questions to it in my journal. Within hours I both felt and internally heard the voice reply. The being, who identified itself as one of my guardian angels, immediately began talking to me about the residual fear I'd been experiencing from a mild case of post-traumatic stress disorder triggered by the car-jacking. When the being had finished speaking, my fear was gone!

I then heard and felt the presence of other angels accompanying my primary guardian angel. As I began focusing on this phenomenon, attempting to understand more and more about it, I soon was able to see the angels that exist around each of us. At first, I'd see only glowing or sparkling lights. Then, just as our eyes adjust to a darkened room, I slowly was able to perceive all the details of the angels' figures and forms.

I have since met thousands of people who have seen the angels, and I have compared notes with them. Our visions are remarkably similar in striking details, including form, height, brightness, coloring, mode of dress, and mode of address.

Angel Therapy

At first the angels gave me guidance only about my own life. But it proved so effective for steering me successfully through the worst of my own difficulties that as a therapist, I couldn't help thinking how wonderful it would be if all my clients could use their sixth sense, too, and have their own source of contact for these heavenly prescriptions.

I was counseling a difficult client one day, uncertain about what I should say to her and thinking that the angels would know how to advise her, when the angels themselves asked me if I wanted them to pass on their advice to her. As a therapist, I had reservations, but I was stuck and didn't know how to help the woman. I felt that neither she nor I could lose from giving the process a try.

For reasons of professional ethics, however, I did not feel I could present anything the angels prescribed as coming from me. I felt I had to be honest with my client and explain the source to her, even if she decided I was crazy and didn't want to work with me any longer. Fortunately, she was a believer in angels, and her curiosity was piqued by the suggestion. She readily agreed to listen with an open mind to anything I had to say.

What she heard that day transformed her life and affected a healing I never could have managed on my own. From then on I began working with the angels to help my counseling clients, always notifying them of the source of the advice I was passing on. Soon I gained a reputation as a therapist who gave "angel readings" or "angel therapy." Clients began to consult me when everything else had failed and they were at last willing to give God and the angels a chance.

The angels gave them clear and effective instructions (what I have been calling Divine prescriptions) that helped my counseling clients to heal their relationships, finances, health, and emotions. Although I have not conducted formal scientific studies of angel therapy, I am content that it is a remarkably effective clinical tool. Therapists whom I have trained in angel therapy report their clients experience greater wellness and peace of mind.

The sheer number of angel therapy cases I've been involved in (which total into the thousands) has removed all doubts from my mind and heart. I've watched skeptics and believers, religious individuals and agnostics become happier and healthier following the Divine prescriptions delivered by their angels. I think this is the reason why so many psychotherapists, medical doctors, nurses, and other healing professionals attend my training seminars.

During a typical angel therapy session, I allow myself to go into a semitrance state, which helps me to connect deeply and quickly with the angels and their Divine prescriptions. In this altered state of consciousness, I am aware of most of the words that come through me at the time. After a session, however, I remember only about half of what is said. For that reason, I frequently tape-record my sessions in case my clients or I want to review what was said. Sometimes the angels specifically ask me to tape-record a session so my client can play it back later. This alerts me that this session probably is going to be intensely emotional. "She won't hear what we're really saying unless she hears it repeatedly," they explain to me.

Near the beginning of each angel therapy session, I describe my clients' angels to them. I've found that there are four primary types of angels (you can read about them in greater detail in appendix A at the back of this book):

- *Angels.* The winged ones sent as messengers from God, who have not lived as humans upon the earth.
- *Archangels.* Managers of the angelic realm who tend to be larger in size and more powerful than angels.
- *Departed loved ones.* Relatives or friends who have passed away but hover nearby to help people, much like guardian angels do.
- *Ascended masters.* Enlightened teachers and healers, such as Jesus Christ, Moses, Mohammed, Buddha, Krishna, Mother Mary, Saint Germaine, and Quan Yin, who help people from heaven.

I then explain to my clients the purpose of each of their spiritual companions' presence. For example, a deceased loved one will arrive at a session just to say "Hello, I love you," or say "I'm with you to help you with your marriage." The angels have more personal reasons to be with us, including helping us to have courage, to learn patience, to stay safe while driving, or to be loving and nonjudgmental to others.

Next, I ask my clients to describe the problem that has brought them to seek out angelic counsel. This usually is focused on a basic question such as, "How can I get my boyfriend to marry me?" or "I'm addicted to catalog shopping. I've run up thousands in credit card bills. How do I stop?" or "My mother and I always fight. What do the angels say I can do to make her stop picking on me?"

Then I ask for guidance from their angels. The angels give their advice through me, delivering their prescription to my client. Sometimes the angels show me a "movie" in which I clearly see my client giving the speech, writing the book, doing healing work, or whatever his purpose is about. Other times, the angels give me audible words that convey the essence of their life purpose.

Typically, the angels deliver their messages through one of the four Divine communication channels: clairvoyance (in which I see pictures of my client's past, present, and probable future life), clairaudience (in which the angels speak to me), clairsentience (in which I receive strong feelings conveying the angels' perspectives), and claircognizance (a form of thought transference from heaven). Everyone has access to these four heavenly "channels," and anyone can tap into her own clairvoyance, clairaudience, clairsentience, and claircognizance. Chapter 1 provides a brief overview of the four communication channels. (If you are interested in learning to receive angelic advice via these four channels, you may want to read my book *Divine Guidance*, in which I provide detailed how-to instructions.)

During sessions I always hear the angels speak in my right ear. For some reason, I've never heard any heavenly message in my left ear. Clients and others have told me that they, too, receive guidance primarily or exclusively in one ear. Some people hear Divine prescriptions equally well with both ears.

To ensure it is truly a heavenly message and not my imagination, I repeatedly pose the same question several different ways to the angels. One of the key characteristics of authentic Divine prescriptions is that the advice is given repeatedly. I've learned that I can ask the angels a question several times, and I'll keep getting the same answer. That's one of the ways I know it's truly the angels speaking, since our imagination tends to give different answers each time.

If the clients have additional questions (and they usually do!), either I or the angels will answer them until they understand their prescription clearly.

People rarely cringe or become upset when the angels deliver prescriptions that call for changing a self-defeating personality trait (e.g., being too aggressive) or letting go of a destructive habit (e.g., compulsive infidelity, smoking). Sometimes, when the angels give me such a prescription to relay, I worry about the client's response, "How can I possibly tell this nice person something like that?," I ask myself. At that point, the angels guide me how to deliver their message in a loving, nonconfrontational way. As a result, my clients receive the remedy in the way it was intended. They feel the unconditional love accompanying these communications. My clients know their angels aren't criticizing, judging, or chastising them. The angels are simply responding to prayers for help. Their answers often ask people to heal. Deep down, most people always recognize the wisdom of their angels' guidance.

When a client's problem involves another person, I always ask the angels to put me in contact with that person.

First, I request that my angels "connect" me with the person. Then, I take a deep breath and mentally repeat the person's first name three times to ensure I focus on the correct individual. That's all it takes. The angels immediately show me a vision of the individual, living or deceased. Each person's name has a vibrational imprint that records all of the information about that person's past, present, and future. It's like the name of a computer file that allows one to access a specific program.

When clients ask me to look into their future, the angels take me through a process similar to watching a videotape on fast-forward. They show me tapes of several different futures the client might have, which I've come to know as alternative futures. Every person has free choice, and these alternative futures represent the course one's life will take depending on which decisions one makes. It's not up to the angels to make decisions for human beings; however, they do try to point out alternative solutions when they suspect someone is about to follow his ego instead of his better nature.

If a client has pent-up, negative feelings like anger, guilt, and blame that are causing problems, the angels work to help her release these blocks. The angels behave like chimney sweeps, brushing and pulling away emotional and spiritual soot caused by negative thoughts and feelings created or collected by the client.

Because I am a psychologist who has worked in marriage and family counseling, I often blend my clinical knowledge with my angel readings. I feel coached by the angels when this is appropriate, and I always let my clients clearly know when I am speaking and when the angels are speaking.

After an angel therapy session, my clients tell me that the Divine prescriptions they have received and the angelic release of negativity they experience make them feel lighter, freer, happier. They usually contact me later via a letter, phone call, or another consultation to report that following their heavenly prescription has resulted in significant and positive changes in their outlook and life.

Heavenly Messages, the Messengers, and You

You don't have to wait to see an angel reader or locate someone with special talents and abilities to receive and benefit from heavenly advice. These messages are meant for you, and God designed them to be easy to receive. Tens of thousands of my clients and workshop participants have already learned how to tap into God's heavenly messenger service, and you can, too. They have learned how to become conscious of the presence of their angels, and aware when the angels are trying to tell them something.

These are normal, everyday people. They don't have any special talent you don't possess. It is my belief that we all have a sixth sense. Further, I am convinced that this sixth sense, which enables people to directly contact the heavenly hosts, is nothing less than the continual presence of God within us. It is something anyone can do (or learn to do) at any time, because what you are attempting to contact is already inside you. We are nothing less than God's and our own Divine communication conduit, our own sixth sense. When you learn to tune in to your own inner feelings, thoughts, visions, and sounds, you can more easily receive and comprehend your angels' advice, too.

Chapter 1 discusses the idea of Divine prescriptions. You will discover:

- What Divine prescriptions are and how they can benefit you personally.
- The three ways prayers are answered: comfort, miracles, and Divine guidance.

- Why people sometimes block or don't act on Divine prescriptions.
- How to overcome fear of angelic contact.
- How to recognize the four channels of the sixth sense.

Chapters 2 through 7 focus on practical, prescriptive advice from God and the angels for dozens of our most universal and urgent human problems. They are drawn from insights the angels have shared with my clients, friends, family, and workshop participants. I've benefited from incorporating many of these prescriptions into my own life, and I believe you can benefit from them, too. Among the problems covered are:

- Personal issues such as addiction, depression, and grief.
- Dating and romance issues: attracting the ideal soulmate, jealousy, fear of commitment, and others.
- Marital issues such as infidelity, sexual incompatibility, and loss of intimacy.
- Family issues including child-rearing, overcritical parents, and other conflicts.
- Financial and career issues: job stress, starting a new business, cash-flow difficulties, and others.

Chapter 8 is filled with detailed instructions on every aspect of asking for and receiving Divine prescriptions for your own personal problems, including:

- How to clear yourself of turbulent emotions so the angels' signals aren't disrupted.
- A simple two-step method for getting Divine prescriptions for your own problems.
- How to tell if the guidance you receive truly comes from heaven.

Chapter 9 provides step-by-step guidance for those who may wish to take the process further and conduct angel readings, helping deliver angelic advice to others. You will learn:

- How to deliver Divine prescriptions to others.
- How to deliver unpleasant prescriptions.
- What to do if people become dependent on you for Divine prescriptions.

This book will put you in direct contact with heavenly counsel. It is my hope that you will then follow through on the guidance you receive. As a therapist, I've observed that those who consult regularly with God, ascended masters, or angels seem better adjusted than those who do not. They tend to be less negative and guarded than those who feel separated from God and the angels, and are less likely to report feeling stuck, as if they're spinning their wheels in life. They also tend to be happier and more optimistic than other people.

DIVINE PRESCRIPTIONS

CHAPTER ONE

Heavenly Solutions for You and Your Issues

You've probably read about or experienced instances of heavenly comfort and miraculous intervention. They're the sort of goosebump-inducing story in which a person's life is saved or healed thanks to the help of some mysterious force, voice, or person. These events help people to have faith that they are watched over and guided by God and guardian angels. The angels intervene when necessary in miraculous ways.

However, God and the angels don't just work miracles to pull people out of life-threatening situations. The heavenly hosts also are full of practical, *prescriptive* advice about how to solve personal problems, heal emotional hurts, and resolve difficult dilemmas. One of the most common, and perhaps most important, ways that heaven intervenes on behalf of human beings is through giving them what I call Divine prescriptions—angelic remedies for the hurts and challenges of everyday living.

In ancient spiritual texts, God and the angels are likewise shown as giving practical guidance for the problems of daily life. For instance, the Torah (or biblical Old Testament) describes sound techniques for conflict resolution among family members and others, healthful suggestions for food preparation, marital harmony, and recommendations for raising both cattle and crops. Heaven didn't stop offering this kind of advice when the Bible was completed. Some 2000 years later, God and the angels continue to offer Divine prescriptions for how people can best handle their personal difficulties.

God's Heavenly "Dear Abby"

If you give the angels permission to deliver remedies to you, and if you learn to open yourself to the four channels of Divine communication (covered later in this chapter) and act on the counsel you receive via your sixth sense, you will ride through life on a cushion of angelic support. The angels' prescriptions are God's gifts to people. When you accept and make use of their guidance, you benefit in countless ways: You achieve success (whatever success means to you), you are more at peace with yourself, and you enjoy more fulfilling romantic and family relationships.

Let's face it. Everyone is presented with difficult, painful challenges from time to time, problems that range from the merely irritating to the overwhelming and devastating. Love, finances, children, health, relationships—who *hasn't* fallen into despair and suffered over one or more of these life areas? You try your best to meet each challenge as it comes. But often it seems as though one problem continuously follows another. And some problems, such as the loss of a business or a major difference of temperament and viewpoint between marital partners, seem impossible to resolve.

Millions of self-help books, therapy sessions, and talk shows later, the human race still struggles with the same challenges it struggled with when the psychological self-help genre was conceived. Though well-intentioned, these human methods have failed to make any measurable difference in helping us become healthier, happier people precisely *because* they are man-made and therefore a product of human limitations and frailties.

The only approaches to psychological healing I have found that produces profound and lasting therapeutic effects involves a spiritual approach. No matter what the struggle is about—an unhappy marriage, rebellious children, depression, addictions, financial challenges, aging-parent issues, a dead-end job—the angels have a Divine prescription for reaching a successful, healing conclusion. As a professional, I have seen their advice help heal my clients. In fact, you might think of angels as the heavenly equivalent of "Dear Abby," dispensing wise, beneficial counsel in response to questions people have asked here on earth.

During my therapy sessions, the angels have given prescriptive and practical advice through me to my clients and audience members on a host of issues. Quite often I've applied these prescriptions to my own life, and they have helped me find solutions to seemingly insoluble problems as well as guide me toward a healthier and happier life. I've also passed along prescriptions that have helped my friends, family members, and other clients as much as it had helped the person for whom it was originally intended. This convinced me that the solutions and strategies the angels provide could be applied successfully by others in similar situations.

In this book, particularly chapters 2 through 7, you'll find nearly fifty Divine remedies the angels have given my clients for resolving some of the most common and painful problems people are likely to face in life today.

I have found these prescriptions to be psychologically sound approaches to problem solving, healing, recovery, and self-growth. Moreover, I've seen those who follow this angelic advice experience greater healing, energy, and peace. They know they are watched over, loved, and protected. The sense of inner serenity this creates draws wonderful people, opportunities, and experiences into their lives.

The Importance of Asking

To receive Divine prescriptions for your problems, there is only one requirement: You must consciously ask heaven for them (whether out loud or silently). Simply think of the angels, then mentally request, "Please help me with [fill in your issue]." Most prayers result in your receiving Divine prescriptions almost at once. When you skip this all-important first step and fail to ask explicitly for angelic assistance, you gag and shackle heaven. You can want Divine counsel, yearn for it, long for it, need it, desire it with all your might, but if you don't direct a conscious request to heaven, angelic guidance won't be forthcoming.

The angels *want* to give you the benefit of their guidance. *Want* is the operative word, since angels are not allowed to violate the free will God granted to you and all other human beings by forcing their help on you. That's why it is so important to ask for their aid and then keep yourself open to receiving it. The only exception is a life-endangering situation—such as an impending car crash—before it's your time to go. Even then, the angels can only help you if you let them.

One evening the angels, with their unique brand of humor, taught me an unforgettable lesson about the importance of consciously asking for their help. I was in North Scottsdale, Arizona, for one of my weekend seminars. Friends dropped me off at a health club on Saturday night. They offered to pick me up later, but I said I'd take a cab back to our hotel. Following my workout, I used the health club's phone and Yellow Pages to call a cab company. The first taxi dispatcher said, "Oh, we don't service North Scottsdale." The second cab company explained they weren't familiar with the street the gym was located on. A third taxi company said, "Well, we're very busy tonight, so it might take us forty or fifty minutes to get out there."

Dejected, I decided to walk to my hotel. After all, I rationalized, I'd spent an hour on a treadmill; what was another hour of exercise? Still, I realized it would be a difficult trek. For one thing, there were no sidewalks in that part of town, and I had to walk over uneven, rock-laden lawns in the dark.

Tripping and stumbling, I decided to search a busy nearby street for a taxi or bus.

The fifty-mile-an-hour traffic whizzed by me, and there was no sign of public transportation. Too residential a neighborhood for buses and taxis, I concluded. I groused silently to my angels, "How come you guys let me down after I spent all day teaching people about angels? I did my part, how come you're not helping me?"

At that moment, I heard the angels' sweet but wry inner reply: *"Excuse me, but did you ask us to get you a cab?"*

I gasped in realization. I *hadn't* asked the angels to get me a taxi. No wonder I was having such difficulty. I was trying to solve the problem on a human level, without requesting aid from above. "Consider this my official request right now, dear angels," I mentally replied. "Please send me a taxi, right away."

No more than two minutes later, I turned around to see a big, brand-new yellow cab in the lane next to me, cruising along at about thirty miles an hour. I reached my hand out as if hailing a New York cab. The driver pulled over immediately.

I smiled as the driver comfortably took me to the hotel. On the way he casually mentioned how lucky it was that he happened to be driving on that street. "Cabs normally don't service this area at all," he said nonchalantly.

Since that incident, I have always remembered to consciously ask the angels to involve themselves in every aspect of my life.

I can't overemphasize enough the importance of asking your angels to help you find remedies for anything that challenges or troubles you. I realize that many people balk at asking God for help with anything less than a life-endangering situation. But remember: During crises, God doesn't need your request or permission to help you. He has already sent angels to you by the time you utter cries for help. It's during the everyday events that God and the angels need your permission to intervene.

Of course, some people hesitate because they are afraid they will do something wrong. They worry that God will ignore requests that are phrased incorrectly, or that there are special ways of wording their question for specific circumstances. To this the angels say, *"You don't need to use formal invocations to call upon us for help. We appreciate the intention of your desire to use what you call proper protocol. However, we are swift to come to you when you call, and to provide remedies for all that troubles you. All that is needed is a thought, a word, or a vision. The words within this request really do not matter. The heart of the matter—that you're asking us for help—is all that counts."*

Although you may feel awkward or clumsy when you first begin asking the angels to help you, please don't worry. As long as your intentions are to connect with God and the angelic realm, you can't make a mistake. Even though it may seem as though they can't hear your question, rest assured that heaven does hear.

Asking for heavenly assistance, sometimes called praying, is a necessity to receiving it. It doesn't matter if your prayers are formal, conducted in a church, temple, or synagogue, or are private, heartfelt appeals to God. No matter what your religious background is, even if you are an agnostic or atheist, whether you have lived a life of blameless service or a life of greed, manipulation, and dishonesty, heaven answers prayers. (Of course, God won't answer the prayers of "bad" people to help them out in their "badness," but the angels will offer advice on how such individuals can find the path to becoming a better person.) Heaven doesn't discriminate in any way and answers all requests for Divine prescriptions.

How Prayers Are Answered: Comfort, Miracles, Prescriptions

In truth, God sends His help in three different ways, depending on what you need or have asked for. Your prayers may be answered in the form of heavenly comfort, miraculous interventions, or Divine prescriptions.

Heavenly comfort. You are depressed, worried, angry, lonely, fearful, or suffering intensely from some other negative emotion, and you ask heaven for help. God and the angels come through for you with a message that is comforting and reassuring. It might be something as simple as a sudden, intense feeling of peace and well-being. Or, you might receive a dream that is meaningful and reassuring to you. It might be a sudden insight that puts the situation into a whole new perspective. Or, a friend might say just the right thing to make you feel better. You might see a sign—a butterfly, a rainbow, or a feather that falls at your feet—that has special meaning for you alone.

Miraculous interventions. You are in the midst of a crisis and pray for help. Miraculously, you are saved not through any effort of your own, but through a fortuitous series of events. Perhaps a stranger appears from out of nowhere to give you directions when you are lost on a lonesome highway, then disappears immediately afterward without a trace. A voice suddenly screams in your ear to "Stop now!" as you approach a green light at an intersection, and you narrowly avoid a collision with a car running the red light. God and the angels always act instantly to try and intervene when mortal danger is imminent.

Divine prescriptions. You have a specific problem—how to raise the money for your daughter's wedding, how to stop smoking cigarettes, how you can help your child improve his math grades, how to get through Thanksgiving with your hypercritical family, how to alleviate your super-high stress level, how to decide which of two seemingly equal job opportunities to take, how to stop meeting losers and find Ms. or Mr. Right—and you request God and the angels to help you solve it. Shortly afterward, perhaps through an inner voice (or an actual physical voice you hear) or through an article or television show, you happen across the exact remedy to your problem. The solution also may be delivered into your hands through something a co-worker says, or through your finding a qualified therapist or recovery group, or through some other means temporarily impressed as a conduit for heavenly information.

Why People Block Out Divine Prescriptions

Some people complain to me that even though they have asked for angelic counsel, heaven has let them down and never replied. Usually, when I ask if they have had intuitions, heard one song repeatedly in their heads, or had intense dreams about the subject of their concern, they answer yes. Heaven has been sending them Divine prescriptions all along, but they have been unconsciously blocking out the message. Rather than God turning a deaf ear upon them, they have been turning a deaf ear upon God's guidance.

Why would people put blinders on their sixth sense and block out anything as benign and healing as God's heavenly remedies? Because, deep down, they mistrust the angels or are afraid of the changes they might be asked to make in their lives and lifestyles. This deep-down part is the lower self, or ego, and it is composed of 100 percent pure fear. It is afraid of everything . . . of God, love, angels, and happiness. Mostly, the ego is afraid that if the person changes or loses his fears, the ego will disappear.

Thus, the ego keeps raising fears. After all, you've followed your intuition before, and it didn't work out. What if you're wrong again, and you make your life worse than it is right now? What will other people say and how will they react? They might laugh at you, leave you, or even sue you. Like a dog chasing its tail, your ego is constantly at war with your higher self, which instinctively trusts and obeys Divine messages, guidance, and prescriptions. Some of the fears that the ego raises to block awareness of Divine prescriptions are discussed below.

FEAR OF OFFENDING GOD

People are prevented from hearing the Divine remedies because of their concern that they somehow will be breaking a rule of their religion. Those raised in religions that emphasize rules wonder whether it's safe or allowable to talk directly to angels. The fear is that by following angelic advice, they will be offending God and perhaps be punished. They ask me, "Is it all right to talk directly to angels, or should I direct all of my requests only to God?"

If you were raised in a religion that taught you to believe that you should converse only with God, Jesus, or some other specific spiritual entity, then simply address your prayers to that entity. The entity will answer your prayers with Divine prescriptions.

For my part, I've never heard of God punishing anyone for going "around" Him and talking directly to the angels. The angels are the first to give all glory to God and say they don't want us to worship them. They also discourage us from praying to them, which is different than talking to them. However, the Bible and other spiritual texts are filled with accounts of people talking with angels, so talking to them is definitely encouraged.

FEAR OF MAKING A MISTAKE

Many people fear they might be led into a disastrous mistake by following Divine prescriptions. What if I misunderstand God's intentions? they ask. What if I change my life for the worse? Heavenly advice is always healing. It will make your life better, never worse. If you ask, the angels also will help you develop trust in the prescriptions, so that you can move forward confidently in enacting them.

FEAR OF NOT DESERVING HAPPINESS

If you were demeaned or abused as a child, you may not believe you deserve a life of harmony, growth, abundance, and love. This is the life God designed for you, and this is the life the angels' Divine prescriptions always lead to. For instance, you might feel unworthy of happiness because of someone you've injured or betrayed, or because you feel you are not good enough, or because of your lifestyle, or because you feel you haven't tried hard enough in life. Naturally, you will fear receiving any form of heavenly guidance.

Though God's love is *unconditional*, far too many people act and react as if it is *conditional*. That's because their love for themselves is conditional. They think, "I don't deserve happiness yet. First I must (fill in the blank: lose weight, graduate, pay off my bills, etc.). Then I'll deserve happiness." This is similar to a person who cleans the house before the housekeeper arrives.

These individuals have it backward. If they were perfectly happy, there would be nothing God could do for them. It is the unhappy whom God and the angels want to help. They want to point the way to a rich, fulfilling, satisfying existence. In short, in order for God to be a giver, He needs someone who needs help. By allowing God to aid you, you allow heaven to fulfill its purpose and give you the Divine guidance it so earnestly wants to share.

FEAR OF GOD-GIVEN POWER

One thing that scares people about God's counsel is that it always empowers them. Most people understand that they are made in the image and likeness of the Creator. Yet they never consider the implications that the Creator is all-powerful. Because you are made in God's image, doesn't it therefore make sense that you are inherently extremely powerful, too?

Too often people behave as if they were hapless and impotent victims of external powers. This is because most people have been taught to fear power. Women, for instance, often are raised to believe that having power equals aggressiveness, which is considered an unfeminine trait. As a result, many women fear being abandoned or criticized if they become empowered. Men sometimes distrust power, because they have seen it destroy their own fathers or other men. Both sexes fear that in the process of exercising power, they might unwittingly make a mistake, causing pain for themselves and others.

If, like many people, you have misused power in the past, the angels remind you that you and your circumstances have evolved since then. The angels say, *"Today, you are more sensitive to the feelings of those around you, and this awareness will prevent you from inflicting pain with your power. You are now actually incapable of abusing your power to the degree you did before."*

When you allow the power with which the Creator has endowed you to come forth, you also have the ability to use it in ways that benefit others. For example, the angels may lead you to resolve a long-standing family dispute, or gain your entire department a commendation from senior management, or leave an abusive relationship, or save your own foundering business. Or, it might be applied to making a success of a service-oriented position, such as being a mentor, teacher, or counselor.

FEAR OF CONTACTING FALLEN ANGELS

Many people fear they may contact a fallen angel if they address their requests to anyone other than God. They ask me, "What if I am fooled by a fallen angel or Antichrist and unwittingly coerced into a life of suffering? After all, doesn't the dark side always lie about its identity?"

The average person, living and praying with good intentions, doesn't have to worry about fallen angels. Those whose consciousness is love-based attract other loving beings into their lives. Those who live a clean life are also *boring* to the dark side. (In appendix A, I've written more about how to recognize and avoid the beings that are called fallen angels.)

The Four Channels of Divine Communication

There's a final reason people sometimes miss out on the prescriptions heaven sends them: They simply don't recognize the answer in the form it takes when it does come. Instead, they dismiss the experience as a daydream, or a weird sensation, or a mood they're in, or an idea they can't get out of their mind. Then, never realizing that their desperately longed-for Divine remedy has come and gone unrecognized, they blame the angels for their failure to answer their prayers.

Although most books refer to people "hearing" heavenly messages, the fact is, that many don't hear their answers as audible words. Only about one-quarter of the people I've surveyed receive Divine prescriptions in the form of an audible voice (either inside their heads or actually spoken out loud). My research shows most people receive angel messages in the form of thoughts or feelings. Still others receive them in the form of pictures seen in their mind's eye or physical sensations. A final group reports a kind of deep knowingness that is beyond words.

Why such a proliferation of channels for transmitting angelic advice from heaven to earth? When you send messages to friends, you aren't limited to a single form of communication; you have options such as telephones, e-mail, newspapers, and personal encounters, depending on which you find most convenient. Similarly, heaven doesn't limit itself to a single way of getting its guidance through to you and me. Instead, it attempts to communicate with you through a variety of methods, depending on which the angels find easiest and best suited to your personality.

Typically, heavenly prescriptions arrive via one or more of the following four channels:

- Clairaudience (words and sounds)
- Clairvoyance (images and pictures)

- Clairsentience (emotions and sensations)
- Claircognizance (a sudden knowingness)

Although everyone can learn to use all four of these modes, science (as well as my own experience) has shown that at least initially, different people receive angelic messages more easily through some modes. Much recent research, including extensive work at Harvard, has tied these four ways of receiving Divine prescriptions to four basic "intelligences," or "domains," of the brain, each of which has its own learning, perceiving, and thinking styles. For some people, it turns out, their visual intelligence, or domain, is dominant. They learn and think better in images than in words.

If your dominant modes of perception and thinking, for instance, are visual, you will find it easier to tune in and understand angelic remedies sent in the form of visual images. If, however, you are more in tune with your feelings about people and situations, the angels will attempt to send most of your messages in the form of emotional intuitions and warnings.

It is easier to be certain you don't miss angelic prescriptions when you are sensitive to your own best modes for receiving them. The better you become at tuning in to such Divine signals, the more confidence you'll develop in your ability to receive them and the validity of the messages they contain. Consequently, your ability to connect with the Divine will increase.

As you read the descriptions of the four channels of Divine communication that follow, you can rate which seem to come most naturally to you. Put a check mark next to each channel for every experience described that you can remember. Then, be alert during the coming week to similar incidents. Add check marks next to each channel as new experiences occur.

Put a check mark even if you aren't sure whether the incident was real or imaginary. Even if you only imagined that you felt an angel's wing brush against you, the fact that you are imagining something that involves your physical sensations shows that you have this orientation. Otherwise, you would have imagined that you saw, heard, or knew the angels' presence. The category that has the most check marks indicates your most prominent channel of heavenly communication.

Clairaudience. Many times, Divine prescriptions are delivered in the form of a soft inner voice that describes the solution to your problem in detail, almost as if you were tuning in to some angelic radio band. (Which is precisely what is happening.) They also can signal you through a catchy tune that comes out of nowhere (especially when you are just waking up in the morning). Or, you might hear the voice of a deceased loved one, hear your name called, or hear a bell-like note. If you would like to hear these sounds more clearly, request the angels to turn up the volume during their conversations with you.

Clairvoyance. The angels also communicate with people by showing them mental images that suddenly pop into their minds. You may see in your mind a sudden, snapshotlike picture of a mental movie, or experience a dream in which a deceased loved one visits you with a message. Often these images are self-explanatory, but if you don't understand what they mean, request clarification. The angels need your feedback to know if the message is getting through or not.

Clairsentience. Sometimes Divine prescriptions are delivered through emotions and bodily sensations. When this happens, the sensations you feel are those of angelic wings brushing against you, trying to nudge you toward—or away from—certain courses of action and ways of looking at things. Tension and feelings of dread can provide guidance as to people and situations you should be cautious of. A warm, relaxed sensation in the stomach or chest area can be a sign that you are on the right course or should go ahead with a new acquaintance. Other examples people have shared with me encompass having a gut feeling that proves correct; smelling the cologne of a deceased loved one; feeling like someone has touched you or sat on your bed when no one is present.

Claircognizance. When you request angelic guidance, the next moment the solution springs complete and clear into your mind, without a consciously worded thought being involved. It's as if God downloaded a computer file marked "Solution to Problem" in your mind. In this wordless and silent knowingness, even complex, abstract concepts are easily absorbed, and everything is understood on a deep level.

Gaining Faith in Divine Prescriptions

Some people fail to follow their angels' advice because they lack faith in themselves, in the angels, in the process. The whole idea of receiving prescriptions from heaven seems outlandish to some. Others doubt God truly listens to and answers their pleas. Still others have difficulty believing angelic advice actually can help them with something as concrete and earthly as their career or finances or marriage.

Yet, the most frequent comment I get during my angel readings is, "I had a feeling that is what my angels would say." In other words, the validity of the Divine prescription I have relayed resonates with my clients at a deep level. They had already received the message earlier and failed to act on it. Now it is being repeated. And yet, some of us still doubt, letting God's precious advice go to waste.

I realize that in the beginning of working with Divine guidance, it's tempting to resist heavenly suggestions. I've learned to trust, purely through experience, that God and the angels really do know what they're doing. When you trust and follow this guidance, your life begins to operate like a well-oiled machine. Once you begin to follow their remedies and regularly experience the profound results, you will begin to build your own strong foundation of trust in heaven's healing wisdom.

Many times, of course, you won't be able to foresee how the prescription you have been given will help you, and you will need to walk in faith for the first few steps. You'll get guidance, for instance, on how to deal with someone who is a thorn in your side, or what steps to take to get that promotion you dream of. Your natural reaction is *first* to look for a *guarantee* that everything will work out right *before* you act on it. God usually doesn't provide people with a step-by-step blueprint of *how* things will work out, however. The only guarantee you will receive is the assurance that everything is in God's hands. Therefore, if you have faith and follow the guidance you will be given as you go along, everything will work out.

Waiting for God to "show you the money" before you take action is the number one reason why people become stuck and fail to reap the benefits of the angels' advice. You must do your end of the work by following the action and guidance you are given. Then, you can leave the rest to God.

An excellent way to overcome doubt is to ask the angels to work with you while you sleep to strengthen your faith in the prescriptions you receive. Just before going to bed tonight, mentally say to the angels, "Please enter my dreams tonight, and clear away any fears that may be blocking me from being aware of and following my Divine prescriptions."

God and the angels are happy to provide Divine prescriptions to your problems, spelling out the steps you need to take to heal, to grow, to cope with crises and pain. The heavenly hosts won't do all the work, though. Heaven wants to give people a road map for traveling successfully through life's minefields. But the angels leave it up to the individual to act on their suggestions. You have to take the steps they prescribe for you or, since you have free will, you can choose to ignore their guidance and continue to suffer needlessly. By following the guidance of this invisible team of helpers that perpetually surrounds us, anyone can heal and grow spiritually, emotionally, and physically, and develop into a more loving and responsible being.

CHAPTER TWO

Prescriptions for Personal Challenges and Crises

We all grapple occasionally with serious challenges and personal crises such as drug addiction, abuse, depression, jealousy, loneliness, or loss of loved ones. We must not feel alone in our struggle. Every day people of all backgrounds—medical doctor and welfare recipient, college graduate and high school dropout, gay and straight, Christian and Jewish, atheist and Hindu—struggle with similar problems. Whatever their outward demeanor, inside too many are suffering silently from one personal difficulty or another. Fortunately, the angels have prescriptions for your personal problems that can bring healing and ultimate success to even the most devastating life experiences. Seeing your peace and happiness is their reward.

You may mistakenly conclude that if you truly have angelic help, you should have a problem-free life. "It's hard for me to believe that anyone's watching over me," a client confided to me once. "I've had one problem after another. As soon as I get one part of my life fixed, here comes another big deal to ruin my happiness. Where are my guardian angels when I need them?"

The angels aren't with you to smooth away all challenges and difficulties, for these are potentially important learning and growth experiences. The angels are, instead, guides who offer suggestions on how best to remedy difficult situations.

These Divine prescriptions are nothing less than God's own blueprint for the self-growth necessary to successfully surmount your inner and outer challenges.

If you ask God or His angelic messengers for a Divine prescription because you are suffering inside or are facing a seemingly overwhelming problem, and you follow the guidance you receive, you can achieve a harmonious life. Peace of mind is a large part of your life's mission, and heaven wills to help you attain this. The angels know that if you wake up in the middle of the night worried, you won't have the energy to help fulfill your mission on earth. Instead, you'll be tense and afraid, which negatively affects everyone with whom you come into contact.

You must act in concert with the angels as co-creators of a peaceful existence. By having the discipline to set your course by heaven's guidance, it is entirely possible to sail successfully through even the most storm-tossed seas. You're like a ship's captain, receiving continuous feedback from directional and weather satellites, who brings her ship to a safe port in the midst of a gale. Typically, though, people forget to consult the angels until they experience turbulence. Then they call on heaven almost immediately for assistance, which the angels will gladly provide, showing them how to carry through to smooth sailing beyond.

The angels know they walk a fine line in guiding human beings. On the one hand, part of your life purpose is to learn how to make responsible choices and to grow from the challenges you overcome. On the other hand, the angels don't want you to waste your life repeating destructive patterns such as addictions or self-loathing. So the angels are in the tricky position of guiding you in an noncontrolling manner.

When you ask for help from God and the angels, whatever the problem, their Divine remedies usually lead to inner changes. As your life heals, it becomes increasingly difficult to tolerate situations, relationships, foods, and locations that are no longer healthy for you. For example, you may feel tempted to join a health club, change your job, sell your possessions and launch that business, or join a recovery support group.

You may start to question every part of your life: your marriage, career path, and home life. Your inner satisfaction seems to hinge on making healthy inner and outer changes.

Prescriptions for Self-Created Problems

When people are unhappy, they seek happiness. All too often, happiness seems to elude them. Yet, the angels say the truth is just the opposite. It is human beings who are eluding happiness.

Although heaven wants everyone to be happy and provides them with the potential circumstances of happiness, some people unknowingly resist the very happiness they seek. They may think that other people and circumstances are making them unhappy, but the angels have taught me that almost every pressure and every problem is self-created.

I doubt there's a person alive who hasn't engaged in some form of self-sabotage. This is probably true of you, too. It might be overspending, or putting your worst foot forward at an important meeting, or failing to exercise, or choosing the wrong mate, or failing to assert yourself at a critical moment, or turning to alcohol to escape the pain of life, or pushing away help because you were too embarrassed to accept it, or screwing things up just as success was within your grasp.

Sadly, this kind of self-sabotage can become a way of life. You unknowingly develop an imbedded habit of creating problems for yourself. Life seems to be one long series of crises (though the angels say life is one long series of learning experiences and opportunities for growth). Unless you are lucky enough to recognize the source, you attribute these self-created difficulties to some outside agency, complaining to friends or your therapist, "God is against me," or "Why do I have so much bad luck?"

No matter what their cause, the wounds of a lost love, an irreparable family breach, or failure to win a job promotion all hurt just as deeply, whatever their source. Self-created wounds are real wounds nevertheless, and they bleed as much as any other kind. Until you become aware that you are the cause of your own problems and begin taking steps to heal the situation, you will likely continue to find yourself trapped in turmoil, trouble, and misery.

Working with the angels has shown me that there are four main reasons why people reject happiness and create their own difficulties.

- They feel they don't deserve happiness.
- They fear happiness will be boring.
- They believe crisis solving gives meaning to their lives.
- They have never experienced real happiness and know no other way of life but misery and unhappiness.

Far too many people feel they don't deserve happiness. This attitude usually is the result of an overcritical parent, or some sort of childhood abuse or trauma. One part of them wants the same happiness they see everyone else enjoying; another part says they aren't worthy of it. Often, when a chance for happiness appears, the latter part shouts louder than the former part. They find some reason or make some pretext, often unwittingly, to foul up their potential for happiness. (The angels tell these people that God made everyone equally worthy, and their faults and mistakes in no way make them less deserving of happiness in His eyes. The angels recommend every potential for happiness they send their way.)

Some people enjoy the excitement of a roller-coaster lifestyle, thriving on the heart-pounding adrenaline rushes associated with chronic relationship breakups or financial crises. They are terrified that stability, peace, even happiness will be boring. The idea of a problem-free life makes them yawn. They say they want happiness, but they are actually afraid it will cost them their edge, that they will lose some of their motivation in life. What would they do with all that free time? How humdrum to have no challenges. (The angels always advise such clients that a peaceful life does not mean an unexciting life. It is merely that the excitement has a different flavor to it. Far from being boring, peace can be filled with a rich abundance of successful projects, friendship, ventures and trips, prosperity, and romance.)

People who reject their own happiness unconsciously feel that solving problems and crises proves the use and worth of their lives. In other words, they unconsciously allow crises to arise in order to make themselves feel useful and needed. (The angels help such clients find more meaningful use for their abilities through volunteer work and mentoring.)

Growing up in a chaotic household causes some individuals to become accustomed to living in the midst of crisis and upset. They are more comfortable in a problem-ridden lifestyle than in a peaceful one because that's all they've known. They instinctively seek out dysfunctional situations at work, with friends, and in their love life. (The angels counsel them to ask for help clearing away the thoughts, beliefs, and feelings that make them cling to a troubled lifestyle and troubled relationships. They suggest joining a charitable service organization dedicated to a cause in which the person passionately believes.)

When it comes to straightening out people who are suffering from self-sabotage, the angels' prescriptions usually call for them to work on changing these patterns to ameliorate the source of their problems. Frequently, clients who ask questions about how to solve their personal problems find the angels respond with messages that sound like spiritual-psychological self-help. Heaven knows that if they heal the destructive personal patterns of thoughts, feelings, and behaviors that cause so many tribulations, they'll be happier. In this way the angels lead people to work on transforming their inner worlds as a way of transforming the chaos around them in the outer world. At my workshops, I poll attendees, surveying what kind of messages they get from God and their angels. Whenever I ask them, "Have you received any guidance to make changes in your life?" virtually every hand is raised.

My client Velda, a trim executive of forty, who works in the private security business, was desperately unhappy because nothing ever seemed to work out right in her life. "I got a great job about three years back," she explained, "but that was right when I was breaking up with this retired cop, and he kept stalking me and causing trouble at work, so I lost that. Then a little later I could have had a great chance with this one guy, but I had just started an affair with this jerk who turned out to be an addict. And then I had another cushy job, but it was me who was the jerk. I just couldn't stand the way my boss talked. Now I'm in this great relationship with this hunk, but every time I think he might be the one for me and start to think about marriage, I get all tense and we begin to fight. For some reason, the bluebird of happiness never seems to land on me."

The angels directed me to ask Velda about her childhood. She described her chaotic and unpredictable upbringing. "My parents argued a lot. My mother was always taking me with her to stay at my grandmother's until she cooled off. My father was in the military and we moved once every year or so. I was always the new kid at school, and every time I'd make new friends it was time to pack up and move again."

"Dearest Velda," the angels responded, *"happiness is not eluding you. It is you who are eluding happiness. Your early life was so confused and trouble-filled that the ideas of peace and happiness seem to be strange, unfamiliar things to you. They are so different from what you knew as a child that you shy away from them and instinctively seek out situations that re-create the chaos and pain of those early years. You believe that life must always be paved with*

difficulty and turmoil. But it is possible for you to live a problem-free life. Do not expect problems to besiege you, and your new expectations will increase your experiences of joy and harmony."

"It's true," Velda mused. "I can see that. I kind of do expect the worst of life. And a couple of times, when I have gotten close to really great guys and the possibility of marriage came up, I did feel panic. But I thought it was just marriage jitters. Yet, when you put it that way, I guess I didn't feel I deserved either of them. But how do I change my expectations when unhappiness is all I have known?"

The angels prescribed, *"Do not accept any pain or unhappiness in your life. Instead, adopt a zero tolerance for pain policy. The moment you become aware of feeling unhappy, please give the entire sensation and situation to us. By surrendering your unhappiness to us, we are placed in a position where we can help you to replace an unhappy situation with something better or heal the situation. Either way, we will help you to attain the joy in your heart that will keep your energy and morale at its highest level."*

"Zero tolerance for unhappiness," Velda repeated, brightening. "That's a wonderful idea. I never thought of it before." Then she frowned. "But when something bad happens, isn't it normal to feel unhappy?"

I told Velda that yes, unhappiness is a natural feeling. I pointed out, however, that if she would ask the angels for help each time she felt unhappy about something, they would quickly send thoughts that would lighten her burden. The angels are wonderful at clearing away negative patterns.

The angels added, *"We suggest you become involved in some group that aids those less fortunate than yourself. This will help put your own problems in perspective and make you more aware of the blessings in your life."*

"You know," Velda said, echoing many of those I've met whose problems are self-created, "I've been feeling an urge to volunteer at the local women's shelter. I wonder if that could have been the angels nudging me." (It was, of course.)

By planting the idea of volunteer work in her mind, the angels had been trying to help Velda out of the mind-set that kept her in her cycle of self-created difficulties. But Velda had been resistant, clinging to the familiar patterns of misery and a chaotic life. When she heard the same thing from the angels through me, it only confirmed what she already knew inside. I counseled Velda to ask her angels to enter her dreams at night and clear away the thoughts, beliefs, and feelings that made her comfortable with problems such as troubled relationships.

Velda promised she would do as I asked. She also followed the angels' suggestion about public service work, and it really did help transform her attitude toward life. The problems she thought were holding her back soon began to seem trivial. She found herself feeling grateful for the many wonderful things in her life she had not appreciated before, like a good job, friends, a comfortable salary. The next time she had an opportunity to advance herself professionally, she didn't let anything deter her and took the position. She hasn't yet found the man she is looking for, but she is certain that, when she does meet him, she won't tolerate any feelings that she doesn't deserve happiness with him. The angels can rearrange someone's priorities more efficiently and quickly than any form of psychotherapy I've tried or witnessed.

The angels say that people are much too tolerant of misery and unhappiness, as if they expect it to be a normal part of life. After all, look at the popular bumper sticker, "S · · · Happens." Why not rewrite this expectation of problems, say the angels, and expect that "Peace and Happiness Happen" instead?

Rx

If your life is a succession of problems, look to why you feel you don't deserve happiness. Then, expect happiness and establish a zero-tolerance policy toward unhappiness.

Prescription for Addiction

Nowadays, addiction seems to be an epidemic. The destruction and suffering caused by drug and alcohol abuse have reached astronomical proportions unprecedented in any age. In addition, hundreds of millions worldwide seem to have fallen victim to more subtle addictions: compulsive spending, gambling, risk taking. Then there are the most subtle addictions of all: too comfortable lifestyles, easy jobs, fine dining, television, media and the Internet, automobiles, mall shopping . . . the list could go on and on.

The consequences of the worst of these addictions—drug and alcohol abuse—cannot be overstated. It has literally devastated society, especially the inner cities, and is now blighting the suburbs, even the most rural of counties. Tens of millions have had their careers, their families, their finances, their physical, emotional, and spiritual health, and their lives destroyed by substance addiction, and the number still seems to be climbing.

The angels understand and feel compassion for the deep-seated sense of what therapists term *existential emptiness* that drives many people to addiction. They also cringe from the havoc these addictions wreak in the lives of all concerned. That is why the angels are so anxious to aid in healing the underlying problems that trigger addictions.

The angels say that addictions and obsessive-compulsive behavior spring from people's inner feelings of emptiness and being cut off from God and His all-encompassing love, which they experienced before birth and within their mother's womb. They explain that since God is omnipresent, He is within every atom of every person and object. People lose this sense of God's love within them, however, soon after birth. The self-deprecating thoughts they learn from parents and society make most people think they are bad or unworthy and block them off from God even more completely.

As a result, people look for something outside of themselves that can create an artificial sense of filling that emptiness or, at the least, dull its pain. They turn to substances like drugs and alcohol, or activities like eating, smoking, gambling, shopping, Internet surfing, or watching television sports, which bring them a temporary high that relieves their feeling of emptiness. Though they are momentarily sated, they soon experience feelings of self-loathing for wasting time and energy in futile, shameful behaviors. This in turn intensifies the original feeling of emptiness, sending people back to the substance or activity.

One client, Barbara, found herself trapped in exactly such a cycle. When Barbara had a miscarriage for the second time in two years, she became depressed and began suffering from insomnia. She and her husband desperately wanted to have children. After five years of trying to have a baby, Barbara feared her husband was emotionally distancing himself out of disappointment. Her doctor prescribed a sedative to help Barbara sleep through the night. Soon, Barbara also began taking the pills during the day. Just to relax, she told herself. Within a month, she had to refill a prescription that should have lasted her several more weeks.

To avoid attracting the suspicions of her doctor and pharmacist, Barbara took fewer sedatives and instead began drinking wine during the day, again, rationalizing that she needed to relax. Barbara's husband found her passed out one afternoon and rushed her to the emergency room. The doctor, himself a recovering drug addict, recognized the signs of Barbara's addiction and recommended counseling. She entered an inpatient center and attended twelve-step recovery groups, and afterward stayed clean and sober.

However, Barbara still hadn't resolved her underlying issues, so her pain manifested in other addictive behaviors. She began smoking and eating compulsively. Her weight shot up alarmingly. Her husband left her.

When I met Barbara, she was an example of what Alcoholics Anonymous terms a *dry drunk*—that is, someone who is not actually taking a drug, but nonetheless is still acting addictively.

"*Beloved Barbara,*" the angels began, "*you have turned to these substances, like so many, because they dull for a moment the pain of the emptiness you feel inside. Your unconscious mind remembers the fullness of feeling loved in heaven by God and your guardian angels. Soon after birth, most people gradually forget about this love and that their guardian angels are permanently by their side, still exuding the same strong love they did in heaven. Like you, they are especially sensitive to the feeling of emptiness that comes when human beings feel cut off from that love. If only you will tune in to that love, your fear of emptiness would vanish.*"

As the angels spoke, Barbara saw that underneath her craving was an emptiness created by the need to feel loved. As long as she had been certain of her husband's love and looked forward to children helping to fill up this need in the future, Barbara had been able to cope. But when she thought her husband was turning away and had lost all hope of having children, Barbara turned to drugs and alcohol to quell the emptiness that closed in around her. Later she turned to smoking and compulsive eating to fill the same desires. She sobbed that she'd always felt empty and needy.

"*The emptiness you are trying to fill is an illusion,*" the angels answered. "*There is no place within you where Love does not reside. You can replace the experience of emptiness with the very Love you are craving. When you hunger for your addictive substance or behavior, take one moment of your time to close your eyes, breathe, and call to us. We will pour over you additional measures of the GodLove, which will warm you through your heart, chest, and belly. Breathe in deeply, fill yourself with GodLove, and your hunger pangs for material objects will cease to control you.*

"*We also beseech you to forgive yourself for the mistakes you think you have made. For we see much addictive behavior perpetuated by the guilt of believing you have 'misbehaved.' You are innocent, dear child of God. Ask us to soothe your guilt pangs, and you will feel their terror no more."*

When our session was over, Barbara promised to begin meditating upon this love daily. She later called to tell me her compulsive behaviors had diminished. I helped her learn how to contact her guardian angels, including her beloved departed grandmother, as a way of experiencing additional love. Barbara wrote letters to her angels each time she felt hungry for love, and she was rewarded with feelings of inner peace. Sometimes Barbara had conversations with her angels by writing down a question and writing down what she heard and felt. She said she felt this process proved extremely healing.

Through my personal and clinical experiences, I know that Divine prescriptions can heal addictions, and I've witnessed dozens of cases where they helped end a person's craving for the drug or behavior. After all, the most tried-and-true addiction treatment model—Alcoholics Anonymous and its twelve-step offshoots—are based on spiritual principles.

Rx

Surround yourself with images of love whenever you feel the call of your addiction. Let it replace the emptiness and pain with warmth and fullness.

Prescription for Depression

Everyone feels blue on occasion. If you are a person who is chronically down, though, it's a sign of trouble. Depression robs you of energy, joy, and motivation. At the same time, your constant depression causes other people to avoid you, which only intensifies your loneliness and sadness.

Studies show depression holds people prisoners in their own home, and prevents them from enjoying fulfilling work, loving relationships, and satisfying lives. It also can cause devastating pain to their loved ones. Children, for instance, can't understand why Mommy or Daddy is so sad all the time. Spouses can sink into co-depression, too, wondering what's wrong with them when all the love they pour on the depressed person is to no avail.

Depression is a major killer through suicide and addiction. It is also a factor in death by self-neglect. It has even been shown to play a contributing role in many accidental deaths.

The angels say that the word *depression* also means a burrow in the ground—in other words, a low point. They understand that depression is a natural behavior when events have hurt people so deeply that they need healing and escape for a time from the world, and so turn inward. In other words, they immerse themselves in an introverted well of depression because they feel dishonored by the world.

The angels say that if people count their troubles in an attempt to justify being isolated emotionally and physically, they will continue on a downward spiral. If they continue to feel sorry for themselves or insist that no one loves or understands them, they protract the length and depth of their depression. Fortunately, though, the angels have a remedy that can help anyone suffering from depression, just as it did my client Bernice.

Bernice is a fifty-three-year-old wife and mother of two who looks ten years older. She complained that everyone she knew—neighbors, friends, and family—seemed to be too busy to see her. As I observed her slumped shoulders, bowed head, and listless demeanor, I immediately recognized the problem, and the angels concurred: Bernice was depressed, and her negativity pushed others away.

Bernice's young adult years had revolved around her family. Her husband, Mike, was always busy with his corporate career, but Bernice hadn't noticed since she'd been busy taking care of her children. Only after her youngest child married and moved out of the house did Bernice feel a void in her life: a combination of grief over her empty nest, loneliness at missing the companionship with her husband and children, and fear over what she would do to fill her empty hours and add meaning to her life.

Within weeks of her daughter's wedding, Bernice felt tired and depressed much of the time. She'd call her children for visits or stop by her neighbors' homes, but everyone seemed too busy to sit and talk with her. Soon she felt bitter, believing her family and people in general didn't like her. Bernice's depression deepened. She began lying in bed all day, and never got dressed. Her husband was worried, but she ignored all his entreaties that she seek help.

One night, she took an overdose of her husband's sleeping pills. After her stomach was pumped and she spent several weeks in a neuropsychiatric hospital, Bernice returned home. Her depression continued. She went on lithium. Then a friend suggested she come to me for counseling.

"Much of your depression stems from a belief that you are alone or misunderstood," the angels told Bernice. *"Be assured that you are never without us, and that we understand you with our unconditional love. We hover even closer whenever we feel you are depressed. It is we, your angels, who seek to pull up your mood and outlook. So do not resist laughter and smiles when you are determined to burrow deeply within yourself. When you feel your heart lilting upward, that is our influence upon you. When you become aware of our angelic energy lifting you up, breathe deeply of our essence. In this way, you draw within you the warmth and reassurance you are seeking."*

Bernice replied, "I've felt that, you know. I had the distinct impression that some heavenly force was near me several times, trying to reach through to me. But I was down so low I just didn't want to hear it."

I told Bernice that when someone is deep in depression, their angels attempt to guide them to see the bright side of situations, to forgive, and to laugh. They attempt to remind people of a funny joke or lead them to turn on the television set just in time to catch a favorite comedy show. I urged Bernice not to resist these angelic efforts to lift her mood.

Then the angels offered their prescription. *"We most strongly urge that you use your moments of darkest depression as a spur to seek for the spark of GodLight that eternally burns within you. See this time as a call to count your blessings. When you are down, take a moment to recall seven instances during the day when you saw love being expressed—a parent and child walking hand in hand, or a kind act between two strangers. If you embark upon this practice, your depression will begin to lighten. If you focus on feeling grateful for what you see, experience, and have, you will uplift yourself and those with whom you come into contact."*

Bernice sat quietly for a moment. Then she smiled, and it was as if the sun had come up. "I just thought of five instances of love I've seen since waking up this morning. The angels are right. It does help."

The angels also advised Bernice to be careful of her choice of words when thinking or talking about her mood. They suggested she avoid possessive phrases such as "my depression" or "I am depressed," which reinforce personal ownership. Instead, they told Bernice to describe the mood as "the appearance of depression," or "I seem to feel down." This way, you don't attach yourself unnecessarily to the condition of depression. In addition, they counseled her to state things in terms of how she wanted them to be, and not in terms of the condition she wanted to change.

Bernice came to see me again several months later on a completely different matter. I could see at once that her depression had lifted. She smiled as she greeted me, and there was energy in her handshake and movements as she sat down. "That was good advice the angels gave me about how to look at things," she announced. "My family and friends are back, and from what my daughter tells me, I am looking forward to baby-sitting my new grandchild soon."

Rx

Review your day, and try to recall seven instances when you saw love being expressed. Each will kindle a golden glow within you, banishing the clouds of depression.

Prescription for Anxiety

Anxiety, like depression, seems to be a fact of twenty-first-century life. Bombarded with television images of violence and disaster around the clock, aware of hot spots of potential war around the globe, faced with AIDS and other biological perils, it's understandable that everyone experiences anxiety more often than before. For some people, though, anxiety runs rampant, a poisonous force that blights every aspect of their lives. The anxiety they experience is all-encompassing and paralyzing, and they become unable to function in the real world.

According to the angels, anxiety begins when out-of-control pessimism is combined with continual worry. The angels say that people are needlessly anxious about their future, not realizing, as the angels put it, that *"God is with you and you are the master of your day."* They also say that present-moment thoughts and emotions create all of our future-moment experiences. Essentially, people are in charge of what happens to them and have nothing to worry about—except worry itself.

Twenty-six-year-old Sarita hardly looked like a candidate for chronic anxiety. After all, she had all that life could offer: an adoring, financially stable husband, two smart and healthy children, and a suburban home. Sarita worked part-time at a bookstore out of a desire to be among people, not out of financial necessity.

So why was Sarita having an angel-reading session with me, asking so many fearful questions about the future? She requested readings about herself, her husband, her children, other family members, and the world in general. She'd ask, "How is the children's health? Is my husband's job secure? Is my mother going to live a long time? Are they angry with me at the bookstore?"

As I gave angel readings for each of Sarita's questions about her family, I'd find that particular person was doing well, with no major problems in his or her immediate future. Curious, I mentally asked the angels why Sarita was so worried when there were no indications of family troubles or health problems.

"She's worrying herself sick," the angels told me. *"She wakes up worrying about her children, then she worries all day about her husband and everyone else she knows. Sarita is a loving soul with intentions of helping others. It's your job to educate her to learn how to stop worrying and start enjoying her relationships and life."*

I asked Sarita if she worried much. She cupped her face in her hands and cried. "I'm frightened all the time. I never stop worrying about the children and my husband and our lives."

The strength of the angels' collective voice and loving energy surprised even me as they delivered their message to Sarita. *"In a sense, your anxiousness arises because you fear darkness in some form and you are trying to escape this darkness. You fear somebody or some circumstance is overpowering or hurting you. Your very fear gives energy and life to a force that actually does not exist in truth. Then, when you fight against darkness by becoming anxious, you give reality to an illusion. You actually create that which you fear the most."*

I explained to Sarita, "Every thought and every feeling is a prayer. You actually draw to you whatever you are focusing on. The irony is that you are worried about losing your loved ones to illness or because they might be angry with you. Yet, your worries are what is creating the problem."

Sarita was still crying. "That's so true. I am always afraid my husband will leave me or that the children will stop loving me, that I am beginning to drive them away. My husband and I are fighting because he is so weary of my incessantly asking them if they are all right or are mad at me. I don't mean to drive everyone crazy. I just don't want them to leave me."

"That's why we ask you to invite us to help you. Instead of fearing dark circumstances, know that we hold you eternally safe and protected. Resist the urge to battle with enemies of your own making, and call upon your friends, both seen and unseen, instead. Nothing outside of yourself threatens you or your family. You merely must adjust your inner circumstances somewhat to create a more peaceful environment within."

The angels also counseled Sarita that by eliminating many of the sources of negative stimulation in her environment, she could ensure her resulting positive outlook. They particularly cautioned her to avoid reading or watching the news and its negative images for a while until her anxieties were stilled. They also recommended meditation as a way of experiencing greater inner peace.

"It is so much better that you invest your time in meaningful and uplifting relationships and activities: laughing with your children, meditating, reading an inspirational book, being outside in nature, or exercising your body."

The angels then began to show me an image of a woman who appeared to be a couple of years older than Sarita. I described this woman to Sarita as having short, dark brown hair and being a little on the plump side. Sarita said it was her friend Patty.

"The angels say that this friend is a source of much of your anxiety," I relayed. "It's as if her negativity is bleeding onto you."

Sarita explained that Patty did tend to become depressed and worried a lot, and that she dropped by frequently for advice about problems.

The angels said, *"When you talk with this so-called friend, her negative outlook is affecting you. Many of your worrying habits come from talking to Patty so much, since she is a worrier herself.*

You spend time with Patty because of guilt and obligation. This is no basis for a relationship, and we ask you to make your choices of how to spend the moments of your day out of love, not fear."

The angels began showing me moving pictures of their Divine prescriptions to quell Sarita's anxiety. *"You must also eliminate the consumption of foods and beverages that are overstimulating you and giving you the tendency to be nervous and high-strung, such as coffee and caffeine. Your current diet is causing some sort of physical reaction similar to your blood pressure being raised. We also caution you to eliminate the consumption of chocolate and sugar, for you are highly sensitive to their stimulating effects."*

When Sarita followed these prescriptions, her life took an immediate turn for the better. (You will find further angelic thoughts about diet and health in appendix B.)

Rx

Eliminate sources of negativity in your life, from television to friends. Engage in positive, fulfilling activities. Eliminate foods that can add to your nervousness.

Prescription for Abuse

People have been abused (and abusing) since the dawn of history. Millions, particularly women, were abused in the name of various fundamentalist religions. Boys often were brutalized by their fathers on the pretext of "making a man" out of them. Girls often were sexually abused by older male relatives with the rationalization that they were "asking for it" or that the perpetrator was "teaching them to be a woman." Workers often suffered at the hands of indifferent or greedy employers on the basis of "efficiency" or "profit."

In the past, abuse was often swept under the rug. Only recently, as psychological understanding of the forces that shape people's emotional growth has broadened, have victims begun to speak up and assert themselves against their abusers.

The angels don't want anyone to remain in or accept an abusive situation, whether it is with a parent, spouse, lover, friend, or employer. If you feel abused in any way in a personal or business relationship, pray for spiritual intervention. God and the angels will guide you to freedom. This might take the form of inspiring you to stand up for yourself, or bringing in someone who can change the dynamic so as to end your abuse, or leading you to a new job or better relationship, or guiding you to professional help.

The angels say someone only needs to be willing to release old pain from the past, and they'll do the rest. The mere willingness to release toxic emotions related to abuse opens the door and allows the angels entry into a person's storehouse of pain. Once there, they go to work, cleaning away bitter memories and self-blaming tendencies springing from the abuse.

When I met Beth and Gary at one of my workshops, I could tell that the sister and brother had endured a difficult life. As Beth stood up for a reading, the angels showed me that her father had emotionally and physically abused her. Even more sadly, they also revealed that she had been sexually abused and molested as well. Gary also had been physically and emotionally abused. Both siblings were fifty pounds or more overweight, a common symptom in abuse survivors who turn to food to stuff their inner pain.

To protect Beth and Gary's privacy, I didn't discuss the abuse the angels showed me during my public reading with her. Instead, I offered to give them a private reading following the workshop. Both of them agreed to postpone their readings.

In our private session, the angels showed me that both Gary and Beth suffered from wounded self-esteem triggered by their years of hearing "You're not good enough!" screamed at them, coupled with beatings and other severe abuse. Brother and sister had repeated this pattern of early abuse even after they moved out of the family house. Beth's first marriage, to an army sergeant several years older—which she had entered largely to escape her father—turned into a nightmare when she discovered he was a domineering, wildly jealous individual who used her as a punching bag whenever he drank. Gary, meanwhile, had become a drug user who somehow always found himself working for abusive employers or making the kind of friends who victimized him, stole from him, beat him up, and then deserted him.

This is typical behavior for abuse survivors. Psychologists have found that when people can't yet forget and forgive, they become mired in the past and keep replicating it around them. That's why unhealed abuse survivors frequently find themselves embroiled in abusive relationships and job situations. By holding on to their resentment this way, Beth and Gary were essentially punishing themselves, not the person they were angry with.

The angels told the two of them, *"We ask that you view your abuse situations through the lens filter of Love. See all situations you've endured as challenges that have made you stronger, and do not succumb to the temptation to close your heart down to the awareness of Love. You have so much to give, borne of your experiences. Those who are struggling from similar experiences need you, and now is the time for you to capitalize upon your treasure chest of experiences, not to stow them away from your sight. Face your experiences, face your feelings, and face yourself. Go forth and share them with others. You'll find great beauty where you thought there was only ugliness or pain. If you need our help in leaving a certain situation, we are happy to assist at your request."*

Like many survivors of abuse, Beth and Gary blamed themselves for the victimization they had suffered. In part, this was because they had been told they were bad by their father and that they deserved the treatment he was meting out to them. He was the adult and they were the children, so they assumed he must know what he was talking about. When the children became adults, they came to feel they somehow should have been able to "prevent" the abuse. Finally, each had concluded, "I must be really bad for Daddy to treat me this way and for Mommy to let it happen to me."

The angels reassured them about this. *"Know in your hearts that the abuse is not your fault and that you never deserved it. God wills for you to be loved and respected in all of your relationships. No matter what mistakes you think you've made, you deserve to be treated only with dignity and kindness."*

The angels shared their Divine prescription for releasing the rage, anger, and depression that results from a history of childhood abuse. *"You must heal through forgiveness. That means releasing anger toward yourself, the abuser, adults who failed to rescue you, anyone who has abused you since. God wants you to release the toxic anger that you hold within yourself. Rage at people and circumstances erases the ability to enjoy the present moment. All the while you are angry with someone or some situation, moments of potential joy pass you by, never to be recaptured in the same way. Waste not your years by counting grievances."*

Initially, Beth and Gary resisted the idea. I explained that the angels were not advocating that they approve of or overlook what happened to them. The angels weren't denying the effect the abuse had upon them, or that their father was in any way right in what he did. The angels say that a person doesn't need to pardon the *actions* of abuse; they need to forgive the *persons* involved, for their own healing growth and not the abuser's.

The angels counsel people to let go of the pain and hatred of the past that trail behind them, "like an ox pulling a plow," as the angels put it. The angels say that forgiveness is a way of snapping the harness of this plow and freeing oneself of its burden. This forgiveness isn't for the sake of anyone but the person who has been abused.

The angels next guided me to show Beth and Gary the following exercise for using Divine energy to release the pain and scarring of childhood abuse. "With a deep breath, allow the healing angels full access into your body," I instructed them. "Allow the angels to come into your mind, your heart, and every cell of your body, and infuse you with Divine love. As they do so, you may notice some tingling sensations, spontaneous movements in your muscles, or an increase in your body temperature. This is a positive sign of angelic intervention and release."

I watched as Gary and Beth allowed their angels to work with them this way. Beth in particular had a blissful expression on her face. She appeared relieved to put the abuse behind her.

"The angels ask you to be willing to release any old anger you may be holding on to connected with being hurt, abused, manipulated, controlled, or overpowered. Just be *willing* to release your own unforgiveness, and let the angels do all of the work."

I saw Gary shudder, a sure sign of release. (I've learned that anyone who is even partially willing to be healed of the emotional scarring of abuse experiences remarkable transformations by working with the angels in this way.)

Rx

Release the pain inside through forgiving the people, but not necessarily the actions involved including yourselves.

Prescription for Loneliness

Feeling lonely—without friends or support, cut off from the warmth and love everyone else seems to bask in—can be one of the most devastating experiences in the world. Most people go through periods when they suffer feelings of isolation.

However, some individuals experience such intense, chronic feelings of loneliness that they can barely function and even consider suicide.

Vicky, a thirty-six-year-old secretary and single parent without any close friendships, complained to me about feeling lonely. It wasn't just romance that concerned her. Though she was a church member and worked at a large company, she simply did not have any close personal friends and at times wondered if it was worth going on in life. Vicky was hungry for a deep emotional connection and bond with like-minded adults.

I saw that Vicky, like all of us, was surrounded by loving angels and people who were potential friends. I also saw that Vicky had an emotional shell around her that blocked her from feeling the warmth that her angels and other people exuded. Undoubtedly, she was unaware of the love that other people felt for her.

I told Vicky, "You are definitely not alone, even though you feel that way a great deal of the time. Your angels send you extra love since they know the hardships you have endured. Some of these challenges have made you guarded against further pain, and this guardedness is misperceived by others as unfriendliness. However, they also see the growth that you have made as a result of these challenges."

Through me, the angels said to Vicky, *"During the times when you choose to lick your wounds from feeling betrayed or abandoned, who are we to break your self-imposed spell? At such times, you deliciously relish the self-pity of believing that no one loves or adores you, even when we are bestowing our greatest love upon you. It is not our intent to redirect your wishes, for you truly are in charge of your dream. However, we do desire for you to know that during those moments that you call lonely, we are closer to you than ever. Even more angels hover near, seeking to awaken you from your nightmarish delusion that God or His children could have abandoned you."*

Vicky bristled as I spoke these words. Clearly, she was uncomfortable with the message. "You know, I hate to admit it," she said slowly, sighing, "but I'm doing the exact thing that I saw my mother do when I was growing up. I never thought I'd be like her in this respect. She always came across like, 'I don't need anyone else,' and as a result, other people left her alone."

I took Vicky's hand and gave her a tissue to wipe her tears. Then I watched her body language reflect a gentle empowerment, as if tapping into the truth had helped her to tap into an inner reserve.

"The message your angels have for you is not to be afraid to let love into your heart," I told her. "They are helping you to be less guarded and more relaxed in letting people get close to you. The angels are working to bring people to you who will treat you with love, respect, and honor, so that you will open up to people who will treat you lovingly."

"If you could, for even one moment, wish to feel our love wrapped around you, be assured that we would make this wish instantly come true. We are also there when you desire us to orchestrate new friends. Seek peace and solace, not through isolation, but through communion with Spirit, which exists within all of us. You are not alone, now or ever. Allow us to materialize this fact for you without delay."

Two months later I received a letter from Vicky in which she wrote, "Our session was life-transforming for me, and I can't thank you and the angels enough. It was difficult for me to face some of the things the angels were saying, especially when they talked about my self-pity. I hadn't seen that in myself at all. But now I know that it was true, that I had the same 'Poor me, nobody loves me' attitude that I'd watched my mother suffer with all her life. But no more. I put my angels to the task of cleaning me up, and practically overnight I couldn't believe the transformation."

Vicky reported that she was actively involved in taking country-and-western dance lessons and was beginning to make new friends.

Rx

Become a friend magnet: Allow yourselves to enjoy meeting and being with other people.

Prescription for Envy

Envy can be a damaging emotion. It has broken up families and friendships. Nations have gone to war and people have engaged in criminal activity in order to obtain things they were envious of. You probably know at least one person who has let envy eat away at him until he no longer feels any joy in life and experiences it as one prolonged deprivation. We learn all this in symbolic form as children when we are told the story of how the giant grew envious of the magical possessions of Jack's father and spirited them away to his castle in the clouds, forcing Jack to climb the beanstalk.

Some people get envy and jealousy mixed up. *Envy* is wanting what someone else has. *Jealousy* is the fear of losing what we have. According to the angels, both envy and jealousy stem from a negative view of life, a pessimistic philosophy of scarcity rather than abundance. Such a view is manifest when you see a couple laughing and wish you had a soulmate; when you see someone with a better job and an expensive wardrobe and wish you had a good job and expensive clothes; when you see someone with an attractive figure and wish you had a nice body, too. You feel covetous, deprived, and envious. You wouldn't experience these emotions unless you first believed that you cannot achieve what the other person has. This belief in turn arises from the conviction that you can never obtain what the other person has obtained, that she has been gifted with some special ability—such as luck, genes, or family connections—that you lack. Envy, in short, assumes that since you were not gifted with that special knack, you can never get the mate, the job, or whatever it is the other person has that you wish was yours, too.

Despite the fact that most people were taught that it is "wrong" to feel envious, it seems to be a normal human emotion that everyone experiences on occasion. Properly reframed, the angels say, the emotion of envy can be a vital motivational tool. Fortunately, the angels have a remedy that can help anyone turn envy in just such a positive direction.

Liliani was envious of people who were more prosperous and seemed to enjoy greater material success than she did. A computer technician, Liliani had to pick up her boss one day a week as part of the company carpooling plan. Each time she drove into the wealthy, upper-class neighborhood where her boss lived, she would wait outside her two-story-with-swimming-pool home, staring at the three gleaming luxury sedans that crowded the driveway. And each time, Liliani burned with anger. "Why does she have everything when I do most of the work that generates the company's real income, and all I have to show for it is a beat-up secondhand car, a tiny apartment, and bills I can't afford to pay?"

Liliani came to me when she found herself beginning to obsess over what she saw as the seeming unfairness of this disparity. It had gotten so bad, that she was beginning to lie awake all night and fume about it until the wee hours. She even found herself carrying her resentment of her boss to the office, where she found it difficult not to be sharp and caustic in her responses.

"Daughter," the angels began, *"our heavenly Father has invested each of you with so many talents that whatever anyone of you accomplishes, the others are capable of accomplishing, too. Instead of envying your employer's success, let it serve as an inspiration to draw you forward and upward in life. In other words, let the intensity of your desire to have all the comforts in life your employer enjoys motivate you to take steps to improve your current situation."*

That surprised Liliani. "You mean I could become as rich as my boss?"

"In the final analysis, that is up to you and the exercise of your free will. As you say, your work is very valuable to the company. It is, in fact, responsible for producing a significant portion of the firm's proceeds. But think. Do you wish to take the risks she took and show the initiative she showed by striking out on your own and starting your own business? That you have it within yourself to do successfully, you should never doubt. But you also like your weekly paycheck, your nine-to-five, your leisure time to call your own. All these you would lose in the years it would take to realize your dream. Both these qualities are in you, and only you can decide which course represents your best interests."

Liliani looked thoughtful. "This is a new perspective for me. I guess I've got a lot of thinking to do. It never occurred to me that I could start a company of my own, become the boss, and be the one with the house in Bel Air, and a Bentley in the driveway. I guess I don't know if I want those things badly enough to change my whole life." She grinned. "But I do know one thing. I know I'm not envious of my boss anymore. She's paid a price for what she has. A high price. Just knowing I could have everything she has, if I truly want it, and that it's my choice if I do or don't, makes me feel a whole lot better."

Rx

There's no need to envy anyone. You were born with all the abilities necessary to get whatever you desire in life. One reason you may not have them already is that to get them, you would have to give up things you value more.

Prescription for Jealousy

Jealousy is another troublesome emotion. It has torn relationships, partnerships, even families wide open. People plot and scheme over it every day in real life, not just on soap operas. Sisters vie to see who will ultimately curry mother's favor and get that priceless family heirloom. Jealous spouses violate their partner's trust because they fear being abandoned or cheated on.

People make fools of themselves over jealousy every day. But the face of jealousy often is uglier. People are stalked, assaulted, even killed every day because of jealousy, too. Jealousy is similar to envy, but with a twist. Instead of desiring what someone else possesses, jealousy is the fear of losing something valuable you already have. It, too, is based in the belief that there is a scarcity of love, money, and good feeling in the world, and that whatever you have must be hoarded, lest someone else take your share from you.

The angels teach that in truth, there is nothing to be jealous of. God will provide His bounty for anyone who asks. The angels say that loss is therefore impossible and that all of a person's needs will be taken care of. They also remind people that part of God's plan involves growth through being challenged by new circumstances, so no relationship or possession is necessarily intended to be a permanent part of one's life.

Jamie, who works as a gardener, was almost out of control with jealousy, fearing that her partner, Robin, would leave her for another woman. "Every time Robin looks at another woman, I feel queasy and angry at the same time," Jamie explained to me. "I know I probably shouldn't feel this way. We are life partners and have gone through a commitment ceremony under the auspices of our church. Still, I keep thinking of those women out there. And Robin is so beautiful. I know they are going to be attracted to her. And look at me. I'm not good-looking. We've been arguing frequently, with Robin accusing me of being untrusting, and me accusing her of being a flirt."

The angels prescribed, *"Our prayer is that by relaxing your thoughts, feelings, emotions, and physicality, you will enjoy the ebb and flow of each moment with Robin instead of bracing yourself against possible future losses. For such guardedness often becomes the catalyst for later losing that which you fear you will lose. The woman you love has no thought of anyone but you. Other women are passing colors in her universe. You are its foundation and core. We assure you that your relationships and possessions cannot truly be lost in any way or form, but merely evolve in the appearance of change. If you seek to guard any situation that you believe you stand to lose, we are happy to assist you and stand watch in all directions. However, be aware that all situations and relationships evolve, so that a static situation is not within our realm to produce."*

Jamie looked shamefaced. "I guess I'm in danger of driving Robin away if I keep up the way I have been going lately. I'll cool it. It's reassuring to hear that things are OK between us from a 'higher' authority like the angels. I guess I got caught up in the illusion that Robin is something I possess and can lose, rather than a gift I should enjoy. Besides, I really don't think she wants to be stolen away."

Jamie was one of those people who come in for a consultation and never return. I always hope that the reason I do not hear from them is that they have followed the angels' prescription, and the problems that were troubling them have been happily resolved.

> Rx
>
> Everything you have is temporal, as is your earthly life. It is all "on loan from God." Nothing can be taken from you unless it is replaced by something of equal or greater value.

Prescription for Grief

Everyone loses a close friend or a family member to death at some time, and it's natural for people to experience devastating grief in the aftermath. This kind of loss can shake a person's foundation of feeling safe and in control, and create a sense of unendurable grief and emptiness. Roller-coaster emotions can leave the grieving person sobbing one moment and screaming angrily the next.

The angels know grief is a natural process everyone must pass through in order to heal after a deep emotional loss. They dislike seeing people suffer, though, and want to help them heal from grief in a timely and peaceful manner. The angels say, *"When your heart is heavy and filled with bereavement from the passing of a loved one, God sends additional angels to fill the seeming void where love seems to be missing from your life. Ask us to help you connect with your loved one, as a communication from heaven is the surest route to healing, once you are reassured of your loved one's safety, happiness, and wishes for your own happiness."*

After twenty-five years of marriage, Arlene's husband had passed away suddenly. She simply couldn't get over the loss. She broke into tears constantly, was unable to function at work, sat around feeling numb and hopeless all the time, and couldn't think or talk about anything else.

When Arlene raised her hand for a reading at one of my workshops, I brought her up on the stage. Immediately, a departed man appeared behind her. I had a strong feeling this was her husband, and when I described him to Arlene, she confirmed it. Her husband, Hank, began speaking to me about how he'd passed on suddenly from a heart condition. Arlene nodded. Then Hank began addressing Arlene. "He says that he's with you when you're gardening," I told Arlene. "He says that when you tend the flowers and pull weeds, you go into a meditative state, and that's when he can communicate closely with you." Arlene began crying and validated his message, saying that she thought she felt Hank's presence in the garden but wasn't sure whether it was her imagination.

Hank showed me that Arlene wasn't handling her grief very well. In fact, at times Arlene considered taking her own life so that she could be with her beloved husband, he told me. When I relayed this message to Arlene, she put her face into her hands and nodded.

"He says that it's not your time yet," I urgently told Arlene. "Hank says that you're together often, more often than you know. He says that you both will be together soon enough, but not yet. 'You have a long and beautiful life to live yet, honey,' Hank says to tell you. "Your children still need you, and you would be angry at yourself if you cut things short."

Arlene smiled for the first time.

Then Hank showed me an image of small yellow butterflies. I described them to Arlene: "They look like little buttercups, not the monarch kind of butterfly." As I uttered these words, Arlene shrieked. "No one knows about those butterflies. There's no way you could have known."

Arlene explained that at Hank's funeral, she and her grown children had noticed dozens of small, pure-yellow butterflies as the casket was lowered into the ground. Since that time, Arlene had seen the same type of butterflies everywhere. She had never told anyone about the visions for fear of being labeled crazy. But now Hank was confirming what she had suspected: The butterflies were a sign from him, that he was OK and was watching over Arlene and their children.

A few weeks later, Arlene called me to say that while she still missed Hank terribly, her sense of devastating loss was slowly lifting, and she was thrilled with the news that she was soon going to be a grandmother.

As with Arlene, when someone passes on, the angels or the departed loved one sometimes sends comforting messages. For instance, you may dream about or see a loved one who tells you she is at peace and doing well, and it is time for you to move on and begin living your life to its fullest again. Or, the angels may give you a sign to remind you that a loved one's presence is with you still, such as Arlene and the butterflies.

One step to healing from grief is to become in tune with signs that might come from your departed loved ones. These signs—such as a physical object that you notice has been moved, a bird or butterfly, a fragrance that reminds you of your loved one, or hearing the departed person's favorite song on the radio repeatedly—usually are accompanied by a strong feeling that the deceased is with you in spirit at that moment. The angels ask that you believe these occurrences are real, and to surrender any temptation to write the incident off as mere coincidence.

Engaging in private conversations with a departed loved one also can speed your own healing. For instance, you can write the person a letter, pouring out your heart. It's common for the living to communicate with the deceased by letter. If you try, don't be surprised to hear or feel replies coming from heaven. Again, the angels ask you to have faith that this is a real experience.

The angels also caution to avoid taking a rosy view of past days with loved ones, dreaming of the good old times when the person was still living. The angels say that the only time that truly exists is *now*. Heaven wants you to squeeze the maximum meaning and enjoyment out of each moment. Therefore, the angels often prescribe fun, relaxation, and other activities that bring you enjoyment and help others.

They also request healing a grieving mind and heart by enjoying the here and now. They love it when people laugh, have fun, and play. Anything you can do that promotes relaxation, such as taking a vacation, getting a massage, or spending time with friends, is a heavenly remedy for alleviating grief.

Throwing yourself into service work, either paid or volunteer, is another angelic prescription for relieving grief and loss. It's an important part of healing to engage in activities you find meaningful or enjoyable, so that you don't sit around all the time feeling sorry for yourself. When you are actively engaged in helping others, you realize how much you truly have to give, which raises self-esteem. This kind of work also helps you to appreciate how much you have and inspires you to count your blessings.

The angels also may guide someone who is grieving to appropriate professional assistance, such as a skilled counselor or a grief support group.

> Rx
>
> Ask the angels to connect you with the person you have lost. Devote some time to helping those with more devastating burdens than yours. Engage in activities that will help you enjoy the here and now.

Prescription for Personal Loss

Sometimes it isn't a deceased loved one you are grieving for, but some other equally shattering loss. It might be a dying love affair, a failed business venture, the loss of your investments, the theft of a valued keepsake, the destruction of your home by fire. These are all things in which you have a tremendous portion of the self invested, and the loss takes a part of you with it.

When this happens, in addition to feeling devastation and grief, you may tend to blame yourself and launch into a detailed review of all the mistakes you made that led to the loss. Instead, the angels suggest that you focus on what you want, not what you don't want. In other words, while it's therapeutic to review past situations and learn from mistakes, it's also important not to overanalyze or wallow in the past.

If you keep your thoughts rooted in the negative experiences of the past, you are perpetually doomed to keep repeating it. That is because your thoughts today create your experiences tomorrow. The angels prescribe that you strive to be flexible and open to change instead of resisting the new changes taking place in life.

Five years ago Eddie had lost the dream home he had designed and built in a devastating fire. Insurance covered much of the cost of repairs, and as the co-owner of a small construction firm, Eddie could afford to rebuild, or even purchase a new home outright. Eddie, however, continued to live in a small room in his retired father's apartment, where he'd moved after the fire.

"I just can't get excited about living anywhere else," Eddie told me, twisting a button on his shirt. "My dad's glad to have me there. That's not a problem. It's a bit awkward when I have a date, but usually whoever I am dating is understanding and we end up at her place. Everybody keeps asking when I am going to get a place of my own or build a new one. But I just can't get excited about the idea. It even upsets me. I put my dreams and hopes, my sweat and tears, and three years of my life into that house. It was perfect in every way. I think only the birth of my first child, whenever I marry, could thrill me more. I was happy every day I lived there. I used to walk through it at night savoring just how right each room and passageway was. Then, bang, it was all gone overnight. What's the use when that can happen?"

This is what the angels prescribed for Eddie. *"Time seems to be a major factor among humans whom we see with grief-filled hearts. They measure past time against present time, and compare wistfully how things once were before the big changes occurred. This focus on the past is, in our perspective, the key component that delays the bliss that could accompany your embracing of the newness which is upon you. When the spring thaws from winter, does the tree grieve the passing coldness? When the blossoms fade and turn to fruit, does the tree's bosom heave with heaviness? You are as much a part of evolving nature as the tree, and we ask you to view each passing change as God readying you for newness and growth."*

"Wow!" Eddie exclaimed. "I have always considered myself spiritual, and, well, I guess that puts me firmly in my place." He sighed heavily, as if releasing a great weight or something that he was dearly loathed to part with. "OK. I guess I can move on. I'm not going to build a home again. I'm not even going to purchase a house. There's a loft space I saw downtown in one of those funky old warehouse buildings you can do so much with. I guess I could take a lease on it. Playing around with the insides ought to keep me busy for a couple of years. By then, who knows, maybe

I will have found the right woman, gotten married, and built us a dream house of our own."

> Rx
>
> Stop focusing on the past. Embrace your new circumstance, with new possibility of fulfillment and happiness.

You are not meant to suffer, and you have a perpetual team of angelic counselors around you who are always available and have your best interests at heart. It's like having a combination of Superman, the Red Cross, and the Peace Corps assigned to you.

Not only do the angels want to help you with your personal happiness, but their assistance also extends to every aspect of your life. In the next chapter, the angels share Divine prescriptions for the problems that can beset you in the search for romance and love.

CHAPTER THREE

Prescriptions for Dating: Seeking Soulmates

No matter who they are or what their background, age, gender, religion, or sexual orientation is, everyone has one thing in common: They desire to feel loved. Everyone I meet—even those who try to appear tough, as if they don't need anyone—eventually tells me that they long for love.

It has long been known that the need for romance—receiving love from someone who is special to you and giving love back to them—is a universal human need. The scientific proof of this emerged with findings that people who are in romantic relationships tend to live longer and be happier and better adjusted.

Moreover, romance is as important to the well-being of men as it is to the well-being of women. Happily married men have longer life expectancies than divorced men. In fact, divorced men represent the largest social group who take their own lives each year. My own survey of several hundred businesswomen identified a good marriage as the main ingredient in their recipe for success and happiness.

This explains why people who aren't in a relationship usually put a great deal of time and energy into dating, dating services, singles groups, and singles bars, searching for a soulmate they can love. Frequently, this search is met with disappointment, heartbreak, rejection, pain, and scalding humiliation. When dating leads nowhere, and when someone cannot find the love he seeks, he wonders what is wrong with *him*, that he is so abandoned by God that he isn't even deserving of the gift of romance He bestows so freely on others.

The need for love is so much deeper than the potential agonies of dating that each weekend night, millions of people are found in restaurants and movie theaters, resuming their quest for romance once again. Whether the person is interested in casual dating, or whether she's searching for the love of her life, heaven wants to be involved every step of the way.

Sometimes, when people look across a table, they think they have found that special person they are looking for, the one, the mythical Mr. Right or Ms. Right. Then, to their disappointment, they later discover that the hunger for a soulmate and romance has misled them. How often have you dated a new person who appeared to be the one, only to find that you were ultimately incompatible?

In contrast to the glamorous social lives depicted on such television programs as *Beverly Hills, 90210*, dating soon becomes an empty and frustrating ritual to most singles. Surveys show many people stay in painful, unfulfilling relationships just to avoid the pain of being alone or the struggle to search for a different partner. Still, they long for a soulmate.

The angels know that you need to feel loved and that a romantic partnership is important in your life. They also know exactly what kind of partnership would truly enhance your life. For these reasons, your angels want to be intimately involved in your love life. They want you to ask them for help in all aspects of your search for potential partners. They can even help you overcome fears of rejection and commitment and tell you the truth about your intended's character.

However, many people who feel comfortable asking God for help in life-threatening situations or in the midst of a personal or professional crisis are hesitant to ask for help with something that seems as trivial, by comparison, as their love life. But, if a harmonious love life is also crucial to health and happiness, as science tells us, how can it be trivial to request assistance with it?

God, who is the source of love, considers your finding a loving, romantic partner so important that He even created angels who specialize in these issues and can be called on for extra help and support at any time. These are the romance angels, and they are God's gift to lovers. The arrow-sporting cherub Cupid is the traditional image of romantic love. There is a certain amount of truth to the Cupid image. As with many mythological creatures, Cupid is based on spiritual reality. The romance angels do appear as childlike cherubs who exude a deep pink glow. When my sixth sense shows me someone surrounded by romance angels, it's like looking at a giant pink valentine. Their presence tells me that the person has asked for angelic intervention in his or her love life, or that new love is on the way and the angels are there to usher it in.

The mission of the romance angels is to help you fulfill your need for romantic love by arranging for you to meet your soulmate or by providing a prescription for saving your foundering marriage. Some romance angels are specialists in bringing new lovers together. Others help to create romance in existing relationships.

Anyone can call on the romance angels. Since they are in abundance, you needn't worry that you are bothering them or misusing their time. It is their pleasure to help you experience romantic love, a necessity for your spiritual and emotional fulfillment.

Ask your angels to guide you to your soulmate, and then be sure to follow your gut feelings as they arise. The angels say, *"You will receive specific guidance, and it may not seem at first related to relationships. Just follow it anyway, because God will lead you to where you want to be."*

In fact, as soon as you utter your prayer, the angels will begin every effort to guide you in arranging a meeting with the person of your dreams. It's like a heavenly to-do list, telling you what steps you need to take to open yourself up to the romance they are trying to bring you, so that you can meet, attract, and enjoy the soulmate you long for. As usual, they will send this guidance to you through feelings, dreams, visions, or ideas.

The job of the romance angels doesn't end when their guidance has aided someone in successfully negotiating the complexities of dating and brought them together with a soulmate. Once the person crosses over the threshold from dating to commitment and becomes part of a couple, the angels work to maintain harmony and keep romance alive during the course of the relationship, as you will read in chapter 4. They are still with the couple when relationships deepen into long-term commitments and marriage, as you will learn in chapter 5.

Prescription for Finding a Soulmate

When you can't find love, the problem often turns out to lie within yourself. You may search desperately for a soulmate, brokenhearted over your inability to connect with the person of your dreams, never noticing that the angels have placed suitable romantic possibilities all around. Instead, you assume that heaven is not answering your prayers, when in fact the angels are all but shooting fireworks to point out potential soulmates.

You forge on, oblivious, pursuing the mistaken belief that there is only one soulmate for each human being, someone you were born to love and be loved by alone, who will share all your interests, make your heart go thump, and love you just the way you are. You will magically recognize this soulmate at first sight, and if you somehow miss this person, you will be doomed to spend the rest of your life settling for second or third best.

Some people put their entire lives on hold, drop or ignore dozens of potentially suitable mates, and subject themselves to years of frustration and loneliness while searching for this mythical beast. Other people pine constantly, believing their soulmate is the one who got away, most likely a past love for whom you now feel nostalgia. Perhaps this perfect lover was married, in the process of divorcing, living halfway across the country or around the globe, abusive, or an addict, or failed to understand the true potential of the relationship. Whatever the reason, this particular relationship is currently viewed through rose-colored glasses, and the fantasy that if only things had worked out differently, they would have made the ideal team.

The angels have taught me that the notion that there is only one soulmate for each person, and that people have to hunt for Mr. or Ms. Right until they find them (or go forever without), is one of the most damaging of all romantic myths. After all, you don't think God really would plant your only potential soulmate in Cleveland and then let you lose out on love because you had taken a job in San Francisco instead, do you? There are literally hundreds of potential soulmates, men and women, who could fulfill you spiritually, emotionally, and physically, waiting for you in every city, occupation, and social group you might possibly choose to be in at some point in your life.

Yet, few people seem to know this, and all too often I find my clients, young and old, women and men, actually preventing themselves from finding the love they seek because they are misled by the soulmate myth.

"When am I going to meet that one special guy?" Rose asked me. Rose, in her mid-thirties, owned an award-winning Italian restaurant she had inherited from her father, whose proud traditions she scrupulously maintained. Usually she was a striking, forceful brunette who could be seen almost any evening of the week at her establishment, fully in command of everything around her.

But today her eager face searched mine imploringly, with an expression of sheer hunger for the companionship she yearned for so badly. Rose was beginning to feel her biological clock ticking. "I feel like time is running out for me. I have looked everywhere. My church, my business, I run into so many people there. I've had my fair share of boyfriends and some of them were serious. But in the end, I was never completely sure about any of them. You know, none of them seemed to live up to my conception of my ideal soulmate. I keep thinking that if I wait enough, I will run into him. We will just look at each other and things will click. And we will make great love, and be an ideal match in every way, and spend the rest of our lives together with few hassles or arguments. I want to be free when he appears. I don't want to find myself married to someone I thought was my soulmate, and then wake up one day and, bang, I run into my real soulmate."

"Rose," the angels answered, *"you do have a soulmate awaiting you, but perhaps not in quite the way you believe. For the truth is that you, like all people, have many potential soulmates, not just one. And each is someone whose love and companionship you would find very fulfilling.*

"Each of these potential soulmates has the ability to nourish and heal a different region of your mind, heart, or soul. You have already passed up several ideal soulmates we have sent your way, because you didn't want to be with them in case there was someone better coming along.

"But be of good cheer. You will find the kind of satisfying, soulmate marriage you seek soon. When the time is right, we will guide you toward the person your soul knows will perform the healing or teach you the lesson you need to take the next step in your own growth and progress. If your soul needs most to learn about freedom, you will be drawn to someone who will encourage you in the effort. Or, if you have hungered for a great, passionate, physical love all your life, you will be drawn to someone who can fulfill that part of your soul. Or, if you need to learn patience, you may be drawn to a very patient man."

Rose looked relieved. "When you put it that way," she said, "I could kick myself for being such a romantic fool. There are a couple of guys I went with, especially Armand, I should have committed to while I had the chance. The angels probably sent him to me. I will be wiser in the future."

Free of the illusions that there was only one right soulmate for her, Rose began to see that there were several men she knew who could be soulmate matches. The last time I heard, she was engaged, and she credited the angels' Divine prescription for her newfound happiness.

Rx

Don't let the myth of the "one perfect soulmate" blind you to the many wonderful potential soulmates the angels have placed in your path.

Prescription for Attracting the Ideal Soulmate

Sometimes you may not find a soulmate because you have set your aim too high. The kind of person you aspire to have as a lover is not the kind of person who would want you as you currently are. The other person is on such a different level that if you were them and they were you, you wouldn't want a relationship with yourself either.

To make this a little more concrete: someone working on anger and communications might dream of a calm, harmonious life with a calm, harmonious mate. But a calm, harmonious person who desires a calm, harmonious life is hardly likely to want a difficult, angry lover. The same can be said of an out-of-shape person who desires a well-defined athlete oozing with health, or, of an addict whose fantasy is of a loving spouse who has it all together.

There is nothing wrong with setting your aim reasonably high. That is precisely what God and the angels desire you to do. Soulmates have many functions, and one of them is to call out your best. Sometimes the ideal soulmate you hunger for attracts you not only because of his own many wonderful qualities, but also because the higher spiritual level calls you to move toward him, and because he represents the kind of person you aspire to be.

The problem comes when you expect something (or someone) far out of your reach to be delivered to you in a neatly wrapped package the moment you envision it. When you lose sight of how absurd this is, you are setting yourself up for disappointment, rejection, and many hours of loneliness, misery, and grief. The law of attraction states you're more likely to pull in a soulmate who is on the same spiritual, physical, and mental range plane as you are. The angels say there are two choices when you find yourself in this situation. You can lower your expectations and settle for a soulmate a little closer to your own level. Or, you can put in the effort to improve yourself and become the kind of person your ideal soulmate would love.

This is always a touchy area for me when working with clients like Carmen, a thirty-five-year-old registered nurse who was practically begging the angels, through me, to tell her how she could make headway with Russell, the hospital's new head of security.

The angels began showing me an almost split-screen movie with images suggesting the two were currently miles apart in temperament and taste. I asked Carmen if she could tell me a little bit about herself.

What came out was the picture of a chronically in-debt woman, prone to squabbling with family, friends, even co-workers, whose emotional and private life had been a series of up-and-down roller-coaster rides. I then asked Carmen to describe Russell.

The picture that emerged was of a well-dressed, well-groomed, college-educated former Navy SEAL, who had a stock market portfolio and was in complete control of himself and his surroundings. "He's so different than the kind of men I have been going out with," she gushed. "Russell is someone a woman could feel safe spending her life with. Tell me what I have to do to land him."

I knew that what the angels were communicating to me was the last thing Carmen wanted to hear. Still, I reminded myself that I was only a messenger whose job was to deliver their prescriptions. I repeated what the angels said: *"Beloved Carmen, what you ask is not impossible. But for it to come about, many steps would have to be taken. You and this man both have in common that you are on the spiritual path, and that is one element in him that calls to you. But you are at two different points on that spiritual path. Neither of you would presently be a good fit for the other. We could bring you a partner now who is on the same level you are. Or, if you waited and worked hard to advance yourself on the spiritual path by making many so-called lifestyle changes, then in a year or two there might be a future for you and this man, Russell, who so attracts you."*

Carmen glared at me. I anticipated an emotional outburst of some kind and asked the angels for intervention. Then she laughed and said, like so many of my clients after they have digested a reading, "I guess I knew that. I was just hoping there was a way the angels could pass some kind of miracle and make me someone he'd want right now. But you know, Russell is worth it. I've been getting tired of the kind of life I've been living and the kind of person I am. I think I would like to learn to be more like him. Calm and composed, but caring, too. He meditates, I know. Maybe I could begin by taking a meditation class. And maybe I could find a counselor or some kind of group to help me smooth out a few of my own emotional kinks. It's not impossible."

A year later I received a phone call from Carmen. She wasn't dating Russell, but she sounded much different, more centered and at peace with herself. Carmen said she was in an anger management group and a yoga class, and had met a wonderful, stable man who worked downstairs in the hospital cafeteria.

Rx

When your ideal soulmate is more ideal than you, take steps toward making yourself a better person, too. Then, through the infallible law of attraction, you will draw him or her to you.

Prescription for Cultivating Realistic Expectations

People date and date, but some never find the soulmate they are looking for even when she or he is right before their eyes. That's because of another terribly misleading myth that seems to have confused many people about the nature of romance: that their true love will be not just a partner, but a twin, someone who is like them in every way. This soulmate will share the same values, love the same music, share the same personal and religious values, enjoy the same recreations, down to listening to Led Zeppelin's "Stairway to Heaven" while eating cold spaghetti on a rainy Saturday night.

The angels say that although you will share much in common with a true soulmate, his purpose is not to serve as your twin or mirror. If your soulmate was your twin in every way, the angels warn, you should soon tire of her and become bored, just as you do of yourself from time to time.

Of course, in the initial phases of a new relationship, every couple tends to focus on their similarities. Your new friend loudly exclaims, "I love *Xena: Warrior Princess*." And you respond, "Really? Me too." Or, they may explain that they are an acrophobe, and you say, "I'm afraid of heights, too." It may seem as though you have found a soulmate with whom you share everything in common. It is only later that your differences with each other begin to emerge and make themselves manifest.

This doesn't mean you and your newfound companion are trying to bamboozle each other into thinking you share more things in common than you actually do. Instead, the two of you are busily searching through your memory banks, trying to find matches that you share. This is a natural process, but it can also delude you into believing that you have found the kind of soulmate relationship you see in the movies, where lovers never disagree on what kind of food they like to eat, or what they think about the next presidential election. Typically, after the six-month mark, most lovers take off their rose-colored glasses and begin noticing their differences instead of their similarities.

Frank, a handsome young newspaper photographer of twenty-seven, came to me in desperation over his love life. His problem wasn't getting women or even getting one to agree to marry him. He was quite successful in the romance department. But none of them turned out to be his vision of the future wife and mother of his future children. Knowing that with this dating history he must have encountered and passed up many who would have made suitable soulmates, I asked Frank to tell me what he thought a soulmate was.

"You know," Frank said confidently, "a feminine me. I guess I want someone who is into all the same things that I'm into. Someone who is outdoorsy, athletic, shares the same values, loves to party, likes to spend weekends watching sports on TV or fishing, digs jazz, is wild about stock-car races, votes Republican, gets along with my friends. I've looked and looked, but I can't seem to be able to find a woman who is all that wrapped up in one package. Once in a while I meet someone who seems like it at first, but later it always turns out we diverge in some important interest or viewpoint somewhere along the line."

His angels said, *"Frank, we do not ask you to compromise in any way. But there needs to be some correction in the way you view what God intends the purpose of a soulmate to be. Like so many, you have made yourself experience needless suffering because you believe a soulmate is meant to be your twin, a mirror image of you in female form, someone who acts, thinks, and talks like you.*

If you had such, you quickly would become bored. After all, do you not have moments now when you bore yourself, when you do not like yourself? Imagine fifty years of sameness without being challenged to think new thoughts or try new experiences.

"Your interests are varied and admirable, and you have many friends of both genders with whom to enjoy pleasure. Do not seek to place your marriage into such a narrow category as being based on unanimity of outside interests. Of course, you should share many interests. More importantly, look for a companion who sets your heart afire and who also leads a compatible separate life with separate interests. In this way, you two will have much to share. So much better to seek complementary interests rather than conduct a lifelong search for identical interests."

After a moment of shock and self-reflection, Frank chuckled. "My friends have been telling me the same thing. I guess everyone is right." Frank decided that his view of an ideal soulmate was unrealistic.

> Rx
>
> A soulmate is not your twin or someone like yourself. We are meant to reinforce each other in ways in which we are similar and to stretch each other in areas in which we are different.

Prescription for Attracting the Right Partner

The old saying "Be careful what you wish for. You may get it," applies doubly to romance. God and the angels are happy to be heavenly matchmakers and bring you together with a soulmate who meets your specifications exactly as you stated them. All you have to do is ask. A word of caution: Take care when drawing up a wish list of what you want in a partner. As I have discovered the hard way, heaven often answers your prayers literally.

Many years ago, when I was a divorced mother of two, I asked God to help me find a soulmate and husband. I wrote a three-page description of what I wanted in a mate, specifying a romantic man who would send me a lot of flowers. I'd successfully used similar types of lists for manifesting career and personal goals for many years.

Within a week I met Johnny the CPA. Without me ever mentioning my love for bouquets, Johnny began sending red roses to my office. Every day my secretary, Donna, would bring me two vases of roses sent from Johnny. I'd get one bouquet in the morning and another in the afternoon. It got to the point of embarrassment to receive this public display of affection at work, when I was the senior therapist and administrator of a conservative psychiatric hospital.

While I found Johnny's attention flattering, I realized that for all the time and detail I'd lavished on my description, I'd left off a vital ingredient. I'd forgotten to specify that I be attracted to him when we met. The truth was, I wasn't even interested in Johnny at all, except as a brotherly friend.

I went back to the drawing board and wrote an even more detailed list. This time I included traits such as "I'm attracted to him" and because Johnny's overintensity had disturbed me, I included, "He wants to get married but is willing to take our committed relationship at a slow pace."

I turned in my love letter to God by feeling the sensation of completely putting it into His hands. This led to feelings and thoughts of Divine guidance, which quickly culminated in me meeting the man on my list. A handsome and talented French Canadian came into my life. We were mutually attracted, and he wanted to get married following a long engagement, just like me. Everything seemed perfect, as it often does in the beginning.

I soon found that his difficulty with the English language was a difficulty for me. His primary language was French, and he was unfamiliar with many English words and phrases. While it was terribly romantic to hear him sing me love songs in French, I craved having a deep and stimulating conversation.

It was back to the drawing board again. This time I went for broke and created a manifestation list: three pages of details about everything I knew I wanted and didn't want in my new husband. I included only characteristics that were important to me. Other things that didn't matter, such as height, I left off the list.

Soon I received Divine directives to go to certain places and engage in specific activities. I followed these orders to a T. The result? Within three weeks I bumped into a man in a French restaurant and our eyes locked. The room spun, as if nothing else existed but him and me. We sat down and "interviewed" each other, rapidly comparing notes to see if the other person was "the one." We were married within three years, and all the things on my list were his natural characteristics.

A few years ago I taught relationship classes for single men and women, in which I spoke about my list and manifestation methods. The students who tried this spiritual approach to dating reported wonderful success.

One woman told me that she had created and carried around a "wish list" about her future husband. She talked affirmatively about the man on her list, knowing that she was going to meet him soon. She even called him her Wish List Man. Months later she met and eventually married the man on her list. She excitedly told me, "Guess what our last name is? It's Wishner. I think I manifested this last name because I kept referring to him as my Wish List Man." So she's now Mrs. Wishner.

To try this approach to manifesting soulmates and other goals, simply take a sheet of paper and write down all the qualities you think your ideal soulmate would have (you can even make a separate list of qualities you don't want a mate to have). Don't rush into it; give yourself a few days. That way, you won't be likely to leave out anything important. Give your list or lists to God and the angels. To cover yourself if you have made any major mistake of omission or inclusion, say, "This or something better, please." You don't want to limit the angels by giving them a restrictive outline of what *you* think will make you happy.

> Rx
>
> When it comes to soulmates, be clear, before you begin looking, about what it is you are looking for. Otherwise, you are likely to find yourself stuck with something you didn't expect or wish you hadn't asked for.

Prescription for Perfectionism

Another way you can be the cause of your own heartbreak in your search for a soulmate is by rejecting ideal candidates because they aren't absolutely perfect. Some people make their lives a living hell, even drive themselves to physical breakdown and suicide, by demanding that their own behavior and work be absolutely perfect. They do not allow any tolerance for making an error or mistake—ever. Other people do the same, with the same self-sabotaging results when it comes to soulmates. They want a soulmate who is absolutely perfect, without a single flaw or weakness. Though their hearts are breaking, they are the ones breaking them. Their expectations are so high that no mere mortal could fulfill them.

These individuals are in the same position as the character in the old Sufi story, in which the man spends his life searching for the perfect wife. When he meets her, she turns him down because she is looking for the perfect man.

This was the case with my client Kathleen, a sales executive in her late thirties who had dated many men over the years but never found one who met her "standards." Kathleen felt pressure to marry while she was still in her childbearing years, yet as far as she was concerned, no real prospects were in sight.

Being in sales, Kathleen was acquainted with a wide variety of men. Many of them were attractive, well-mannered successes who seemed to be any woman's *beau ideal*. But as Kathleen cataloged them for me, she pointed out a fatal flaw in each one that prevented him from fitting the bill. He might have been too short, too tall, too fat, too skinny, too romantic or not romantic enough, too good a lover or too poor a lover, too absorbed in his career or not absorbed enough, too tight with his money, too much of a free spender. "In short," she said, "every time I meet a guy who I think at first glance could be the one, when I get to know him better he's got ten other girlfriends, or he's on my case about my weight all the time, or he's a workaholic."

Kathleen was practically panicking about her future when she blurted out, "Do you think I'll ever meet the perfect man?"

The angels explained, *"This perfectionism is your shield against actually finding a mate, because of your fears of commitment and rejection. You believe you desire a deep, intimate soulmate relationship, but deep inside, Kathleen, you are frightened to commit yourself to such a relationship. Insisting that your soulmate have no imperfections or human foibles is the excuse you use for not committing yourself to a relationship. Many times you have been with someone who might have been the man of your dreams, but you have searched for some flaw, then retreated, feeling justified that you have found one.*

"To bring a soulmate into your own life, you must heal your feelings of being vulnerable and hurt. We can help you to mend your heart. Merely ask us to enter your dreams and carry away all your fears of love and intimacy, of sharing and mingling yourself with another. Ask us to help you forgive your parents, past lovers, and yourself for old wounds that they have caused you and that you have caused them. Invite us to help you release the fear of being loved and of giving love. With our assistance, you'll soon be willing to let go of your perfection-

ism, opening the way for a relationship with a man who genuinely loves you, and whom you love as well."

Kathleen's expression showed relief. She was clearly pleased by the news. Right away, the angels began showing me a movie of Kathleen with a future partner. I narrated what I saw to her. "Yes, I do see a soulmate," I said. "I don't see, though, that he is one hundred percent perfect by your present standards. He's got glasses, a good sense of humor in a private way, but is shy as opposed to outspoken. He's got some mother issues, but hey. You meet this man out of the house, such as at a library, bookstore, or a place of study. I feel a lot of books around this man, as if he's an avid reader. He's not Fabio or anything, but you definitely find him attractive.

"I see you both traveling together because of his job. I also see a train, and it feels like a European rail vacation. I do see you could be very happy with this man and very fulfilled in terms of companionship, mutual respect. I sense warmth that you would call romantic, but not fiery passion and gaga romance. It feels like a good relationship that is committed and loving."

Kathleen sighed deeply and said, "Well, I must admit that when you were first describing him to me, I was frightened. He doesn't sound like the gorgeous, with-it, Mr. Perfect I've been dreaming about. But you know what?" She sat up straighter and said earnestly, "This sounds absolutely wonderful to me. I think I am beginning to be able to live without perfect. I'm beginning to realize I am more in need of someone who can be my best friend and a romantic lover. This man sounds like just what I need."

Kathleen was transferred to New Orleans a few weeks later, and I haven't heard from her. I know that if she stuck to her resolve and asked the angels to help her overcome her perfectionism, she will have found a soulmate the angels think is perfect for her by now.

Rx

Don't hold your breath waiting for someone who is absolutely perfect. Someone might be the soulmate for you and still have a few imperfections.

Prescription for Those Who Can't Find Anyone

The saying, "God helps those who help themselves" holds true when one is searching for a soulmate. You can't expect God to steer a likely soulmate into your arms if you aren't placing yourself where a likely soulmate is to be found. The angels want to fulfill your romantic wishes, but you have to help get the process in motion by first contributing a modicum of faith and effort. The angels can then start working to bring your desires to fruition in a most amazing way. Rather than being a passive activity, as some people think, the angels say enlisting the assistance of heaven requires human participation.

Too many people decide they want a soulmate, then sit back and expect God and the angels to do the rest. They stick to the same habits and routine that have previously failed to bring them into contact with a soulmate, and wait for a miracle. When nothing happens, they feel let down and disappointed. They bemoan a fate that keeps them mateless. They even begin to lose faith in God and the angels. "I've prayed and prayed for a soulmate," they tell me, "but where is my soulmate? I thought you said God and the angels always fulfill our prayers. Do the angels have it in for me? Or is it all a fake?"

I am really reminded of the old joke in which a man prays each week that he will win the lottery. He sits by the phone every Friday waiting for the call that will announce he has hit the jackpot. After weeks of disappointment, he looks up angrily toward heaven and complains, "God, what's wrong? Every week I pray to you, but I never win the lottery." And God answers, "So buy a ticket already."

You can't expect to find your soulmate unless you become actively involved in the quest, too. What do you want the angels to do? Drop your soulmate at your front door? That's fine if you want to marry the pizza delivery person or the mail carrier. If they were your soulmate, you'd already be hitched.

If you have been praying for love and no one seems to be answering your prayers, you may be clinging to habits and routines that are restricting your opportunities and creating barriers that prevent you from encountering a soulmate. After all, a lonely man who never dates a woman taller than himself, or a lonely woman who spends all her free time cleaning her apartment could be wasting tears on their single status. They need only to make an effort to meet the angels halfway and venture outside their normal routine. Both could be denying themselves the very opportunity that would lead to their dream relationship. This is what the angels told my client Emmanuel.

During our session, Emmanuel, a thirty-eight-year-old printing foreman who had never married, complained that his problem wasn't finding a soulmate; it was finding any woman at all. A quiet and unassuming man who considered himself spiritually minded, Emmanuel explained that he had been looking for a potential wife and mate for years with no success. He couldn't seem to find anyone to date.

"I really think I'd make a good husband and father," he remarked, "but lately I'm wondering if maybe God isn't hearing my prayers or if I'm just not meant to have a wife and family. I haven't been out on a date in years, and I never meet any women at all."

After a few moments, the angels responded, *"We have heard your prayers for help for many years, and we are trying to assist you. We have been urging you to leave your house more often during your time away from your work so that we can arrange for you to meet your love. However, you are resisting this guidance. You go straight home after work and watch television, and you wonder why you are lonely. When the weekend comes, you sit down in front of the TV and have your meals delivered to your door. When co-workers invite you to gatherings, you always tell yourself you will attend, but then you decide you are too tired, and hibernate in your home again. Indeed, we believe you may be somewhat shy and fearful of venturing forth only to be turned down by someone whose love you might very much like to have. In this way, you have missed meeting a number of women who would have made you happy for life. We are unable to help you unless you assist us by following the guidance that we are sending through your thoughts and feelings."*

Emmanuel's mouth fell open and his eyes grew wide as he listened to the angels. "That's incredible. I saw a flyer about an exercise class in my neighborhood. A couple of times I almost went and signed up for it. Each time I talked myself out of it."

"You won't be alone for long," his angels prescribed, *"but you must make alterations in your normal pattern of activity in order to meet the soulmate we would like to bring into your sphere. We ask you to attend that exercise course; we arranged for you to receive its flyer. Yes, that was us urging you to go. We also desire you to act on your co-workers' invitations. Otherwise, you will never place yourself in a position to encounter the love you seek. "*

Emmanuel called me several days later, wondering where "she" was. "I've joined the exercise class, but I haven't met anyone yet," he said.

I chuckled and advised him to give the angels time. After all, he'd been on the playing field for only a week. The angels were indeed working, pulling all the strings required to place his soulmate in his path. They added, *"You not only have to leave your home, but you also must extend yourself to people you meet by making friendly eye contact, with a smile and a greeting. The woman you seek is sensitive and shy like you. She won't approach you, especially with your present standoffish manner. You must extend warmth to others. You can easily do this by telling yourself that each person you meet has God within them. Feel your love for God each time you see or talk with anyone, and your warmth will radiate automatically. You will attract many friends, including the woman you seek."*

Emmanuel promised to be more patient and to make an even greater effort to get out and mix with other people. Apparently that was all he needed to do, because the next time I heard from him he proudly announced that a very promising woman had recently joined his class. They had dated, seemed attracted to each other, and had a lot in common, and it looked as if things might become serious. "I guess the angels do know what they're talking about," Emmanuel admitted.

Rx

If you are failing to encounter a soulmate, don't stay in your well-worn rut. Find a way to be wherever you are most likely to find the kind of person with whom you would like to be.

CHAPTER FOUR

Prescriptions for Romance: Connecting with Soulmates

If you're like most people, your romantic difficulties don't end when you find a soulmate. In fact, they are just beginning. Once you are coupled in a committed relationship that defines you and your partner as a twosome—whether it's an informal, silent understanding or a formal engagement—you often find yourselves facing conflicts you never imagined when you were first dating.

The better the two of you get to know each other, the more your rough edges are likely to rub together and create friction. Or, you may see your soulmate in everyone you meet and devote all your time to attempting to make a committed relationship out of what is often only a sexual or emotional convenience for the other person. Some of you even waste years of your lives trying to change a partner you have "settled" for into the soulmate of your dreams. Or, you seem to "wake up" when it's too late and find yourself in relationships with destructive, abusive lovers. For many, the problem isn't so much finding someone to be with, as it is finding someone who will commit. For a rare few, the difficulty lies in finding too many soulmates and dealing with the conflicts that result.

When it comes to the romance that follows finding a soulmate, the possibilities for heartbreak and suffering are tenfold. After all, now you have moved beyond a casual relationship and invested much of what you are, something of what you hope to be, and almost all of your heart in what you are now seeing as a partnership. When anything threatens your love affair, it threatens not only something that means so very much to you, but also the deepest parts of your self. Those who have experienced this—and that includes almost everyone—know just how horrible and devastating such a threat can be.

I can't emphasize enough that the work of the romance angels doesn't stop when they help people acquire a soulmate. It continues throughout the relationship till death do them part, whether it's the death of the partnership or of one or both partners. The angels say that each person you fall in love with or who falls in love with you is here to teach you one or more important lessons (and vice versa). If the lesson is simple and can be quickly absorbed, you may turn out to be only a temporary part of each other's lives even though you both feel passionate love for each other. If there are several lessons, or if they are lessons that are difficult to absorb, you and your partner may be together for years. The angels remain by your side, attempting to guide both of you toward the maximum possible healing and harmony.

Prescription for Relationship Friction

How often has this happened to you? Your search for a soulmate is over. At long last you have found Ms. or Mr. Right. The two of you settle down and begin a life together. Then the friction starts. You and your partner are like oil and water. The two of you turn out to have habits, needs, and ways of communicating that are very different, in some cases seemingly antithetical to each other, in other cases destructive to each other.

The friction such relationships create leads to unnecessary arguments, shouting matches, hateful words, hurt feelings, and guilt. Often it results in explosive, painful breakups.

Occasionally, when passions run high and partners do not allow the angels to intervene, it explodes into physical violence. Many people think that the course of soulmate relationships will always run true, that there never should be any friction or conflict or butting heads. The angels say this delusion is based on the wrong idea of what a soulmate relationship is all about.

Think of a soulmate as an earth angel (a person who has been unknowingly selected for a Divine mission). If you're arguing with your soulmate you may think of him as anything but angelic. Yet, however aggravating he is, however much you might drive each other crazy, heaven has sent this earth angel to you to carry out a certain mission. He can help you grow, heal you, show you how to find your inner strength, or teach you the true meaning of patience, kindness, loyalty, and love (sometimes by possessing these qualities, sometimes precisely because he lacks them).

In this sense, soulmates also function much like guardian angels in that they nudge you to carve out time for your priorities, inspire you to be your very best, to follow your passions, and to make a difference in the world. The ways a soulmate accomplishes this can sometimes make you wish you'd never met the angel in the first place. Just as you become irritated at your angels when they push you to improve your life, so you often become furious with your soulmate when her motivational efforts as an earth angel make you feel controlled and bullied.

My neighbor Brad knew that his wife, Lisa, wanted to finish her master's degree so that she could begin a teaching career. Brad saw Lisa procrastinating and putting off working on her thesis. He looked for ways to gently but clearly motivate Lisa into action. He cut out magazine pictures of people graduating and put them under Lisa's pillow; he created a mock M.A. degree and hung it on the refrigerator; he offered to do the laundry and dishes so that Lisa would have extra time at night. Lisa constantly told Brad to back off. She felt pressured by his incessant hints to get to work on her writing.

"Doesn't he know that I'll work on it when I'm good and ready?" she complained to me. Lisa seemed about to explode. "It's not like I'm a child. Sure, I keep putting it off. And sure, I'm sick of working part-time in the library. But I'll get around to it eventually. I just need more time to think about it and get myself together."

The angels were quick to respond. *"We can understand your annoyance. But put yourself in Brad's shoes. He knows how badly you want to change your present condition and begin your work as a teacher. He hears you voice that longing every day, though you may not be aware how often you voice it. And then you are annoyed when he does everything he can to help nudge you along the way. Brad does what he does because he loves and cares about you. You have a tendency to become stuck and afraid to go forward. Helping give you the all-important push to get started is one of the purposes Brad serves is in your life."*

Lisa looked somewhat mollified. "I guess that's one reason I was attracted to him. He supported me in everything. I guess I wasn't looking at what I could be learning from his presence in my life."

Lisa was determined to be more responsive to and appreciative of her soulmate and earth angel. Something must have worked, for a year or so later Lisa successfully completed her thesis and received her degree. Perhaps she simply was motivated to finish it because she was tired of Brad's prodding. Still, Lisa hugs him publicly whenever people congratulate her on her degree.

Rx

Before you write a soulmate off because you butt heads with each other, look for the lesson.

Prescription for Soulmate-itis

You may find yourself so filled with the image of the soulmate we all long to find that you project it onto every new person you date. You become instantly convinced that this love is "the one" and announce it to all of your friends. In doing so, you are setting up your life and that of your partner for tragedy and suffering by devoting all your efforts toward making the relationship work. You have been misled into believing that, because that person is your soulmate, it must be worth it. I call this soulmate-itis, a pernicious romantic disease that has been the cause of much unnecessary heartbreak.

When soulmate-itis strikes, you act impulsively, pushing the other person to see the relationship your way and to commit herself long before the two of you can truly know one another. You suffer painful consequences when you realize you are committed to a fantasy of what your partner potentially could be. Instead of waiting for Divine timing and the angels to help manifest a soulmate relationship, you rush into whatever partnership seems readily available. Breakups and divorce are the painful result of this haste.

My client Terri is an attractive young television reporter who doesn't flaunt her natural beauty. During our session, she gazed at me intently and asked whether marriage was a possibility with a man she had just met. "I feel like I've known Marcus my whole life, even though we've only known each other for a couple of months," she began. "We can talk to each other about anything and we have great sex. I am sure this man is my soulmate. I've been prodding him to rent a house together. Do you see us living together and marrying in our future?"

Guided by the angels, I asked Terri if she had ever had this experience before. "Oh, yes," she replied. "I met a wonderful man last year. I thought we were star-crossed lovers, fated to be together forever. But we were like cats and dogs once we got to know each other. And there was that weatherman last spring. I would have sworn we were soulmates." Terri blushed. "Actually, I guess I've felt that way a time or two before. Is that what you're getting at?"

"Dear Terri, you are searching for a soulmate so hard you are beginning to see them in everyone around you. You are just beginning to know Marcus. As yet, you cannot know him well enough to be certain he is a soulmate. Instead of convincing yourself he is the man you are looking for, use these early months of your relationship with Marcus to discover more about him and about yourself. Set a solid foundation of continued friendship, respect, and trust, and allow things to evolve slowly along their natural course. Do not force the relationship to be anything other than what it naturally becomes. If you force a rose to open instead of allowing it to bloom naturally, you will destroy its beauty."

Terri looked deflated. "I suppose what the angels are saying is that I am just going to have to be patient and wait until the right man comes along on his own. I can't make it happen all by myself."

"This relationship looks like it could very well last for a long time," the angels elaborated. *"Whether this is your last and permanent relationship is not the point. This relationship will help you with your self-esteem, and any future relationships will be enhanced because you were part of it. Marcus is one of your soulmates, yes; however, we must remember that we all have several soulmates for different purposes. A part of his purpose is to allow you to know that you are lovable. One of the reasons why you continue rushing into relationships is because you desperately want to be loved and feel insecure about whether someone would love you. We say to you that Marcus will help you to heal this fear, but only if you allow it to naturally occur. Otherwise, you will never believe that he or any man truly loves the true you. You will always suspect that you manipulated them into a relationship or marriage, and you will never have the opportunity to learn how lovable you really are."*

"Do the angels mean that my relationship with him won't be permanent?" Terri asked.

"We're not saying that at all. The future is not written. The choices you both make will determine it. We are simply asking you to enjoy each moment now with this man, instead of trying to capture the future and put it into a tiny little box. Such capturing actions deaden your love energies and are a chief reason why humans turn to another partner to recapture the magic that is lost once a relationship becomes contained. When you attempt to trap the whole of a relationship, you yourself begin to feel trapped. Keep your mind focused on enjoying each moment that you are together, and the future will automatically take care of itself."

Terri's eyes grew moist and her jaw fell open as she realized the truth of her angels' words. Terri knew she had been focusing too hard on seeing Marcus as her soulmate and needing to be with him forever. She hadn't been appreciating their time together. She left the session with a new resolve to stay in the moment and not get caught up in the fantasy that every new man she met must be her soulmate.

Rx

Don't push to make someone your soulmate or to bring a soulmate relationship about. Let nature and the angels take their course. You may later remember that there was a "sign" of some kind when you met your lifetime soulmate, but remember that you also had a "special feeling" about many people you met along the way who weren't.

Prescription for Too Many Soulmates

For a conflicted few, the lack of a potential soulmate isn't the problem—it's having more than one potential soulmate and not knowing which to choose. I've found that when you can't decide between several lovers, it means that none of them is right. Each prospective partner embodies some of the qualities you are seeking in an ideal love. Your physical needs, for instance, are met by Shawn, but you find conversation with him dull and boring. You love your intellectual repartee with Nelson, but he doesn't light your physical fire. Leonard is a terrific partner for backpacking and tennis but is only fair in bed or as a conversationalist. You wind up dating all three, wondering which you should choose, or if there's one lover out there somewhere who could meet all of your needs.

This may sound like a much lesser evil than having no prospective soulmate in sight. But when many hearts become entangled with one person, someone is bound to have his heart broken. If all involved are caring, compassionate people, then everyone will experience pain before the situation is resolved. Perhaps the most devastating consequence might be to marry one of those prospects, only to find that because he lacked all the qualities of your ideal soulmate, the relationship did not work out.

When you find yourself torn between two or more potential soulmates, each with different qualities that touch you, the angels' prescription is not to settle for less than the whole of what you want. Look for one partner who meets all of these needs. The angels have difficulty understanding why people compromise in their love life with a partner who is almost good enough, rather than manifesting one who truly mirrors their desires. Nobody has to settle, because your Divine heritage as a Child of God means you deserve the best.

Thirty-three-year-old Carl, a successful young architect, was dating three women, Caroline, Deborah, and Sui Lee. "I'm kind of in love with all three of them. Or, I think I could be," Carl said. "There are things I really value about each of them. I think all three would make great mates and mothers. Sometimes I think I want to make it permanent with Caroline. Then I think no, it's Sui Lee. Sometimes I think Deborah is the one. I just can't seem to make up my mind. How do I know which one is right for me?"

I took a deep breath and mentally repeated the names of the three women, telling my angels to connect me with their guardian angels. My angels and their angels presented me with a lot of information rapidly, and I repeated it to Carl as it was given to me.

"None is right for the romantic goals you seek to fulfill. They are right for someone who is looking for women with their special qualities, but you have your own needs for a soulmate who combines certain qualities each of these wonderful women possess. This doesn't mean that anything is wrong with Caroline, Deborah, or Sui Lee. It's simply a matter of none of them having all the specific styles, outlooks, and goals that you seek. Trying to force yourself to settle down with any one of them would not solve the problem; it would just lead to pain and frustration."

Carl sighed. "So I have to begin my search all over again?"

"We don't recommend pursuing any of these women at the present time. All have genuine feelings for you, and they would try to change to keep and please you. However, they are not capable of providing all the needs you have romantically. You would only be wasting your own time and theirs and end up causing each other much grievous pain in the end.

"Instead, retreat a bit from all three women and spend some time alone in nature, which is so important to you, and in meditating about the qualities in these women that you want to see incorporated in the woman you dream of spending your life with. We urge you to write a letter to your future soulmate's guardian angels. Don't worry—by merely writing it, you will ensure it is delivered to that future love's angels. Ask them to help bring you together."

Carl was intrigued by the idea of writing the letter and agreed to try it. I told him to sit down with a pad of paper and write to his future soulmate's guardian angels, asking to bring the two of them together. I told him to pour out his heart and not worry about grammar, spelling, or formality, that the most important ingredient was sincerity. I suggested he might say something like the following, but in his own words:

Dear Guardian Angel of My Future Soulmate,

I ask your assistance in helping me to meet and recognize my soulmate. Please help me to attain the health and happiness I need in order to be a compatible partner to my soulmate. Please arrange for circumstances so that we can find one another. Guide me very clearly with explicit instructions so I will meet my soulmate without delay. Please help me to stay peaceful and serene during the time before I meet my soulmate, and help me to stay filled with peace and inner love.

Thank you.

Carl must have written that letter, because I received a letter from him recently. He is married to a woman he brags has all the qualities he wanted wrapped up in one package. He is glad he didn't settle for less. And he is the proud father of a one-year-old.

Rx

When you are torn between potential soulmates, each with a part of what you are looking for in your ideal soulmate, don't compromise in this most important of all the areas of your life. Continue seeking until you find one person who meets all these needs.

Prescription for Trying to Change People

Have you ever broken your own heart trying to mold someone into the ideal soulmate, only to fail completely and lose the person in the end? Most people have done that at one time or another in their search for love. They meet someone with both lovable and not-so-lovable characteristics. They fall in love with a fantasy of what that person could be like instead of what he or she actually is. Leaping headfirst into the relationship, they attempt to cajole, bully, or seduce their partner into conforming to their ideal image.

If you are suffering from soulmate-itis, as discussed earlier in this chapter, you imagine how perfect the relationship would be if only you could entice your partner into wanting sex more often. Or, you fantasize how successful your partner could be if only he saw all his own good qualities and developed some ambition. Or, you believe you and your partner are a perfect match physically and mentally and could move to a farm to raise corn and children, only if you could just love your partner enough to make her give up gambling, drinking, cheating, trying to make a living as a stock-car racer, doing crack cocaine, or some other undesirable lifestyle habit. When nothing changes, and your partner resists your attempts to make her over into something she is not, you experience frustration, disappointment, anger, hostility, heartbreak, and even fear.

The trouble here, the angels say, is not with your seemingly recalcitrant soulmate, but with the fact that your love for your "soulmate" is only conditional. In other words, your love for the other person is conditional on him changing to please you.

Most people, however, don't want to be changed. They can sense a partner's love is conditional when they find that person trying to change them in a significant way. Emotional pain, breakups, arguments, and power struggles are the inevitable results.

The angels say that when you try to change another person, you do yourself and your partner a grave disservice. You waste your time, and you also miss out on the possibility of being with a partner better suited to your needs. You also rob your present partner of the opportunity to be with someone who might have unconditional love for her. Better to accept your partner as she is, or move on, rather than harm both of you in a fruitless effort to change the other.

What the angels find sad is that while all human beings dream of a warm, all-embracing unconditional love, they too often place conditions on the love they have for others. This is what happened to Theresa, a forty-two-year-old divorcee who scheduled a session with me because she wanted to know how she could keep her boyfriend, Charles, from constantly cheating on her. Theresa closed her eyes, in obvious emotional pain concerning the relationship. As she spoke, she pulled her graying brunette hair back in a ponytail to keep it from falling onto her tear-streaked face.

"When we are together, Charles treats me like I'm very special," she began. "But he's constantly cheating on me with somebody new. This has happened over and over. When I confront him, he cries and says he loves me and doesn't know why he did it and promises never to do it again. But then a few weeks later I'll find a phone number on the back of a woman's business card, or a condom in his wallet, or smell perfume on him when he comes home. Then there's the mysterious phone calls that always hang up when I answer the phone, and I know it's happening all over again. I think he may have had this problem with his other girlfriends, too. I love Charles. I know we'd be perfect together otherwise. I knew he was perfect for me when I first saw him. In many ways he is the best person that has ever come into my life, if he'd only stop cheating. What do the angels say about how I can keep him faithful?"

Before I could answer, Theresa continued. "I love him with all my heart and soul. He is the first man I've ever been completely compatible with and enjoy being around. It's what he does when he's not around that's killing me. I hurt so much when I discover he's cheating that I just want to die. I love him, but sometimes I hate him so much for treating me this way, I could kill him. I know I shouldn't feel that way, and I try not to have feelings of jealousy and anger. What can I do?"

At this point Theresa stopped talking and looked directly at me. I spent a moment gazing back at her before I felt myself slipping into the semitrance in which I more easily hear her angels' Divine remedies. Within seconds I heard her angels begin talking into my right ear. *"You are being much too harsh on yourself, dear one. Your jealous feelings about Charles are normal. He has shown you warmth, love, and acceptance, and your heart is swollen with appreciation and love. Please don't judge yourself for having feelings of anger, jealousy, or shame over his affairs. These, too, are a perfectly normal reaction in the face of knowing a bond that is sacred to you is of so little importance to him. However, Charles is showing you that he cannot be faithful to you or any woman right now. Are you willing to accept this in your relationship with him?"*

Theresa answered, "No, but can't you tell me how to change him?" She was clearly surprised at the angels' message. She had expected them to reveal a plan that would make Charles fall monogamously in love with her.

The angels then confronted Theresa about the conditional nature of her love toward her so-called soulmate: *"You are trying to change Charles into being something very different than he is now, something he does not desire within his heart to be. Remember that true Love accepts people as they are. How would you like to have someone who loved you spend time urging you to give up your interest in art? If you cannot accept him as he is with a willing heart, then you must look elsewhere for your soulmate."*

Theresa struggled through her tears. "I feel like I just heard the honest truth from my best friends. Deep down, I guess I knew that Charles didn't feel the same way about me as I do about him. It hurts and it'll probably take me a little while to feel OK with it. But at least now I know that I shouldn't give any more of myself to a relationship that's not going to give me what I need."

The angels concluded their prescription. *"We know that what you truly desire is a soulmate who will see love as a sacrament as you do and will share his love exclusively with you. Someone who has Charles's good qualities but is capable of the fidelity you need. If you were to meet someone who treated you wonderfully, who was compatible, and who wanted to be with only you, would this make you happy?"*

"Of course," Theresa said.

Theresa understood that she had deliberately blinded herself to all the signs that Charles was not interested in a monogamous relationship. He may have loved her, but he wasn't ready for anything beyond sex. Theresa had been putting herself through hell by ignoring these cues until her angels intervened to help.

Rx

If someone needs changing, he or she isn't the soulmate for you. Trying to change a person who seems in need of change is always a waste of time. If you can't accept someone as they are with a whole heart, then that person is not the soulmate you seek.

Prescription for Finding Commitment

For many of you, finding someone to love is not what stands in the way of a fulfilling soulmate relationship. The problem is that all the people you find happen to be either unwilling or unable to commit; they never seem quite ready for marriage or even an exclusive relationship. Inevitably, no matter how desperately you search, you always end up in love with partners who are determined to remain unattached, are already married, have a different sexual orientation than yours, are facing jail time, or otherwise are not prospects for marriage or partnership.

God and our angels become concerned when you place yourself in situations like this. The angels know these paths are a direct route to needless suffering. The angels have to stand by and watch while you agonize and despair over a lover who can't invest fully in a relationship. They also have to watch when you squander your time and energy on these dead-end relationships, while missing out on heaven-sent opportunities for true romance. The angels don't want you to suffer endlessly over someone who is never going to be there for you. Like good therapists, their prescription says you need to focus not on pressuring a partner to commit, but on why you keep picking partners you can't become completely close to. Heaven invites you to consider whether the problem might not lie in your own fear of intimacy and closeness, or the possibility of losing these if you have them.

Brenda, age 37, consulted me about Stephan, her newest romantic interest, even though Brenda constantly referred to him as her boyfriend. Stephan was two years older than Brenda and had never been married, although he had had a succession of long-term, live-in girlfriends before meeting Brenda.

Before Stephan, Brenda had had a live-in relationship with Drew, a medical student at college whom she had loved passionately, but who had broken up with her because he wouldn't consider marriage until after he graduated and established a practice. Then Brenda fell in love with one of Drew's former roommates, "a really sweet boy when he wasn't drinking, but he ended up in prison for excessive DUIs." After that, she had a long affair with her married boss, who swore he was going to divorce his wife and marry her, but kept finding reasons to put it off. One day he informed Brenda that he was going to break off their relationship and stay with his wife. Brenda then fell head over heels for Ernest, a single man looking for a wife, but after six months she discovered he actually was already married and had lied to her. Next came her current love, commitment-phobic Stephan, who said he loved her, but wasn't interested in anything permanent, and had the relationship history to prove it.

Brenda refused to take what Stephan said seriously. She was convinced he was the one and just needed a little pushing. "We have so much in common," she insisted. "I'm the right woman for him and he's the right man for me. But why do I keep falling for men who can't see that and commit?"

"Beloved, Brenda, believe him when he says he is not ready for a relationship," the angels said. *"What we wish you to understand is that it is not that the men who are attracted to you are unwilling to commit. It is that you are, on one level, attracted to men who are unavailable. Though one part of your heart seeks love and intimacy, another part seeks the safety of relationships where you cannot fully open your heart to another and run the risk you, like so many, are so terribly afraid of—being hurt, rejected, abandoned."*

I asked Brenda if this could be true, if there was anything in her past that might have made her afraid of losing true love if she had it.

Brenda explained that when she was seven, her parents had gone through a lengthy, bitter divorce. To Brenda, her father simply disappeared from her life one day, and she rarely saw him. Only years later, as an adult did she learn that her mother had done all she could to block her father's constant attempts to contact Brenda. By then, sadly her father was dead. Brenda had never shaken the feelings of abandonment, depression, and guilt that she'd carried ever since her parents' divorce.

"We can help you heal these hurts so that you lose your fear of being in a relationship of true love. We will do the work. You merely need to be willing to allow us to help you clear them away. Will you consent?"

Brenda took a deep breath. "OK, I'll try. What am I supposed to do?"

"All we ask is that you be willing to release any unforgiveness that you may be holding toward both your parents. Be willing to release all pain associated with your love for them. Be willing also to release your fear of giving love, including the fear that you could be hurt in any way. And be willing to release the fear of being loved, including the fear that you could be abandoned, rejected, found unlovable, or hurt in any way. Be willing to trade all pain associated with love in exchange for peace."

As the angels spoke and performed clearing work, I watched Brenda's posture relax and her breathing slow and deepen. "I seem to feel lighter now," she said. Then she scrunched up her face, as if thinking hard. "But isn't there some chance with Stephan?" she pleaded. "Couldn't he change his mind? I mean, we're so good together."

"Beloved daughter," the angels reassured, *"trust that the parts of this relationship that you do enjoy are waiting for you with another man who is able to commit to and love you. It is not a personal rejection of you or a statement about your attractiveness. It is because Stephan still lacks the maturity to enter into something as serious as marriage and knows it. His past history should show you that he is correct in this estimation of himself. He loves you to the greatest degree that he is capable of loving anyone right now. Yet, Stephan is still a long way from being someone who would make you a faithful, supportive, loving husband in a marriage partnership. You would wait a long time before he is ready, and meanwhile miss the opportunity to form a soulmate relationship with a loving man who is ready for marriage and commitment. Is this truly what you desire?"*

Brenda admitted it was not. She and I talked a while longer, and by the end of our session she seemed clear-eyed and strong in her resolve to end her relationship with Stephan. Brenda said she was grateful that he was so honest about his feelings, and that it was she who had been dishonest with herself.

Rx

If you become willing to release the fears that hold you back from finding a partner who is available for commitment, you break down the barriers that keep you from finding a soulmate who also wants to make it permanent.

Prescription for Destructive Love

For a tragic handful of people, the search for a soulmate continually turns into a nightmare. Instead of finding love and happiness, they repeatedly end up in relationships that fill them with frustration and pain. They pick partners who are incompatible or unavailable, indifferent, abusive, destructive, or exploitative. They often find themselves in therapy or, in extreme cases, in the hospital or a battered women's shelter. They blame their partners, themselves, even God, wondering why they are such losers at love, and why they can't seem to find a decent relationship.

When this happens, the angels say, the problem lies—to paraphrase the Bard—not so much with the person's stars as with their taste in mates. Wonderful, caring soulmates have been around them all along, but they have stared them in the face without noticing. Instead, these people allow themselves to be attracted and excited by qualities that are unhealthful for them.

The result is the same: These individuals seem to be turned on by and fall in love with only the most inappropriate, often harmful, of partners. It could be something as simple as falling for someone who doesn't want children when it is the most important thing in the world to them. Or it could be something as serious as a fatal fixation on lovers who turn out to be addicts or other dangerous, violent people.

The romance angels say they are always trying to answer prayers for a soulmate, but some people are caught in a pattern that will lead them to constantly reject partners who are ideal for them unless they first heal their own preference in soulmates. That was the situation for Renee, an executive assistant to the head of a small publishing firm, who came to me in tears. Renee had been asking God and her angels to guide her to the loving man of her dreams. But each time she found herself in the arms of a man who made her feel like he might be the one, he instead turned out to be a batterer and often an alcoholic.

"I keep looking for my soulmate," she sobbed, "but all I ever seem to attract are losers and abusers. My boyfriends have been both physically and verbally abusive to me. I just keep stumbling on men who look promising at first, but when I get to know them they have a violent streak, drink, or are addicts or gamblers, and they sneak around and cheat on me. Looking back, I think the signs are always there early in the relationship, but the chemistry between us is always so hot, I blind myself to them. What am I doing wrong? I want a decent guy who will treat me right and who I can trust to be faithful when we have children. Why do I keep winding up with jerks?"

I relayed the romance angels' reply: *"With regard to your request for a soulmate relationship, we have butted heads with you many times about mate selection. We continually send you men whom we feel would make perfect partners to you, but you continue to overlook them. We are trying to help you with your preference in men. But you are resisting us. You must change this aspect before you will be able to see your true soulmate when next he arrives."*

Renee admitted that she had always been attracted to what she called the macho stud type, the strong, tough, dangerous man. Just looking at them turned her on, and the sex was great. They always eventually revealed themselves to be controlling and abusive, however.

The angels said, *"We're working with you to reconcile these differences, because what we want for you in a partner is a little different than your desires."*

The angels knew all along that Renee, being a sensitive soul herself, could only be happy and fulfilled in a relationship with a more sensitive type of man who showed and expressed his affection. Whenever they arranged for her to encounter decent potential soulmates, however, Renee had been blind to their existence. She was letting herself be turned on to the wrong type of man, and turning herself off to the right type.

Renee told me that she'd had gut feelings similar to what the angels were telling her. I explained that those feelings meant that she was receiving angelic guidance through her intuition. I added that the angels needed her to heal her present, unhealthy yen for macho men before she'd be open to the kind of fulfilling love match they were eager to arrange.

The angels added, "*You were abused verbally by your father, who was a strict, demanding man. You began to believe he was right and you merited abuse. Soon you magnified your every small imperfection, as he did, and convinced yourself that the way you were treated was justified. This led you to attract other people who abused you as well. Finally, you became uncomfortable in a relationship with any man who wasn't abusive, thinking he must be a fool or a nebbish if he didn't see how much you deserved his abuse. When we presented a proper soulmate to you, you looked down your nose at him.*"

I counseled her, "Be sure to ask the angels to help you to be willing to change. Because right now the angels tell me that you're not willing to let go of the kind of image of manhood that currently gets you excited. So there's nothing they can do to help you. You've tied their hands. You understand that, don't you?"

"Yes, I do," she replied, "but what about sex? I know the kind of guy the angels mean, like Moshe over in accounting. He's the stable, homebody type. Everybody says we'd make a great match, and he's asked me out several times. But I don't know. He just doesn't ring my chimes. I'd rather go out with Ralphie in the marketing department. He's more my type. But I guess I'd just find out the hard way that he was another abuser or alcoholic, too. But, gosh, if I married someone like Moshe, I'd be condemning myself to a dull life in the bedroom, wouldn't I? How can I get turned on by the kind of man who turns me off?"

I told Renee that it wasn't a case of all or nothing. The angels didn't want to deprive her of an intense and satisfying sex life, and there was a heavenly prescription to her dilemma. She could have the kind of man she could safely and comfortably. share a life with as well as enjoy highly charged sex.

"So if I develop healthier tastes in men, then those kind of men will become what turns me on? I'll get steamed up by them?" Renee asked.

"Bravo, Renee," her angels applauded. *"When you are ready for these men, they will stir the passion you desire, yet treat you with the loving kindness you deserve. But first you must cease, or significantly decrease, the self-criticism that misled you into believing you have merited the abuse all these men have visited upon you. Only then will you no longer find yourself attracted to such destructive relationships.*

"We ask you to become more aware of these thoughts by noticing whenever you feel any form of pain, whether physical, emotional, spiritual, or intellectual. Anytime you feel badly, begin to notice what thought you are thinking. We ask you to write that thought in a journal and ask yourself, 'What positive thought could I choose to replace it?' In time you will soon begin to recognize self-hating thoughts and replace them with self-loving thoughts. You may not need the journal very long, but use it as a tool in the beginning to propel you and your life to a new experience of love."

I added, "Remember, your angels don't want to control you. They want to help you to fulfill your true will, which is for a very happy and harmonious long-term relationship with a quieter excitement than the roller-coaster kind you've had in your love life before. Does that make sense?"

Renee nodded. The last time I heard from her, she was taking this Divine remedy to heart. She had split from her abusive boyfriend and was journaling her thoughts daily. Renee reported feeling happier, freer, and lighter. She was beginning to feel better about herself, and the fact that she could be turned on by a different kind of man. Renee felt so much better that she didn't feel any special need to rush into a relationship. As I spoke with her, I heard Renee's angels say she had already attracted the interest of a man who could be her genuine soulmate. I have a feeling Renee will soon find sparks flying with the exact kind of man she would have rated "boring" before.

Rx

You attract the kind of partners you believe you deserve. If you believe you merit abuse, disrespect, indifference, that's the kind of relationship you will have. If you believe you merit love, respect, cherishing, that's the kind of love you will find.

CHAPTER FIVE

Prescriptions for Marriage and Committed Relationships

If seeking and finding romance is perilous, filled with the pitfalls of rejection, unhappiness, and pain, then it is easy to understand how much worse the pain can be when a marriage or long-term relationship encounters troubled waters. There is nothing like the joy and contentment of partnership when all goes right, and there is nothing like the suffering and agony of love when things go wrong. It's hardly surprising that misunderstandings, the friction of living together, hurtful acts from each partner's dark side, and external threats—such as financial pressures and infidelity—to the partnership itself cause people more concern than any other aspect of life.

The pain and guilt of divorce and the disintegration of committed partnerships fill more therapists' offices than any other problem. They also are a leading cause of suicide and, sadly, even murder, as each evening's news headlines attest. They are so agonizing that often we will suffer through a nightmarish relationship rather than end it.

That's why the angels are so quick to help when you ask for assistance with intimate relationships. Perhaps your partnership is sailing along smoothly at the moment, but you're interested in finding out what the angels prescribe for common marital problems you might encounter along the way. Maybe you and your partner are beginning to enter troubled waters and want to smooth things out before they grow choppy enough to become a threat to your relationship. Or, you could be facing a major marital crisis that only a prescription from heaven could mend. Whether you're faced with marital boredom, infidelity, sexual issues, chronic arguments, or some other relationship challenge, the angels have practical solutions for you and your partner.

Again and again, the angels have demonstrated their ability to give my clients advice that has literally saved marriages that seemed beyond all possibility of healing. The angels are deeply concerned about saving committed relationships and marriages for many reasons. For example, the angels, who were probably instrumental in bringing you together in the first place, may know that you and your partner—as much as you sometimes irritate each other—have been joined for a healing purpose that ultimately will make you both stronger and happier people. The angels also often intervene to prescribe better approaches to marital power-sharing and communication for quarreling parents whose children are traumatized by their mother and father's arguments.

Although the angels do their best, sometimes both partners want out or are unwilling to change. When marriages dissolve, the angels can help make the transition more harmonious, clearing away bitterness for the partners, their children, and other family members. While I believe that any relationship can be spiritually healed, I also have seen many instances where two partners were clearly no longer meant to be together. When they divorced or broke up, their lives significantly improved. As long as we're following Divine guidance, there is no reason to feel guilty if a divorce comes about. It isn't a sigh of failure; it is a learning and growth opportunity. Of course, when children are involved, divorces become a deeper topic because of the potential harm to the offspring. Yet, I've also seen children benefit when they are removed from parental battlegrounds.

My clinical, personal, and angel experiences have taught me that each marriage and each family is subject to its own set of rules, rather than one carte blanche guideline. I do know that when people ask God and the angels for healing and guidance about relationships, everything always improves, even when a breakup is the result. Their Divine remedy for a "Should I stay or should I go?" syndrome is to ask your partner's guardian angel to heal the situation. But they caution not to specify how you want it to heal. Leave that to God and the angels. They will know which course will produce the happiest outcome for both of you.

(If your relationship is in need of even deeper help, the archangel of emotional healing, Uriel (see appendix A) is the angel to call to your side. Uriel heals wounded hearts and punctured pride so couples can communicate without a wall of hurt coloring their perceptions. He also leads troubled couples to appropriate outlets of human help, such as skilled marriage counselors, support groups, or loving friends.)

Prescription for Letting Go

When a relationship is over, you know it's unfair to you and the other person to hold on out of feelings of neediness, guilt, or obligation. Yet, a part of you hurts and aches at the thought and is devastated by the end of a love that has meant so much to you. Your every instinct is to hold on at all cost, not wanting to let go or acknowledge that there is nothing left for either of you. You continue to cling to the relationship, perhaps even after your former lover has given up on it, denying all the signs, hoping it isn't as bad as you think or that it can somehow be fixed or put back together again. Instead, by grasping too hard at what is gone, both of you suffer more and cause each other pain; anger festers, and hurtful, unforgivable words are spoken and actions taken.

The angels don't want to see either of you hurt. When there is still something positive left for both parties in a relationship, they will supply Divine prescriptions for healing it.

But sometimes, despite the love between two people, their relationship simply can no longer be made fruitful or fulfilling. When this happens, the angels can show you the best way to let go and save what's positive and loving between you.

Elyse, director of an Internet-based adult-education facility, had been unhappily married for several years. With her children grown and herself firmly ensconced on the spiritual path, Elyse longed for a deeper and more meaningful marriage. She had turned from academics to what she felt was more fulfilling work: coaching people on how to achieve their life goals. However, her husband, a professor of engineering, had no interest in the inner life and disapproved of the income loss caused by Elyse's change of career. He also declined to read any of the books that were influencing her or to attend any of the classes that interested her. The two grew increasingly distant, arguing violently and regularly.

Prior to consulting me, Elyse had tried more traditional approaches to handling the situation. She'd suggested counseling to her husband, but he refused. Elyse also had raised the idea of divorce, since they both seemed equally unhappy. Her husband was very much against that step, too.

One evening Elyse attended a lecture in which I discussed how the angels look at divorce and relationship breakups. The angels, I told the audience, say that everyone who comes into your life comes for a healing purpose. Ultimately each person becomes your teacher and conveyer of heavenly messages. The person might give you a specific angel message, teach you a hard-won lesson such as patience, or provide you with an opportunity that brings you closer to your purpose. Some of these friends will enter your life for a short period and then exit. Other people will be part of your life for years.

When you've done your work with the other person, the purpose has been served, and you won't feel the pull of attraction toward him or her any longer. The angels say that it's important, once you suspect that a relationship is over, to pause for a minute of peace. They say, *"Please don't label yourself or the other person as being good, bad, right, or wrong. Labels not only are inaccurate; but they also create painful feelings for you and the other person. If you feel guilty withdrawing from a friendship, you will create pain. After all, guilt always expects punishment and creates it as a self-fulfilling prophecy. Instead, hold the thought and attitude of gratitude for the good times you and the other person have shared. Mentally say to the other person, 'I forgive you, I forgive myself, and now I release you without attachment.' Then let Divine guidance take care of what happens next."*

I closed by offering the angels' Divine prescription for those who were wondering whether they should stay in or leave an unhappy relationship. "Talk to your partner's guardian angel," I advised, "and ask the angel for clarification about the future of the relationship. Ask the other person's angel to help heal the situation so that it either ends peacefully or is resolved."

Elyse described her reaction to me during our session some weeks later. "I was very clear that the healing I was asking my husband's guardian angel to provide did not necessarily mean a decision to stay within the marriage. I was asking for something much bigger: a healing of all the negativity and pain around the relationship.

"So I followed the angelic guidance and spoke to his guardian angel in my mind, although I didn't see any angel and it felt very much like talking to myself. I shared the level of pain that I was in and asked for a holy solution. I told the guardian angel that it was no longer acceptable for me to stay stuck in this unconscious relationship and that I was determined to be part of a spiritual partnership. I wanted a rededication to my marriage or I wanted my husband to let me go. I surrendered the idea of whether to stay or to go and focused on receiving a healing of the situation."

Elyse continued praying for a healing, with no attachment to what kind of healing. She talked to her husband's guardian angel daily. Less than two months later, Elyse said a miracle occurred. "My husband, in total clarity and warmth, told me, 'I will always love you in my heart if not in my head. You are going in a different direction than I am and I've spent a lot of time seriously considering what it would mean if I went in your direction. I've decided that it is not right for me. It is time for us to let go.' I was flabbergasted. We had never spoken about this subject on this level. I was in shock that he could have gained this level of clarity and peace without any external influence from a counselor. It was like talking to another person who had actually heard all of my conversations with his guardian angel.

"Since then my husband and I have amicably separated, and we are treating each other far better now than in the last years of our marriage. We mediated a divorce settlement with a great deal of angelic guidance that I asked God to send. Our children are handling the transition beautifully because we have found love for each other once again, in the form of loving each other enough to let go."

Rx

Appeal to your own or to the other person's guardian angel. Seek healing without being attached to a specified outcome or form of healing.

Prescription for the Grass Is Greener Complex

After a few years of living together, it's common for one or both partners to fall into the grass-is-greener trap, wherein a potential new partner looks better than the current one. I've counseled many people in committed or marital relationships who believe they have recently found their soulmate, and it isn't their current lover or spouse. They all want advice on what to do next, and many secretly hope for confirmation that their new flame is the one true love they were destined for, and that I'll tell them it's spiritually OK to dump their old love for the new one.

Most often, however, what these people have done is to look at that new someone they have just met through rose-colored glasses, projecting their ideal fantasy onto that person the way they did onto their present partner when they first met. If they were to live with the new person every day, the exciting new romantic prospect eventually would fall off the pedestal, too.

One long-married client, Ursula, an advertising copywriter, found herself in just this situation, wondering whether her current spouse was an obstacle that was preventing her from being with the ideal love, when she met "a wonderful man who totally changed my life." "I feel like he is my angel," she gushed.

The problem was that her angel, Victor, a marketing executive, was also married, and not happily, either. Both also had children. Neither felt comfortable with the situation, and they hadn't become intimate yet. They were meeting frequently for secret lunches and dinners, however, and Ursula knew she wouldn't be able to postpone the physical aspect of her relationship with Victor much longer.

Ursula explained to me, "I have tried to stop thinking about Victor but I really think he is perfect for me. I don't want to do anything wrong, but I wonder if maybe staying in a loveless marriage is what is wrong, not being with Victor. My husband is a good person and deserves to find his soulmate, too. Maybe I would be doing us both a favor if I set him free."

Then Ursula asked the question that had brought her in for an angel reading: "Is Victor part of my future life? Should I get a divorce and leave my husband for him?"

I could tell that Ursula wanted some sort of Divine permission to leave her family, marry this other man, and live happily ever after. I usually am very aware of what my clients want me to tell them, and it's never fun to deliver what they don't want to hear.

I was already in my semitrance state and the angels were busily communicating with me while Ursula was speaking. Many times in my sessions, I'm called upon to split my awareness between what my client is saying in the physical world and what her angels are saying in the spiritual world.

When Ursula asked her question, I took a deep breath and felt the angels kick in, as if they had picked up a speaker phone and were talking directly to Ursula through me. The angels said, *"Allow us to help you make decisions based upon the love within you, and not from any fear or guilt. You don't feel that your needs are being met in your marriage. You long for great love and to be held and appreciated. We know this.*

"You are enjoying the feeling of unconditional love you receive when you are with this new man, and it's important to remember that the source of love isn't another person—it is your spirit within. Though many have soulmates, you don't necessarily need to marry your soulmate to benefit from and enjoy the relationship. Some soulmate relationships are best left unconsummated, as sex can sometimes complicate or even ruin a wonderful soulmate relationship."

Feeling the urge to confront Ursula lovingly as a psychologist, I said, "This is me talking now, Ursula. I feel guided to say this: Before you make any decisions, you must be very clear and sure. I'd wait three days after you make a decision, just to be certain you still feel that way. Dating a married man is often the quickest route to heartache. Very few married men leave their wives, especially if children are involved. The angels and I both conclude that perhaps your better option would be to keep this man as a dear friend, and look to other options to fulfill your romantic needs."

Ursula looked relieved. I got the sense that she was very concerned about doing the right thing from a moral and spiritual perspective. Ursula had felt justified in leaving her husband, since she was unhappy in her marriage. But she also had been worried about the effect on both spouses and on the children. And, of course, she had been concerned about what the long-term prospects of her new relationship might be. This solution seemed to give her the best of both worlds without hurting anyone.

"We won't bring you any relationship where you would need to compromise your ethics," the angels explained. *"However, we will help you to face the truth about yourself and your present marriage."*

At this, Ursula squirmed uncomfortably in her seat. Nevertheless, she understood and accepted the truth of the angels' remedy. She had a new reserve of strength to come to terms directly with the problems in her marriage, instead of avoiding the issue by leaping into a hasty affair and possible divorce. She still didn't know if she wanted to be with her husband or with Victor. But now she knew she had the option of keeping him in her life without a physical relationship.

The angels never moralize, but they do discuss commonsense concerns when it comes to moral issues. They say that if someone violates his own code of standards, he will experience painful guilt. In Ursula's case, they never slapped her hand for considering an extramarital affair. They simply outlined their remedy for getting her needs met in a way that wouldn't cause pain to herself or others.

Rx

Come fully to terms with your present relationship before you jump the fence into a pasture where the grass is greener.

Prescription for Being Overcontrolling

When we try to solve our problems or make a bad situation better, we sometimes try so hard that we make things worse instead. Overcontrolling a situation is just as dangerous as oversteering a car. Rather than going straight and smooth, the course of things veers wildly from side to side.

Once you get into the habit of being overcontrolling, it can be difficult to break. Even when you ask for Divine assistance in turning things around, you may still continue to try too hard to make the situation better, which interferes with the efforts the angels are making on your behalf. Once you request angelic assistance, you should get out of the angels' way so they can do their job. The angels liken it to being a member of a sports team: You need to pass the ball before your teammates can help you. So many times people ask for spiritual help, but don't truly allow it to happen because they fear losing control of the situation.

My client Patrice came to me for help with her marriage to Keith, her husband of fifteen years. "All we ever do is argue," she told me. "My husband and son are constantly battling. When I try to intervene to keep the peace, then Keith and I end up fighting."

She explained that although Keith was never abusive, she felt he pushed their son a little too hard. "Keith says he's trying to motivate Bradley to improve his grades, but I think there are other ways to inspire someone instead of riding them constantly. I have tried praying, but that doesn't seem to work. What can I do to create the peaceful household that I'm craving so desperately?"

Through me the angels said to her, *"Detach, Patrice. You are too involved in trying to control the situation. You must release the situation, so that we can intervene to bring harmony. If you detach, there will be harmony and healing."*

The angels saw that Patrice's overinvolvement was actually worsening the tension. Keith could feel that Patrice didn't trust his judgment, and Bradley could sense that his parents weren't getting along. The situation was exacerbated because of the additional stress, and Patrice's angels said the only solution was for her to back off.

"The angels ask you to allow them to help you, Patrice," I said. She looked at me with uncertainty, afraid to trust, yet afraid not to. She said she could understand where the angels were coming from, but she was afraid to detach because she feared her husband would then totally overwhelm and dominate her son emotionally.

Patrice's forehead wrinkled, indicating her strain as she struggled to surrender control of this family conflict. Again, the angels spoke up. *"We ask you to take some deep breaths, Patrice."* She did and noticeably relaxed.

The angels reassured Patrice about her son's emotional safety, and she agreed to give their approach a try. That's when she ran into another barrier. "But *how* do I detach?" she asked. She wasn't asking for the mechanics. She genuinely didn't know how to back away emotionally from a situation in which she was so deeply enmeshed.

A large male angel appearing over Patrice's shoulder gave me visual cues as to how to handle the situation, as if he were holding a television screen in front of me with a video of the family's ideal outcome. I looked at him, received instructions through his combination of charadelike motions and clairvoyant imagery, and then translated these visual cues into verbal instructions. "Patrice, ask your angel to help you to be willing to release the situation. He will help you to desire detachment."

Patrice nodded, pleased that her angel understood her mental impasse. Audibly, she mouthed the words, "Please help me to desire releasing my family situation to God."

I watched Patrice's body shudder, a sure sign of angelic intervention. Her body relaxed and she breathed slowly and deeply. "Something just happened," was all she could say.

I went on, "Your guardian angel now asks you to visualize your situation in a symbolic way, such as imagining a mental picture of Keith, Bradley, and yourself during one of your altercations." The angel nodded, indicating that I was hearing him accurately. He continued motioning instructions to me. "The angel is placing a large bucket in front of you, and asks you to visualize yourself placing the picture of the situation into this bucket."

Patrice frowned for a moment as she followed these instructions. Suddenly she smiled and looked as if a great weight had been taken off her. "I think it's working," she said, obviously feeling better.

When I saw Patrice a few months later, she couldn't wait to tell me the news. "I was able to detach, just like you and the angels suggested. And guess what happened? My husband and son began to be palsy-walsy with each other. At first I could tell they were a little suspicious, waiting for Mom to intervene in their squabbles. When I didn't, I guess the energy of their arguments fizzled, because they've hardly crossed swords since. It's truly a miracle that our household is now so peaceful after just one angel-reading session."

Rx

Release the situation. If you have difficulty letting go, ask the angels to help you want to surrender control.

Prescription for Marital Miscommunication

Miscommunication may cause more marital problems and breakups than any other single factor. Only therapists may know just how many arguments and separations have taken place because one partner misinterpreted or misunderstood something the other partner said or did. Whenever two people explore their deepest feelings and beliefs together, there are bound to be differences and misunderstandings. When miscommunication and misunderstanding become severe enough, partners often grow afraid to share their true feelings with each other. Although they still share the same roof, they become more like roommates than married lovers.

Over the years I have seen the angels heal relationships even where there were severe communication problems or communication had broken down altogether. Their Divine remedy is to encourage estranged partners to share their vulnerable feelings of love and fear with each other—in other words, to be totally honest. That is how they healed the marriage of my friend Mary Ellen, author of *Expect Miracles*.

Mary Ellen has been married to Howard for more than twenty years. Eight years ago they began developing separate interests and grew apart from each other. When they discussed important, emotionally charged topics like money, children, sex, or the course of their future lives, they began to disagree more and more frequently. Finally, all they seemed to do was argue. Hurt feelings resulted; each became convinced the other did not love him or her, and while they continued to share the same household, theirs was a marriage in name only. Both had retreated into silence.

For the next six years, Mary Ellen and Howard lived in separate bedrooms in a celibate relationship and had little communication with each other. Mary Ellen decided that was the way her marriage was going to be. She tried to ignore the fact that her needs for intimate communication weren't being met, and channeled her desire to communicate into writing poetry, a newsletter, and a book.

Mary Ellen attended a weekend angel retreat that focused her mind on her angels' messages of love and healing. The day after she returned home from the retreat, she woke up with the phrase "Teach only love" in her mind. She thought, "Gosh, how can I teach love in my newsletter if I don't live a loving life in my own home?"

As far as teaching love went, the angels were asking her to live with integrity and to do as she taught others to do. She called Howard at work and told him the truth. She explained how much she loved and missed him. Howard started to cry and said that he loved and missed her, too.

Mary Ellen credits the angels' guidance with healing her marriage. She says, "We are now a couple again. Howard moved back into our bedroom after nearly six years. He is so kind and gentle, talking and sharing with me. Both of our hearts have totally opened as a result of following the angels' prescriptions to be honest with one another."

The angels say, *"Truth heals in many ways. For instance, if you feel confused or angry at your mate's words or actions, immediately ask your partner to clarify what he or she means. Don't assume negativity coming from your partner where none may exist. At the same time, let your partner know how you are emotionally affected by words and actions. If you feel hurt or afraid, admit these feelings immediately. Holding these emotions in will result only in further misunderstandings and additional pain and confusion.*

"Begin by telling your partner whatever is true for you at the moment. Claim the truth for yourself and don't blame your truth on another. In this process of sharing and caring, two partners can mend eons of anger and an eternity of rage. If you like, ask us to help guide your words so they are aligned with your truthfulness. We will let you know if you are veering off from your center of truth."

Rx

Communicate your feelings of love and fear for the relationship honestly with your partner.

Prescription for Waning Passion

At the beginning of every intimate and romantic relationship, you and your partner share intense passionate feelings for, and a deep bonding with, each other. You are intensely attracted to each other, want to be together all the time, and can barely keep your hands off each other or take a break from the deep spiritual and emotional bonding of lovemaking. Each partner is truly and genuinely concerned for the other's needs and happiness.

Later, however, unless you know what to do or avoid, boredom, disinterest, and discontentment can set in. It's as if each partner becomes burned out on the relationship. The passion gone, you stay together out of habit, financial need, guilt, children, or obligation.

When you stick with a partner after the passion is gone, you often begin to resent each other, making belittling remarks, withholding affection, or acting out in other passive-aggressive ways. Your lovemaking becomes routine and unexciting, if it exists at all. You may even pursue extramarital affairs or fantasize about having one.

The angels say it is natural for passion to go through periodic fluctuations. When it is low, however, you can boost the overall level through will and conscious intention. This desire to lift your mind and heart out of the low spots and rekindle ardor is the angels' Divine prescription for a deadened relationship. The secret is that you have to strongly desire the passion to increase.

You also can ask the angels to help you increase the energy level of your relationship. The angels will directly intervene into your heart and mind, clearing away any boredom or overfamiliarity that may be lowering your passion, and flooding you with their own Divine passion. The angels also can give you direct guidance that will elevate your energy, such as forgiving your partner the slights you think you've suffered, or giving you a new perspective on the relationship.

When Janie and Lynda first met and dated, sparks of passion flew. All of their friends remarked that the two seemed meant for each other. Janie, 37, had never been in a long-term, committed relationship before. Lynda, 40, was divorced four years and new to the lesbian scene when she met Janie. When they moved in together and donned rings symbolizing their commitment to the relationship, everything seemed wonderfully new to the couple. They were heads-over-heels in love, and both went out of their way to express themselves romantically.

Two years later, when the couple came to me for an angel session, they were on the verge of breaking up. Janie told me she wanted to begin dating other people, and Lynda felt hurt and confused, unsure whether she wanted the relationship to continue or not. Both partners were anxious to hear the angels' opinions on what they should do.

Janie's angels began speaking first. Her primary guide was her deceased grandfather on her mother's side of the family. He was a no-nonsense man who had been successful in business ventures, mainly because of his social skills. He said to me, *"Janie's always been prone to boredom, and she's itching for some excitement in her life right now."*

Both Janie and Lynda nodded in agreement. Then he directed his message toward Janie: *"You're dreaming of the dating scene as if it's a panacea that will bring you new excitement. But honey, you'll soon become bored with that. From my perspective, you and Lynda have a good thing going."* Despite Janie's best efforts to remain stoic, she wiped a tear from one eye.

At that point Lynda's angels chimed in. *"We, too, see that this partnership has many benefits for both. We ask that you give it a fair chance by introducing some new elements of romance as essential components. We see the two of you have succumbed to a routine that is dull and lifeless, with a focus only upon the basics of life, which for you, Lynda, are mostly about paying bills. When was the last time you left the house for an evening? Could you enter into a new phase of your relationship akin to starting over, like dating each other? From what we see, the answer is yes. There is still considerable love within this relationship, and we see that with a minimal effort, you will fan its flames once more."*

With the angels' help, Lynda, Janie, and I came up with plans for starting anew in their relationship. Each Wednesday and Saturday night would be considered a date night, and Lynda and Janie would take turns being in charge and planning each date. The date didn't need to be elaborate; going for a picnic, or a walk, or to a movie would do. Because Janie missed listening to live music at the nightclub where they'd first met, the two agreed to attend concerts at least once a month. Janie agreed to stay loyal to Lynda, and Lynda agreed to widen her scope of interests beyond mundane concerns.

I received an e-mail from Janie and Lynda six months later, reporting that they had rekindled their passion. "It's different than before," Lynda wrote. "We're definitely in love again, but in a very mature and stable way that I like better than the head-over-heels love we had in the beginning. I think that both of us needed to be confronted by the angels to remind us to put effort into the relationship in order to receive what we wanted."

(By the way, my gay and lesbian clients, and some of my straight ones as well, often ask what the angels say about homosexuality, since some religious groups and individuals hold negative views of same-sex partnerships. They're often surprised when I tell them that the angels are entirely neutral about the topic. They see no distinction between a heterosexual and a homosexual relationship, and never make negative judgments about the latter. As long as there are two willing partners and no one is being hurt, the angels are always happy about any two people being in a loving, committed spiritual relationship.)

Rx

Desire an increase in passion and make an effort to reignite the feelings that originally brought you together.

Prescription for Impatience

Like almost everyone, you probably have wanted something so badly that you pushed too hard to get it, ultimately ruining the situation. You set your sights on a goal, then put all your focus and energy into getting what you want as quickly as possible. As a child, you may have been so anxious for a puppy that you turned your parents off to the idea completely. Or, as an adult, you may have been in such a hurry to get married and start a family that you fell into the trap of committing to the wrong kind of partner.

When you go crazy with impatience to get what you want from a lover and partner, the only result is to drive an ever-widening gap between you. The more you push, the farther she withdraws. The more emotional you become, the cooler he turns. You begin to resent her for not meeting your needs, and she resents you because you keep pressuring her for something she clearly does not feel comfortable giving.

The angels, on the other hand, never rush or get impatient. They know there is an optimum rhythm and an ideal time for every event to occur, and they are willing to wait until that moment arrives. In fact, it is part of their job to help synchronize events, sometimes called Divine timing. Instead of pushing to make things happen when *you* want them to happen, the angels counsel that you make the best progress toward your goals when you have patience, keep your eye on the ball, and allow events to manifest in their own, more natural—and often slower—order. This is especially true when marriage or an intimate relationship is involved. That's how the angels counseled my client Gregor.

At first Gregor glossed over the problems he was having in his marriage. He said meekly, "My wife and I have been getting along and, for the most part, things have been pretty good."

But Gregor's angels gave me an entirely different picture, telling me that there was strain. Gregor gulped, realizing that he couldn't fool his angels. "In the last couple of weeks, we have been arguing quite a bit," he admitted. "I don't know where that's coming from, because I'm actually feeling a lot of joy over what's coming up in both of our lives and careers. Both of us have decided to start home-based businesses part-time after work. What's exciting is that we'll both be engaged in doing what we love to do. We're hoping that within a year, we can both quit our regular jobs and work full-time at home. Maybe we are experiencing tension over the change."

Gregor's angels were not to be fooled. They were very loud and specific. *"This difference between you stems from a difference in your desires for children. You want children, and your wife does not."* (The angels weren't betraying Gregor's confidence, but helping so that the truth could come to the surface.)

Gregor nodded and explained how he really felt. "Yes, that's true. We have been having tension over that. We've been married seven years, and I'm really starting to feel the desire for children. I really, really want to have one now. Katherine doesn't feel like she wants to, or doesn't know if she will ever be ready. It has added to our problems in and out of bed."

The angels offered their prescription. *"This would not be a good time to start a family. When you're in the middle of a career transition, you don't want any additional financial stress on you, and that's what having a child would be for you right now. There needs to be a readiness for it. As soon as you get to a comfortable plateau with your new career, in roughly two and one half years, then you'll both be ready."*

I looked at Gregor to check on his reaction. He seemed intrigued, both to know when his finances would stabilize and that there would come a time when he and his wife would want a child together. He scribbled notes on a little pad of paper.

Gregor relaxed considerably, feeling more confident that he and his wife would negotiate the optimal moment to begin having children. His relaxed outlook, in turn, had a positive result on his relationship, and the arguments between the two of them began to abate. In the interim, both are happily focusing their energies on their new businesses.

Rx

Relax and let things happen when they come. Pushing impatiently only drives them farther away.

Prescription for Feeling Trapped

Most relationships reach a point when, although each partner would like to stay together, both partners know each other's faults, foibles, and dark side well enough to wonder if they would be better off on their own or seeking a new partner. Often this stage is reached after prolonged, unresolved marital conflict, anger, and hateful words have created great hurt and driven the couple apart. The result is the infamous "can't live with them, can't live without them" blues. It leads to the pain of feeling trapped in an unhappy relationship with a person who has hurt you. You don't want to stay, but you don't want to leave either. (It's rare that just one partner in a relationship sees things this way. If a partner is unhappy, we always sense it. Yet, as a therapist, I have discovered that unless the partners have some opportunity to compare notes, such as in therapy, each believes he or she is the only one who can't live with or without the other.)

Lucy, a forty-five-year-old business owner, sought angelic advice when she began to feel trapped in her marriage. She worried that she and her husband had suffered too much pain to salvage their once happy twelve-year relationship. "We've had many problems. Both my husband, Chandler, and I had previous marriages," she related to me.

The couple initially had had custody of all the children from both of their previous marriages. After Chandler and Lucy married, they had two children together. Everything seemed ideal until they began having problems with Chandler's ex-wife, Ally. "Ally was very jealous during the time the boys were living with us, even though she chose to leave them," Lucy explained. "She made our lives miserable with her constant intentional disruption and lies. My husband feared standing up to her because she twisted everything to the boys for pity. I became very resentful of her and my husband. His boys are all gone now but the pain is not. My husband and I have also had many problems in our personal relationship, and this one issue in particular has become a very uncomfortable situation and has caused me a lot of pain that I cannot seem to forgive him for."

Lucy closed her eyes, jaw, and fists tightly with anger. "I guess I am looking for some guidance on the correct path to take. Right now I am feeling trapped and don't know what to do. I have considered divorce but am still uncertain about that. I love him and I hate him at the same time. Maybe if I could forgive him for all the ways I feel he has failed me, I would find peace and once again be able to love him. I just can't see the man I married in him anymore."

As she talked, I smiled to myself. It was wonderful to hear Lucy use the word *forgive* since that is such an integral healing point emphasized by the angels. To the angels, *forgiving* means *"releasing the pain associated with an event. You don't need to forgive the action, just the person. Your reason for forgiving is to heal yourself, not because it is something that you are expected to do."*

I relayed the angels' message to Lucy. "You are most certainly receiving guidance accurately from your angels. All you can see of Chandler now is his shortcomings and faults. In fact, you have very loud angels, and it is a joy to work with them because they are so clear." Lucy beamed at the realization that she had correctly heard her angels' remedy.

"Yes, forgiveness is very important for you here," the angels continued. *"You don't need to forgive Chandler's actions or faults, just forgive him as a person. He is in a strange situation right now because he sees you as being unhappy and it makes him feel badly about himself. Even though he is not responsible for your feelings, he takes responsibility for them.*

"If you'll give us your permission, we will help you to forgive him and his ex-wife. We can help you want *to forgive them, and this is what you should ask us for."*

Through me the angels then clearly told Lucy that they preferred the marriage to endure for a number of reasons. First, love still existed between Chandler and Lucy. Second, a divorce would divert both partners from their life's purpose and spiritual path. Finally, the children would suffer emotional pain that would profoundly and negatively affect them in adulthood. Still, the angels shrugged their shoulders and said, *"We can't* force *you to stay together, nor would we want to exercise our will over yours, but we would ask you to at least make the attempt."*

Lucy nodded thoughtfully. I could see that what she was hearing was in line enough with her own inclinations for her to be willing to try. Lucy agreed to incorporate the angels' prescriptions to save her marriage. "I want to care about my husband and marriage," she confessed, "and I realize that I'll need the help of God, Jesus, and the angels to let go of all this baggage we've been carrying around, baggage that has probably made us feel very, very tired of everything, including each other."

> Rx
>
> Heal yourself by forgiving not the words or the deeds, but the person.

Prescription for Lack of Intimacy

At some point every couple finds themselves estranged, on two different sides of a seemingly unbreachable gulf. If you and your partner know how to reach out immediately, you can close the gulf and return to your former closeness and intimacy. When you don't know how to do this, the gulf can widen, the relationship can grow more chilly, and you and your partner can drift in different directions. Sadly, such is human egotism that each partner frequently feels it is the other who has withdrawn. The angels say that you never lose an intimate connection with another unless you have taken actions or spoken words that helped cut you off from them in some way, as Carolyn discovered.

After twenty years of marriage, Carolyn complained that she and her husband didn't know each other anymore. "We have both changed," she explained. "I more than he. We don't seem to have anything in common anymore. We almost never hug or kiss, and we never make love. We might as well be strangers, and I can't imagine growing old with him."

A few weeks earlier, Carolyn's employer had announced the relocation of their company. Carolyn emphasized that she didn't have to move with the company; she had other employment options locally. She wondered if she should use the move as an opportunity to separate from her husband, since she'd dreamed of being single for some time.

"The kids are almost grown, and I am sure they would adapt to new surroundings. I would like to start fresh: new location, new life," she said anxiously, as if begging for my blessings. "In my business, I meet so many interesting people who have much more in common with me, and sometimes I hate going home. I need a soulmate and a partner, not a financially secure legal arrangement, which is all I feel I have now with my husband."

I scanned Carolyn's energy level, both within herself and within her marriage. "You are right," I said, "the angels show me that the energy in your marriage is quite low right now. Your company's relocation is also stirring up a lot of emotions for you and draining you further of energy. Are you sure you want to make such an important decision about your marriage in the stressful midst of this other change?"

Carolyn told me that she was afraid she would lose her nerve if she didn't take the job transfer. She conveyed a now-or-never attitude that I knew stemmed from her fears and not from true Divine prescriptions. Guidance from the angels always counsels people against impatience and cautions them to wait for Divine timing to bring what they want to them at the right moment in their development. In addition, Carolyn hadn't yet made a firm decision. She was asking for guidance.

A large female angel above Carolyn's head showed me a movie that I saw in my mind's eye. The angel looked six feet tall, and her eyes and smile radiated so much love that I thought she would burst from the strength of the emotion. In the mental movie projected by the angel, I saw a review of Carolyn's childhood. Carolyn's father had set high standards for her behavior, always making it clear to her whenever she failed to live up to them—which, being a child, was frequent. Carolyn felt her father didn't like her because she wasn't good enough. She began to hate herself and assumed others would too. She began to spend many hours alone in her bedroom, reading and writing. She was quite shy and lonely, uncomfortable around other children.

I felt the depth of Carolyn's incredibly painful loneliness. Carolyn had unwittingly held herself apart from others her entire life, not feeling she deserved their friendship and company. She felt that even if she sought out friends, they would ultimately reject her, once they got to know her better and found how undeserving she was of their affection. At the same time, like all of us, Carolyn craved a sense of love and connectedness with others.

When Carolyn married Harold, she thought her solitude would end. But after a while she noticed a chilliness between them. They weren't talking as often and each spent more and more time in his or her own personal study, Carolyn working on her doctorate, her husband attending to his paperwork. Carolyn was feeling as isolated as she had in her childhood.

A ray of hope cheered her up, though, when she received the news she was pregnant. After the birth of their child, she figured she'd feel better. Carolyn did find comfort in being a mother to not one, but three children, two sons and a daughter. She developed very close relationships with her children in which she finally felt loved and accepted. Now that the children were nearly grown, however, Carolyn feared being alone with Harold. She knew it would only emphasize the distance between them and her own sense of isolation.

Her angels said through me, *"Rationalizing your loneliness as a condition brought about by outside circumstances will only make the situation worsen. Remember this: We live with you daily and we see within you the kindness that you are seeking. The very qualities you are unwilling to explore within yourself, you are instead searching for in your outer world. And since you cannot recognize them in yourself, you cannot recognize them in others. But we say to you that if you will stop, notice, and appreciate these aspects of your inner nature, you will soon find them in your outer world. All your relationships will deepen and grow the more that you focus on the flowers that sprout within your own self."*

I watched Carolyn shudder with truthful recognition that her husband and others hadn't run away from her. She was running away from herself. She told me that she now saw how her sense of not being worthy of being liked, that she would ultimately be rejected, had led her to pull away from her husband in the early years of their marriage. She'd convinced herself that he soon would be pulling away from her. The very expectation of rejection had created the experience she feared the worst, and consequently, Carolyn felt alone and unloved much of the time.

The angels consoled her: *"The energy level within yourself and your marriage will rise substantially as you allow yourself to like yourself. We're asking you to look for what's worthy and likable in yourself. You will see more of it in others, too. We are also asking you to look for the love in yourself for your husband. As you find it, you will begin to notice his love for you. Come out of your room and into his and spend some time with him. You will be surprised at the change. He has been waiting for you to do this all these years. Your life will take on a greater sense of purpose."*

Carolyn reached for a tissue and dabbed her moist eyes. "You're probably right," she said. "I really don't want a divorce. I just want to be close to my husband. I'm willing to try."

I spoke with Carolyn one month after our session. The change was remarkable. She told me she had indeed stopped hiding in her study and had begun having discussions with her husband when they found themselves together in the kitchen or living room and even the bedroom. He had responded and soon no longer spent all his evenings locked away with his paperwork. "At first I waited for him to reject me. But I tried to believe I was lovable and likable, and began to discover positive traits I have never realized I possessed. And you know what? My husband already liked me. And I saw so many wonderful qualities in him I had forgotten. Both of us are so much more relaxed and happier, and we really like spending time together. And that's a miracle, let me tell you."

One year later I saw Carolyn and her husband at one of my workshops. I barely recognized her. She radiated an inner happiness, and she'd also dropped several pounds, which she attributed to her newfound peacefulness. During the entire seminar, I delighted in watching the couple sitting hand in hand. Her willingness to like herself and reach out toward her spouse had been the Divine remedy that brought the intimacy back into their ailing marriage.

Rx

Reconnect with what is good and lovable in yourself, and you will reconnect with what is good and lovable in your partner.

Prescription for Infidelity

Perhaps nothing is more painful than discovering a partner you trusted to be faithful has been having an affair. You feel cheated and betrayed, and that there must be something wrong with you that has made you undesirable. Anger and pain levels go off the Richter scale. You experience the devastating sense that something terribly important to your life and well-being being is destroyed beyond repair.

Often the pain of an affair is a two-way street. The person doing the cheating suffers as well. There's the remorse of hurting their partner, parents, and children, and there is tremendous guilt about the action and shame over letting libido control one's actions.

Yolanda and Jose had been married for seven years, and everything seemed fine in their relationship. Then Yolanda noticed some strange occurrences she couldn't explain. For instance, Jose began working later hours, but his paycheck didn't reflect any overtime pay. He'd also come home from work and not want any dinner, when normally he was starving. Jose had also purchased new underwear even though he'd never before shopped for any of his clothing. She suspected an affair but wasn't ready to admit the possibility to herself.

One Saturday afternoon Yolanda noticed the telephone cord trailing into the bathroom. Listening outside the closed bathroom door, she heard Jose speaking in hushed tones. Yolanda thought she heard Jose saying, "But I do love you, baby." Her heart dropped as she rushed to another phone and quietly picked up the receiver in time to hear Jose and a woman clearly having a lovers' quarrel.

Yolanda was beside herself and wasn't able to confront Jose for several days. He admitted the affair promptly when Yolanda asked him directly. He cried and begged for forgiveness, promising that the affair was over. Yolanda desperately wanted to believe Jose, but she was too hurt and confused to know what to think. She came to me for an angel reading, hoping for answers and guidance.

Yolanda's angels asked me to tape-record our session. *"She won't hear what we're really saying unless she hears it repeatedly,"* they explained. This alerted me that this session probably was going to be intensely emotional. I grabbed a box of tissue and turned on the tape recorder.

"We begin by asking you to see this situation from our perspective," the angels said. Yolanda had a large group of beings delivering this message to her, including Jesus, with whom she had a very close bond, standing right behind her, his face beaming love. I also saw Yolanda's maternal grandmother, a tough-minded but loving and spiritual person. This group spoke to me collectively in a unified voice. However, at times Jesus would speak alone, as would Yolanda's grandmother.

The angels explained that Jose loved her very much and that he did not consciously desire to leave or cheat on his wife. Without justifying the situation or placing blame, the angels gently explained that Jose's affair was a by-product of two factors: his wavering self-esteem and their floundering marriage. *"You need to know how much control and say-so you have in this situation. Do not perceive your marriage as being in the complete control of Jose or another woman. You, too, play an important role in determining the future of your marriage."*

Yolanda had not realized she still had any control over the situation. *"You also want a guarantee that Jose will never betray you again, and that we cannot give. However, if you decide that you desire this marriage to remain intact and be a partnership of great happiness and reward, you both will need to make some changes in your lives. It's not just Jose who will have to change, dear one. You, too, will face some consequences in your outer life if your inner life is not examined and altered."*

"I don't understand that part about changing," Yolanda interrupted. "What kind of changes do I have to make?"

The angels answered in no uncertain terms. *"First, from our perspective, we see that your marriage is devoid of fun and is focused on fear. Your personal fears, Yolanda, are twofold: You are fearful about your housework, whether everything is clean and straightened; and you are fearful about money, whether there will be enough. Your relationship with Jose has become centered around these two fears, with most of your conversations on these two topics.*

"Since Jose shares your fears about money, your conversations on this topic are extensive. However, you must know that he views himself as inadequate with regard to money, and this feeling of inadequacy has kept him from loving himself fully. His relationship with another woman was more about his desire to boost his sense of adequacy than it was about sex. He never worried about money when he was with her."

Yolanda closed her eyes, squeezing out tears. "Thank God. That makes it easier to bear. I thought he didn't love me anymore or blamed me for our money problems."

"We do see the two of you continuing your marriage, since you both share a deep commitment to it. You will both enjoy tremendous growth as you begin to speak from your hearts to one another, and not from your intellect so much of the time. You need to worry less about your house and more about the human side of life. Take time to laugh and love. It will make you a better partner and potential mother. Let go of your money worries, and let Jose know that you have. It will take off the pressure that helped him to stray. Trust us to see that you do not starve and have a roof over your head. Be willing to forgive Jose, the other woman, and yourself. We ask you to allow us to help you, and to recommit to a true marriage."

I then saw the spirits of two babies around Yolanda. Clairvoyantly, I've seen that prior to their birth, children attach to their mother like helium balloons, vying for dibs on the opportunity to be born to that mother. Children's spirits do not appear unless there is a chance for their birth. I mentioned the children to Yolanda, and she confirmed that she'd always dreamed of having two children.

Both Yolanda and Jose visited me nearly one year later. They were holding hands and displayed a youthful exuberance. Jose patted Yolanda's belly and announced that they were expecting a child. The couple and their angels reported to me that through Yolanda's efforts to change and Jose's love for her, they'd recaptured the closeness they'd felt during their courtship and healed the damage caused by his affair. The angels told me that Jose was faithful and that Yolanda was more relaxed about her home and money.

> Rx
>
> Forgive your partner and look to the changes you need to make in yourself if you want to go forward together.

Prescription for Disputes About Money

As in Jose and Yolanda's story, conflicts over money can be terribly destructive to a relationship. Money is cited in survey after survey as the number one cause of tension and arguments in intimate relationships. It has been called the root of all evil, but more correctly it might be called the root of all marital disputes.

Surprisingly, because many people have been taught to think of money as being the opposite of spirituality, neither God nor the angels want anyone to suffer from a lack of money. They see money as a tool that, used in the right way, can empower people to fulfill their Divine missions here on earth. Conversely, the angels understand that when people are pinched financially or know actual want, they are too busy worrying about survival to focus their attention on spiritual matters.

At the same time, the heavenly hosts feel doubly sad when couples, rather than using money as the resource for happiness it is meant to be, fight over it instead. Raymond and Selma had been married for six months and had lived together for two years prior to their marriage. Both held executive positions at large corporations in the San Francisco Bay Area, he in the insurance industry and she in the computer industry. They were both well dressed and highly educated, the kind of couple you might refer to as double income, no kids.

As I gazed at the couple, the angels showed me images that made me wince. I saw them screaming and throwing things at home in heated disputes. "The angels show me that you frequently fight about finances," I said. Both partners nodded.

"It's Selma," Raymond blurted. "She spends everything we make on things we don't need. Look at her right now, for instance. This suit she's wearing cost us a grand, and her shoes were over three hundred dollars. I won't even go into what her jewelry cost. Here we are, trying to build an investment portfolio, and she—"

"You mean, *you're* trying to build an investment portfolio," Selma interrupted angrily. "It's not my idea to throw money away on the stock market. Why can't we just have a 401K and a home like everyone else?"

"Because you've got the credit cards maxed out to the point where all we do is pay interest," Raymond screamed.

I could see we were getting nowhere, and I hushed them down. It was time to bring in the angels to get a sane perspective on the situation.

"Neither partner has heard the other one speak," an angel whispered in my ear. I intuitively knew what the angel meant: Raymond and Selma were each hiding behind a wall of angry words instead of listening to the other person. The angels guided me on how to help the couple.

"You have both judged the other as being in the wrong. We guide you to relinquish this tendency, as neither deserves blame. You have different styles of handling money; that is all. Your only error has been in not being open to having a tolerant conversation about this topic until now. We therefore recommend that you see situations through the eyes of the other person."

Raymond and Selma looked at me blankly. Clearly they were so caught up in their own viewpoints that they could not understand what the angels were telling them. Finally Raymond asked, "How do I see things through Selma's eyes? Isn't that impossible?"

"You've asked the angels for help," I said, "and I'll need your trust and cooperation to do this." Both nodded vehemently, and the thought crossed my mind that they were competing with each other to be the "best" client. I then fell back on a technique I had learned during my training as a psychotherapist. "Raymond, I'd like to ask you to imagine that you are Selma for a moment. Would you please, coming from Selma's perspective, talk to us about money?"

Raymond smiled, apparently thinking this would be easy. "Hi, I'm Selma, and I love to spend every dime that my husband and I make on Saint John knits. And, of course, I have to buy every shoe that Nordstrom carries, even if the charge card is maxed to its limit."

I put my hand on Raymond's shoulder and asked him to take a deep breath. I saw Selma, her arms crossed defensively over her chest, scowl at Raymond. Mentally I prayed to the angels for extra help. "Let's try this again, even if it seems awkward or silly. Raymond, please let yourself imagine that you are Selma and again, talk about money to us," I requested, reassured by the angels that this method would work.

Raymond cleared his throat nervously. Like a method actor, he moved his shoulders and neck muscles to relax into the part. He glanced at Selma and visibly relaxed as she smiled approvingly at him. "My name is Selma and I work for a Fortune 500 company as a midlevel executive." He settled into the role rapidly as he continued speaking. "Mostly men work in my department, and I sometimes wonder if I can ever get ahead. Even though I've got an excellent education in business administration and computer sciences, the company seems to promote men to upper management. I need to be taken seriously to get ahead, so I'm dressing for the position that I want. There are only two women at my company who are in upper management, and they dress to the nines. I've taken my formula for dressing from them. Otherwise, I'll always be relegated to looking like I come from the secretarial pool."

Both Raymond and Selma were silent for a long time, deep in thought. Finally Raymond said to Selma, "Are you really looking at your wardrobe as an investment?"

"That's what I've been trying to tell you," she snapped. She quickly apologized. "You think I want to dress this way?" she asked as she lifted the hem of her knit suit. "I much prefer jeans and a T-shirt, but I'll be stuck in my job forever unless I dress for success."

"The angels are asking you each to see the other's point of view," I interjected. "Selma, could you now pretend to be Raymond and talk about money?"

"OK," she said eagerly. "I'm Raymond and I inherited a small trust fund, but the bank interest rates are nothing compared to what I could make in the stock market. My father and his father before him both made a fortune in stocks. I almost feel like I'm letting down my dad by not investing in stocks. If I had my druthers, I'd cut out all the fat from our monthly budget and use it to buy commodities. It drives me crazy to read the *Journal* every morning and see that the stocks I should have invested in are peaking. The extra two thousand that Selma spends on clothes and shoes could be doubled easily through careful investing. We could both retire comfortably and live on interest and residuals within ten years if we played our cards right."

Just as when Raymond impersonated Selma, I could tell Selma was reeling from the words that had popped out of her mouth. She turned to Raymond. "I'm sorry that I misjudged you, Ray."

The angels spoke again. *"Beginning today, negotiate your stances about money through careful listening of the other's perspective, and through promising to allay all angry words and actions. It is helpful to pray before beginning a conversation on this topic. We would suggest that you hold your individual money in different banks, and pool only a portion of your income in a collective account. In that way, you are each beholden only to yourself in your spending and savings habits, and you are committed to joint resources of a fixed amount that shall be used in careful investing."*

The couple hugged each other tightly, with Raymond repeatedly saying, "We can work this out, honey."

> Rx
>
> Try to understand how your partner feels about money by seeing things from his or her point of view. Only then can you begin to resolve your financial disputes.

Prescription for Conflict Over Sex

Right after money, sex is named as the prime source of marital disharmony. Although people don't enter intimate relationships only for sex, there is the expectation that it will be an important part of the relationship. When partners have different sexual wants and desires, both feel frustrated and cheated. For instance, one partner will want to experiment with different techniques and positions, while the other will feel reluctance and perhaps aversion. Both become angry and unhappy, blaming the other partner, and the path to breakup has been paved.

In another example, one partner will feel a much stronger urge for physical sex than the other and want it considerably more often. Therapists call this "sexual desire discrepancy." Typically, the man's desire for intercourse exceeds the woman's, but this is by no means always true. I have seen the reverse, in which the man's drive is low and the woman is the dissatisfied, frustrated partner. No matter which partner is hungrier for sex, though, sexual desire discrepancy creates misunderstanding, unhappiness, and anger that can undermine the entire relationship.

Chantall came to me for an angel reading about her relationship with her live-in boyfriend, Felipe. "I want to know if he's the man I'm supposed to marry," she said. Felipe had proposed twice, but on each occasion Chantall stalled for additional time. "It's our sex life," she admitted to me.

Chantall explained that Felipe had a much stronger sex drive than she did. "I'd be very satisfied making love two or three times a week," she explained, "but Felipe wants it every day, sometimes two or three times. I love him, but he's wearing me out. When I say no, we get into these huge arguments, which take more time and energy than if I'd given in and said yes in the first place. I want to know what the angels have to say about our relationship."

"There is love in this partnership," the angels said to me, which I relayed to Chantall. *"The expression of that love is what is in question here. From our perspective, we see that Felipe expresses the depth of his love through actions and not by his words. With his physical expressions, his message to Chantall sends a confusing signal. He intends to show love and passion with his actions of physical love. Felipe is a man of great passion, both high and low, and it frustrates him to hold these emotions inside. To Felipe, physical expression is an outlet and a way to convey his messages to you, beloved Chantall."*

The difference in sexual desire between Chantall and Felipe was really the difference in the way they communicated their feelings of love for each other. Felipe tried to express his love by showing it through actions that he considering loving (sex). When he was rebuffed, he felt his love was being spurned, and he shut down. Similarly, Chantall tried to express her love by telling Felipe how much she loved him. When this didn't satisfy his craving, she felt inadequate and pressured.

I related all this to Chantall as she sat with her arms crossed and a scowl on her face. "So does that mean I should marry him and put up with his pestering me for sex all the time, or not?" she pressed.

"From our vantage point, we see that you will marry and have children, just as you desire. We caution you, however, not to rush

into such a union. To do so would not be beneficial to either yourself, your spouse, or your children."

Chantall was growing impatient. "So, you're saying not to marry Felipe?"

"Not at this time. It is not advisable, no. There is a strong need for the two of you to sit and talk with a third-party adviser, someone who is able to translate your love for each other into language that you both can share and understand, and feel the love. As it stands right now, your verbal expressions of love fall upon Felipe's deaf ears, and his demonstrative expressions of love fall upon your blind eyes. You speak different languages, and you therefore need an interpreter before you enter into a contract of marriage."

"I'm not sure whether Felipe would be open to going to counseling. Can't we just discuss this between the two of us, on our own?" Chantall asked.

"Because of your sense of time urgency in resolving this matter, we again recommend a third party, a counselor, to initiate the conversation that you eventually could have on your own, but will have much sooner in a counseling setting."

I came partway out of my semitrance state and said, "Your angels are strongly recommending that you and Felipe sit down with a counselor, and I'm going to give you the names of three licensed relationship therapists who blend spirituality with psychotherapy."

Several months later, I heard from one of the counselors. She had seen Felipe and Chantall individually and as a couple on a regular basis, and said they were learning how to deal successfully with their sexual differences. Some couples can learn how to translate each other's mode of communication through trial and error. In Felipe and Chantall's case, through counseling each learned the importance of recognizing and acknowledging his or her partner's unique expressions of love. Once Felipe felt his love acknowledged, his need to be reassured of Chantall's love through sex diminished. At the same time, the less she felt pressured for sex, the greater the desire Chantall felt for Felipe. She soon saw sex as a way of expressing her love for Felipe as well. Eventually the couple fell into an emotional and sexual pattern that was satisfying for both. Chantall later told me they were planning to marry in another year if things continued smoothly.

> Rx
>
> Learn each other's language of love by discussing your differing ways of expressing love and why you see that as a way of showing your passion. Try to translate your love for each other into language that you can share and understand.

Prescription for Spritually Unbalanced Relationships

Around 1990, in my private psychotherapy practice, the main subjects of anger and argument among couples were money, sex, and child-rearing. What a difference a decade makes. As a result of society's present spiritual renaissance, a common cause of relationship conflict has become spiritual differences, not sexual differences. It emerges when people on the spiritual path are married to or living with a partner who isn't.

Typically, the spiritually minded partner feels unable to discuss her true interests with the other person, and her attempts to bring up the issue often are met with skepticism and disdain. So she ventures out on her own attending study groups, lectures, and workshops. When she returns home, she must keep silent if she wants to avoid a fight. She cannot share her thoughts and insights with her nonspiritual partner, creating a sense of loneliness and resentment that makes her drift apart from her partner.

The situation is difficult for the nonspiritual partner, as well. If he was raised in a conservative religion, he may have been taught to fear and mistrust metaphysics and spirituality as something dark and evil not far from demonology. Even if the nonspiritual partner isn't prejudiced against the spiritual path, he may have common fears such as: What if my partner gets involved with a cult leader? What if she gets brainwashed? What if her self-esteem rises to the point where she wants a divorce?

I call these spiritually unbalanced relationships. If you are currently in such a relationship, you're likely unhappy and frustrated. The gulf of interest and understanding between you and your partner may seem well nigh uncrossable. You may be considering divorce, wondering if it's time to trade your current partner in for a more spiritually minded model. I meet hundreds of people each month in similar situations.

A student of mine, Sue, became interested in angels and psychic phenomena following her mother's death. Raised in a traditional Christian home, Sue had always been a conservative person. She'd never given much thought to life after death or other lofty philosophical concerns, however. Sue was much too focused on daily responsibilities to think about heaven, an afterlife, or other esoteric matters.

Sue fell into despair when her mother passed away following a sudden illness. One night she awoke from a sound sleep. There, at the foot of her bed, was a bluish white glow. In the middle of the light stood her mother. Sue rubbed her eyes and thought she was dreaming, but her mother was as real as life in front of her. She spoke telepathically to Sue Ellen, conveying a sense of peace and calm that instantly healed much of her grief. After her mother's apparition vanished, Sue looked over at her sleeping husband, Dan. He was still sleeping soundly.

The next morning at breakfast, Sue wanted to tell Dan about the encounter, but she worried what Dan, who'd always scoffed at such notions, would say. Summoning up the courage, Sue gently broached the subject of life after death, and Dan rolled his eyes. "Look," he said, putting down his newspaper, "when a person dies, they're gone. Sorry to break the news to you, honey. But life is sweet, short, and then it's all over."

He got up, walked over to Sue and put his hands around her shoulders. "If this is about your mother, let's get you into counseling, OK? I know you miss her so much."

As Dan walked away from the kitchen table, Sue felt like she'd been dismissed. She still wondered about her encounter. It had been so real, not like any dream she'd ever before experienced. "Maybe someone has written a book on the topic," she thought as she got dressed. An hour later Sue purchased three books on life-after-death. She found great comfort in reading the case studies of people who'd had near-death experiences and people who'd seen apparitions of departed loved ones. She concealed the books from Dan, knowing he would only put her down for reading them. She found a local bookstore that held various classes related to her new interest in metaphysics, including a class that I taught.

The only trouble was, she couldn't share her interests and experiences with the husband she had been so close to for so many years. Sue felt guilty, as though she was leading a double life, sneaking out to metaphysics classes behind her husband's back. She began to wonder if divorce might be the answer.

Finally Sue worked up the courage to come to me. The angels said, *"View your partner as a spiritual person, since everybody is a child of God, and therefore is a spiritual person in truth. Avoid thoughts that create separation and difference such as, 'He's not as spiritual as me.' Whether he knows it or not, your husband is as spiritual as you, and if you are able to see that quality in him, it will be easier for him to recognize it, too."*

"I never thought of him as a spiritual being before," Sue mused. "But it fits everything I have learned. We are all spiritual beings."

The angels then told her, *"Surrender the entire relationship to heaven. Ask God to help you release your emotional grip on the situation if you find yourself clinging to judgments or pain about your relationship. Unless you let go and allow God and us to help you, we cannot intervene. However, if you hold the intention of releasing your love life to heaven, it opens a door for Divine light to stream in and illuminate the situation. Either the relationship will heal in a miraculous, unforeseen way, or it will end in a harmonious way, and a new relationship will replace it when you are emotionally ready."*

Sue looked concerned. "I'd like to let go of the situation, but how do I do it?"

The angels offered the following Divine prescription. You may want to try it yourself. *"Picture yourself holding the relationship in the hand with which you normally write. This is your releasing hand. On the count of three, open your hand and visualize an angel carrying your relationship to the light, where treatment can ensue. Feel the sense of relief and lightness that comes with saying to God, 'Here, I give this entire situation to you. Please take over this situation so that I can unburden my mind, which is tired from always trying to think and decide what is the right thing to do.' Know that the situation is already healed in truth, and you will soon experience evidence of this. Expect a miracle."*

Sue took this advice to heart. Instead of despairing because she was stuck in a spiritually unbalanced relationship, she set about healing her own thoughts and feelings about the situation and trusted the angels to set the spiritual balance right in her life. Eventually she and her husband did separate, but on amicable terms. Sue has since met a spiritually minded man, and they are considering marriage.

Rx

Try and understand that your nonspiritual partner is nevertheless a spiritual being. Don't think thoughts that create separation. Perhaps he or she will discover spirituality in time, or you will both go your separate ways, opening the way for you to meet someone who will share the spiritual path with you.

Prescription for Dealing with Troublesome Ex's

Today many marital conflicts stem from prior relationships and marriages. With so many marriages and domestic partnerships ending in separation or divorce, the blended family has become an accepted part of life. In addition to the typical stresses and strains of marriage, these families—made up of stepparents, stepchildren, and half siblings—face unique stresses surrounding custody, visitations, and arguments with former spouses or partners.

Thirty-three-year-old Kirsten was trying to deal with a problem that arose out of remarriage. She and Kirk had been married to other people when they first met and fell in love. Kirsten had been unhappy ever since she discovered her husband had been secretly using cocaine and refused to seek treatment. Kirk also was unhappy because he wanted to have more children and his wife did not. Neither Kirsten nor Kirk had experienced much affection at home for quite some time, so they were emotionally vulnerable and romantically starved when they met. Their affair was practically inevitable and led quickly to a steady relationship.

Both decided to leave their spouses so they could be together as a couple. Kirsten's divorce was final, but Kirk's wife was dragging her heels in signing the divorce papers. "We love each other so very much," Kirsten told me. "Frankly, I have not experienced such serenity with anyone." Her smile turned to a grim frown. "Our biggest concern is his ex-wife's bitterness. She is constantly trying to poison their nine-year-old daughter's mind against both her father and me. She calls up at all hours to scream at me and at Kirk. She shoves into our house every time she comes to pick up their daughter from visitation and picks a fight with me. It's having a horrible effect on us as well as on Kirk's relationship with his daughter. We need some spiritual guidance here. What can we do to resolve this before it destroys us all?"

I took a deep breath and focused on the angels' messages for Kirsten. "Yes, the angels show me a peaceful resolution to this situation," I said.

"You can speed up the healing process by writing a letter to Kirk's ex-wife's guardian angels. Ask them to help you have a peaceful resolution, and her own angels will whisper in her ear and remind her of the importance of acting in the spirit of Divine love for the sake of her child."

Kirsten was busily writing down this remedy in her notebook. "Okay, I'm willing to try that," she said.

The angels continued relaying Kirsten's Divine prescription. *"It's important for you to hold a loving viewpoint of Kirk's ex-wife. If you expect her to behave negatively, you will actually send her negative energy that will manifest in her acting negatively."*

Kirsten looked at me, eyes wide, as if the words surprised her. "That makes sense. I've been getting a strong feeling that I needed to forgive his ex-wife. I guess I've been hearing my angels after all."

Kirsten's case reflects the prescription I've heard the angels convey in many similar situations. Their primary remedy is to hold a loving viewpoint of your ex, whether it's your ex-lover, ex-spouse, or your ex-in-laws. If we hang on to blame or unforgiveness, we harbor toxic feelings that further intensify any hostility they may harbor against us. The angels saw that Kirk's ex-wife could feel Kirsten's negative energy and expectations, which elicited even more negative behavior from her.

A year later, Kirsten had a follow-up session with me, this time to get an angel reading for the baby she and Kirk were expecting. I saw how Kirsten's changed attitude toward Kirk's former wife had eliminated a lot of stress in their household and had helped her stepchild to adjust to the divorce. The angels also said that Kirsten's unborn baby was happy to be coming into such a loving family situation.

Rx

Hold loving thoughts of the other person. Don't send negative energy that can be manifested back to you in the form of additional troubles and headaches.

CHAPTER SIX

Prescriptions for Children, Family, and Loved Ones

The angels have more than just insightful advice on how to resolve your personal challenges and romantic relationships. They also have effective prescriptions for problems with children, parents, siblings, and other loved ones. Sibling rivalry, blended-family issues, marital arguments, parent-child clashes . . . sometimes it seems that conflict within families is inevitable. According to the angels, though, with their assistance you can enjoy peaceful interactions with every member of your family.

From time to time, everyone has difficulties communicating with others, especially those closest to them. Unless these misunderstandings are nipped in the bud, they rapidly cause family rifts that worsen over time. Fortunately, when people learn to listen to and heed angelic suggestions, the angels can teach them how to have honest and loving family relationships. The angels' greatest wish for human beings is peace, and it is their great pleasure to shine light upon all human interactions.

Prescription for Unhappy, Withdrawn Children

When a child who has been normal and happy suddenly becomes withdrawn and distant, a parent becomes paralyzed with fear that something is dreadfully wrong. This fear can in itself worsen the situation, making the child even more unhappy and solitary.

The angels say that parents' positive expectations create positive results with their children. On the other hand, worry is a negative prayer that creates self-fulfilling problems. The angels counsel that children are sensitive and can feel when an adult is worried. Children then react negatively because the knowledge that their parents are afraid of something makes them feel afraid and insecure.

Ilona was worried about her oldest daughter, Kim, age 15. She wondered why Kim, who had always been a sunny, happy child, had recently grown sullen and distant. Ilona's imagination conjured up images of sexual activity, pregnancy, drug use, and worse.

"Kim keeps pushing me away whenever I try to talk with her. We were so close until just a few months ago. Now she barely responds when I talk to her and spends most of her time at home shut in her room. Do the angels say that Kim suddenly hates me for some reason? Or has she started to use drugs? I have to know why she has changed and grown so distant."

"Think about the way you viewed Kim during your moments of closeness," the angels replied. *"You held her in the highest regard and expected her to do the same. The mutual respect and the friendship was expected, and it therefore was your outcome. Think of it this way: Don't you behave differently around people who obviously like you? Doesn't it bring out the best in you when you sense that someone has high regard for you?"*

"Of course," Ilona answered.

"And conversely, don't you behave awkwardly around someone who seems to disapprove of you?"

"Yes, I suppose I do," Ilona admitted.

"Your daughter, Kim, is merely responding to your expectations. You took it personally when she began to need greater solitude and privacy to work out her thoughts now that she has become a teenager. You changed how you viewed and interacted with her. This situation is compounded every day, as the negative expectations with which you reach out to her drive her further into herself."

Ilona raised an eyebrow. "You mean that *I'm* causing Kim to behave this way?"

"In the ultimate sense, everyone is an extension of you and is affected by your positive or negative expectations. Just as you behave differently around a positive person than you do a fearful or disapproving person, so it is with Kim.

"We know that you desire a deeper and closer relationship with your daughter. We ask you to see and feel the relationship that you desire every time that you talk with or think about Kim. Imagine the two of you at the movies, shopping, talking, and having a wonderful mother-daughter friendship. When you slip into negative expectations, ask us to catch and correct your thoughts so they are aligned with your desires, not with your fears."

"I can do that," Ilona said.

Two weeks later I had a follow-up session with Ilona. "It was difficult at first to remain optimistic when Kim gave me the cold shoulder," she began, "but I prayed for help and that seemed to give me some strength. I refused to give up because I love my daughter so much. I just forced myself to visualize the two of us palling around like we used to. It seems to be having a somewhat positive effect on Kim. I know I feel a little better; hopeful, I guess."

A month or so after that conversation, I received an excited phone call from Ilona. "You'll never guess where I just returned from," she said breathlessly. "Kim and I went to the movies and had a great time. It was just like I'd visualized, and she really is starting to come around and treat me as if she likes me again. She has stopped spending so much time alone in her room, and we have been getting along fine."

It is important to state here that when a child withdraws and opts for isolation, it *could* be a warning sign of something deeper such as substance abuse, which is discussed below. If you suspect drug use, get professional help immediately. However, in the above case history, the essential cause was Kim reacting to Ilona's expectations.

Rx

Hold a positive attitude toward, and positive expectations of, your child. Positive energy will always make him or her feel closer to you and respond positively, too.

Prescription for Helping Children Adjust to a Move

A family move to a distant city can be devastating to children. The emotional wrenching of being separated from their familiar environment and friends is painful enough. Add to this the uncertainties of adjusting to a new school, schoolmates, and town, and without strong support from adults, children can suffer into adulthood from the trauma.

The angels know children often have a difficult time adjusting to a major relocation. They also understand that a move often is unavoidable and beneficial for the entire family in the long run. They have a Divine prescription for parents that will help them help their children to adjust and thrive.

They shared this remedy with Betty, a forty-four-year-old widowed mother of three. Since the accidental death of their father two years earlier, Betty's children, ages 7, 9, and 11, had slowly adjusted to life without Dad. Now, Betty had accepted a position as an office manager in a different city. The new job came with a high starting salary and generous benefits and would make life much easier for Betty and her children. Initially, Betty was thrilled. Then reality set in. When her children learned they would have to move 250 miles away from their roots and their friends, they burst into tears. Betty felt agonizing guilt. That's what brought her to me.

She asked for guidance. "I feel like I've made the best decision for all of us. But now I'm concerned about the damage uprooting my kids might do to them at this point in their lives. They've already been through so much with losing their dad. Now I'm asking them to lose their friends and familiar surroundings."

I saw a group of beautiful angels surrounding Betty, among them her deceased husband, Ed. They showed me a movie of Betty with her children in the near future, and the children were smiling happily.

The angels reassured Betty. *"Your children will be fine with the move. However, they will need some extra attention from you in the beginning while they adjust. Since they will be removed from the nurturing of their friends, they will look to you for extra nurturing. Be prepared to spend more play time with them, as this will be very important in ensuring a smooth transition."*

Betty smiled and said, "Ed always used to play with the kids a lot. It always calmed them down, and me too. I just get so busy sometimes that I forget to make the time to play with them. These days, I tend to shoo them out the door or set them down in front of the TV and tell them to go amuse themselves." She hung her head and said quietly, "I guess I need to make more time with them."

I assured Betty that her angels were not trying to make her feel guilty. They were instead offering a Divine remedy that could help her children adjust. The angels emphasized that if Betty devoted additional time to her children, they would feel safe, loved, and reassured. The children would then bring these feelings with them to school, and their happy outlook would attract new friends, and quickly help them get over their sense of loss and disruption and the longing for their old home town.

Rx

Give the children additional time and loving until they make friends and adjust to the new surroundings. Because they have lost the nurturing of their school friends, they will need more nurturing than usual from you.

Prescription for Hyperactive Children

Over the last few years, the number of children diagnosed with attention deficit hyperactivity disorder (ADHD, formerly known as attention deficit disorder or ADD) has skyrocketed. These children have inordinate amounts of excess energy that causes them to rush from one toy or game or thought to another, talk a blue streak continuously, and disrupt everyone around them. Parents of children with ADHD can be at their wit's end with frustration from their inability to communicate with their offspring, and often profoundly exhausted from the attempt to keep up with them as well.

In some U.S. schools, 20 percent of students have been diagnosed with ADHD. More disturbingly, that number continues to rise. The standard medical response to treating ADHD is methylphenidate (Ritalin). One medical researcher has estimated that as we crossed over into the twenty-first century, "some 8 million American schoolchildren" were being treated with Ritalin.

This was the case with one young man, whose mother, Maria, had consulted me about a different issue. The angels had their own agenda in mind that day. Instead of answering the question she asked, they showed me a picture of the young man living with her. When I described him to her—a tall, thin, brown-haired adolescent with wire-rimmed glasses—Maria said with surprise that this was her son, Ricardo, Ricky for short.

Suddenly I felt the intense energy of Ricky's angels as they talked to Maria through me. They were loud and vocal, anxious to get their messages to Maria. "Does your son have some sort of extra nervous energy? An excess of energy?" I asked her. "Because this is what the angels show me."

Maria picked up a stuffed bear that was on my sofa and hugged it tightly to her chest. "Yes, definitely. The school psychologist has diagnosed him as being hyperactive and put him on Ritalin. I'm very worried about how the drug is affecting him, but I don't know what else to do."

The angels said, *"Within Ricky are high ambitions. Even when he appears not to be ambitious on the outside, inside he is deeply concerned about his future. Please allow his artistic side to flourish. This is a very strong message that we emphasize to you. Artistic work is an outlet for him. Encourage him to draw, sketch, or play music as an outlet for all that extra energy. He is being prepared for leadership and a form of management role in the future. Don't worry about your son."*

Maria said that Ricky did have musical interests and talents, and that he played the piano. Maria said she would encourage and support Ricky's creative outlets and also pray for guidance as to other activities he might enjoy. The angels said that if Ricky channeled his energy into these outlets, he'd be calmer and more focused at home and school.

"We ask that you not target Ricky's energy levels with drugs in your therapeutic efforts, but instead help him discover how to focus his young mind. We see that those youths who have outlets in creative pursuits, such as music or the arts, tend to calm their minds from the whirlwind of mental activity. Involve your children in projects that truly interest them, and everyone will benefit."

I saw the ethereal body and spirit of a tall man appear next to Ricky. I said, "There is a male deceased relative with him who is tall and thin. Is this Ricky's great-grandfather?"

"Yes, that sounds just like him," Maria replied.

I continued describing what I was seeing and hearing. "Ricky's great-grandfather shows me his teeth and says there was something wrong with them as a way of helping you to identify that this is your grandpa."

Maria shrieked with delight. "He had no teeth. That is him!"

"Your grandfather is very, very close to your son, so your son definitely has a strong male influence in his life," I went on. "He shows me that Ricky doesn't always listen to you, to his angels, or to him. In fact, he shows me that Ricky's ears are often plugged, as if by wax. Anyway, Ricky's great-grandfather says to let Ricky daydream, because it is his way of working out his issues. Don't worry about him. It's all being handled. He's in God's hands."

Maria smiled and sighed with relief. "I had a feeling he was in God's hands."

I saw Maria and Ricky a year later when they both attended one of my workshops. Ricky struck me as a calm, mature young man. His mother pulled me aside and said that she'd enrolled Ricky in music lessons and that he'd also taken up photography. He was completely off of Ritalin within a few months of concentrating on his artistic abilities, and his school grades were flourishing.

What the angels prescribed for Ricky corresponds to suggestions from the prestigious National Foundation for Gifted and Creative Children. "Many gifted children are being falsely labeled with ADHD," the foundation says. "And many parents are unaware their child could be potentially gifted." According to the foundation, gifted children typically possess all the characteristics shown by Ricky and other children diagnosed with ADHD, including high sensitivity to their environment; excessive amounts of energy; becoming bored or easily distracted due to the quickness with which their minds work; becoming easily frustrated due to lack of resources to bring the creative ideas they have to fruition; and the inability to sit still unless absorbed in something of deep personal interest to them.

Rx

Children diagnosed with ADHD are often hypercreative and settle down when they are supported in finding a creative outlet for their energy.

Prescription for the Angry Child

Parents are horrified when a happy, loving child suddenly turns angry or destructive. A family's closeness is disrupted by the tension of the child's continual outbursts, and the home's loving atmosphere is marred by loud screams, slamming doors, or thrown objects. Everyone is hurt: Parents blame themselves; siblings are subjected to what is little less than emotional abuse; and schoolmates, even the school system itself, suffer. If initial efforts to turn the behavior around fail to work, parents may grow panicky, blame each other, and even divorce.

The angelic realm Divinely prescribes physical exercise as a way for children to channel their inordinate amounts of anger. The angels particularly recommend Eastern forms of exercise, such as yoga and t'ai chi, since these movements teach how to focus the mind as well as the body. This is the prescription they gave to Dianna, whose young daughter's behavior had become a serious problem.

Dianna's ten-year-old daughter, Teri, had started getting into trouble at school and exploding with anger at home. "Teri's teachers say she tries to be the center of attention, and when things don't go her way she gets very upset and lashes out both physically and verbally at the other kids," began Dianna. "They don't want anything to do with her anymore. When we try to talk about it to her, she does the same thing to us. Sometimes an angry outburst begins for no apparent reason at all. My husband says it's my fault for spoiling her. I think it's his for being too hard on her. We've been fighting with each other a lot. What happened to the sweet, affectionate little girl she used to be? Can the angels tell me where her anger comes from and how we can help her to control it?"

I instantly saw a clairvoyant image of Teri in which she was rapidly moving from activity to activity. The angels took me inside Teri's thought and emotional processes so I could truly understand her. I saw that her thoughts bounced back and forth between topics faster than a metronome measuring a minute waltz. Teri's emotions were volatile, constantly churned to a high degree that obliterated her ability to listen and concentrate.

Another set of images followed in which Teri was practicing martial arts. Far from the violent martial arts films of Hollywood, this movie depicted Teri in yoga poses. I saw her serenely stretching her arms and legs, feeling very much in control of her posture and muscles. Inside her mind and heart, I felt the tremendous difference: Teri was focused and extremely serene, almost sedate. To Dianna I said, "The angels show me that your daughter has a lot of energy, and that it isn't just anger that she has in excess. They show me that your daughter definitely needs a physical way to focus her energy, such as t'ai chi or some other Eastern practice."

The angels added, *"Your daughter is very strong and energetic, and we don't want to see her energy shut down or discouraged. She needs to feel good about her energetic nature, because she will be a powerful leader as an adult. Eastern practices are preferable to team sports, since your daughter would benefit from learning to center her mind and energy. Competitive sports would exacerbate her aggressiveness."*

Dianna perked up. "I've thought of enrolling Teri in t'ai chi classes. That is so amazing." Clearly the angels had been trying to get the same message across to Dianna, but for some reason she hadn't followed through with their guidance.

Dianna was determined to place her daughter in t'ai chi classes right away. She called me two weeks later to report a remarkable change in Teri. "For the first time since she was a small child, she's a pleasure to be around," Dianna gushed. "Her schoolteachers say that she's getting along better with everyone, and they're seeing a definite improvement in her homework and test scores. I think Teri feels much better about herself and is taking pride in her work now. Thank you, angels."

Rx

Try physical exercise as an outlet for extremely angry children, particularly Eastern forms, such as yoga, t'ai chi, and aikido, as these help focus the mind as well as the body.

Prescription for Adolescent Drug Addiction

Many family arguments arise over teenage use of drugs, cigarettes, or alcohol. The use of these substances by adolescents has become astronomical. Parents naturally fear substance abuse will negatively affect grades and employment opportunities, and lead to involvement with life-threatening behavior or criminal activity, such as driving under the influence, vandalism, gangs, stealing, or worse.

What few parents understand is the *cause* of adolescent drug abuse. The angels counsel that substance abuse typically stems from feelings of emptiness and fear. That's what they told my client Loretta about her son's marijuana smoking.

During our first session, Loretta, a homemaker and mother of three, confessed, "I'm concerned about my son, Lester. He smokes a lot of marijuana. I'm afraid he's addicted."

I repeated Lester's name several times. I find it easiest to access information about a person other than my immediate client by saying that person's name over and over. When I tuned in to Lester, I heard his angels say, *"He's being much too harsh on himself. He beats himself up mentally."* I relayed this message to Loretta and added, "He's also got some rage, the angels are telling me."

I heard Lester's angels talking loudly in my right ear. "They're telling me that Lester is using marijuana to try to escape his feelings about himself, so they ask that you have compassion with him for the time being. The angels are working on him and with him regarding his addiction."

Loretta looked surprised, as if she had expected the angels to thunderously denounce his marijuana use and instruct her to take action right away. The angels explained that those who are addicted are searching for the feeling of God's love. Addicts feel empty inside and believe they are unloved and unlovable. They then begin searching for their desire (God's love) outside themselves. Hoping to connect to God through the essence contained in substances, they overeat, drink, use drugs, gamble, spend excessively, or smoke in an attempt to infuse themselves with the full feeling of being loved.

The angels said, *"He's terrified to let go of his habit because of his fears of emptiness. Asking your son to let go of marijuana is like asking him to give up the center of his universe. He has some issues with his dad. He has felt picked on and now he picks on himself. We hold compassion for this person. He doesn't know how to love himself right now, and so he masks these feelings. It has nothing to do with you."*

"But what can I do?" Loretta pleaded. "I'm afraid he'll get involved with more dangerous drugs if he goes on like this."

The angels offered this prescription: *"It would help him to be away from city stresses and such. If he could be on a ranch or somewhere out in nature, this would help him to let go of his unhealthy ways of looking at himself and life."*

A lightbulb seemed to blink on over Loretta's head. "My brother has a ranch, and Lester loves to go there," she said excitedly. "We had planned to send him there this summer."

I told her the angels say that living on the ranch would help Lester to heal his mind. I am always thrilled when I encounter people who are ready to listen to and follow their angels' prescriptions. "So you've already been receiving Divine guidance on how your son can heal. The angels counsel you to just keep praying for him," I reassured her.

The angels then showed me a happy resolution in the form of a rainbow around Loretta and her son as a sign of a potential happy ending if their remedy was followed. They showed me the word, *worry* in a circle with a line crossing through it, to tell her not to worry.

Loretta brought Lester to see me a year later. He had stopped using marijuana while at his uncle's ranch. After he returned home and his friends offered it to him, however, he was tempted to start using it again. Lester confessed this to his mother and asked her what to do. As they talked, Lester began to describe the same feeling of emptiness the angels had described to her during our session. Loretta knew then that they both should come to me for a reading. Lester had eagerly agreed.

"The only way to banish this feeling of emptiness and experience the feeling of fullness and love is through becoming consciously aware of your oneness with God, Lester," the angels said. *"This can be accomplished in many ways: meditation, time alone in nature, a loving religious setting, or by asking us to help you. If you'll ask, we will enter into your mind, emotions, and cells and infuse you with the very high that you are seeking: the feeling of being deeply loved.*

"God's love is everywhere, since the Creator is omnipresent. Therefore, everything has the essence of God's love within it. You must create quiet time to really feel this Divine love. After all, daily noise can obliterate your awareness of our presence. That is why we angels were so adamant to your mother about your need to spend time outdoors. It is much like the adage 'One is nearer to God in a garden than anywhere else on the earth.'"

Lester expressed that he had felt full of wonderful, positive energy on his uncle's ranch, and that when he experienced this feeling, he no longer felt the craving for drugs. His mother asked Lester if he would like her to write his uncle and ask if Lester could spend all his time at his ranch. Lester brightened immediately. Today he lives full-time on the ranch and spends summers with his mother. For Lester, as for many children, the great outdoors was the angels' preferred setting for healing his feelings of emptiness.

When I talk to parents whose children might be involved in drugs, I point out that the angels emphasize the importance of intercessory prayer when dealing with the addictions of loved ones. The term *intercessory* means intervening on behalf of another. Scientific studies show that people who are prayed for have higher recovery rates from operations, illnesses, and diseases than those who aren't prayed for.

Rx

Ask the angels to help you steer the child toward meditation, spending time alone in nature, an activity dear to his or her heart, or a supportive religious setting.

Prescription for Conflict with Parents

As children mature and prepare to leave the nest, there comes a time when both child and parent discover the child's ideas about what is the best course for her future. Often, what the parent feels is best and what the child feels is best are entirely different. The enlightened parent, heeding his angels, resolves the conflict in a peaceful, healing way, launching the child off in life with love and support.

Some parents and some children, however do not instantly find their way to a harmonious solution. Instead, they butt heads and send off sparks, creating resentment where there should be only love. When this happens, the angels are eager to intervene if we will let them, and proffer many suggestions for healing the conflict.

Allysa, a nineteen-year-old college student was undergoing a major crisis. She enjoyed art and wanted to become a professional artist. Her father refused to consider the possibility and had insisted she enroll in business school instead. He'd even refused to pay for her schooling unless she did so.

"I feel so pulled to focus on art," she explained, "but my parents insist that I need something to fall back on. They're paying for my tuition, so I don't have any say-so in my curriculum. My dad is making me get a degree in business administration because he says it's practical. Every time I even suggest studying art, my father blows his top."

Allysa then confessed the terrible price bowing to her father's will had cost her. In the second semester of her freshman year, she'd begun to drink heavily, gained over twenty pounds, and become involved in a number of abusive relationships with men. Her relationship with her parents, already strained prior to college, became a battle zone each time she came home to visit.

During our discussion, Allysa asked for advice from her angels. They told me, *"This situation is an opportunity for great growth, as Allysa breaks through her long-standing fears of being open and honest with her father. He is a more advanced soul than Allysa gives him credit for, and he is open to negotiating the situation."*

I talked with Allysa about the angels' advice, quizzing her about how she'd handled past discussions with her father on the subject. The more she told me, the more I understood what the angels had meant. Allysa's attempts to communicate with her father had been more like a fencing match, in which she would thrust an angry demand at her father, then retreat to complete silence when he defended his stance.

The angels and I asked Allysa to talk with her father as if she were talking with a beloved friend or mentor. Through me, the angels said, *"Suggest to him this compromise approach, which is highly suggested for you: Add some art classes to your schedule, and defer one or two business classes until a later date."*

They were proposing a double major. When I suggested this to Allysa, she was struck by the simplicity of the solution. She and her father had been looking at her college career as an all-or-nothing proposition. Allysa went home and had a rational discussion with her father. They talked about how valuable it would be for an artist to have business skills, and vice versa. Her father agreed to adding two art classes to her schedule and dropping one business class.

When next I heard from her, Allysa reported feeling happier and more positive about her future than she had in a long time. The extra weight was gone, as were the family disputes.

Rx

Expect others to be more evolved than you think they are. Suggest compromise and you will get it.

Prescription for Adult Sibling Rivalry

Conflicts between siblings are inevitable. Parents are human and have only so much time and energy and money to go around. Each child is bound to experience moments when he yearns for parental attention or resources, only to see them go to his sibling. The resulting tension, jealousy, and hostility lead to flare-ups, resentments, and rivalries that do not always end with childhood. Unless resolved, they may continue to play out through adulthood, with one or both siblings fighting the other at every possible moment, or missing no opportunity to disparage or demean the other.

Fahri's sister Nedi was constantly putting Fahri down. Fahri, a shop owner, was the eldest of three daughters. Their father had died when they were very young. Fahri's mother had gone to work following his death and had little time to give to her children. Nedi, the middle child, had always resented Fahri's status as the eldest, as well as the attention her mother gave to the youngest sister. As a result, Nedi constantly put Fahri down ever since they were children, and continued to do so at every family gathering now that each had grown up and married.

"Nedi is always insulting me," Fahri fumed. "Just this week she said I was probably so bad in bed my husband would eventually leave me. When I complain, Nedi says that I'm too sensitive and that she's just joking. But her jokes hurt my feelings, and I don't know how to get her to stop."

The angels taught Fahri the most effective conflict resolution method I have ever seen. *"To heal conflict, hold the intention of talking with the guardian angels of any friend or family member with whom you have a concern. Then, either have a mental conversation with this person's angels, or write the angels a letter. Pour out your heart to these angels and ask them for help in resolving the conflict. You can be certain that the angels share your goal of peace. After asking these angels for help, pay extra attention to your feelings, hunches, dreams, or visions. These are the channels we will use to send you guidance toward a loving resolution with your sister."*

Fahri was willing to give the method a try, but she wondered whether she'd be successful in contacting her sister's guardian angels and whether they could turn Nedi's attitude around.

"You don't need to be psychic in order to talk to another person's guardian angels," I explained. "You may not even hear or feel the angels replying to your request. But you will see the evidence that they heard you, because they'll intervene in bringing peace to the situation quite rapidly. In fact, close your eyes right now. Take a deep breath and hold the intention of sending a mental message to your sister's guardian angels. Then, mentally tell the angels how you feel and that you'd like to have a peaceful resolution."

I watched as Fahri followed my instructions. She opened her eyes and smiled. "I feel better," she announced. "More hopeful that Nedi and I can have a normal sisterly relationship."

Two weeks later Fahri sent me an e-mail. She'd had dinner with her sister. Nedi had arrived at the restaurant looking sheepish. "I've been seeing a therapist," her sister admitted before Fahri could say anything, "and I have come to realize I haven't been a very good sister to you. I directed a lot of my anger and resentment over our father's death, and my jealousy that Mom spent more time talking about household matters with you, at you. I know now that was wrong, and I was wondering if it is too late for us to begin all over and be sisters again."

When Nedi asked for Fahri's forgiveness, both sisters burst into tears and reconciled. Fahri called the change in her sister nothing short of miraculous. Her guardian angels must have been talking to her from above. I can't explain it otherwise.

Talking directly to the other person's guardian angels also works well when you realize you have injured others by saying or doing things you later regret. Ask their angels to intervene and help the person you have hurt forgive you for your trespasses. The angels are happy to help you correct your mistakes and to learn from them so that you do not repeat them.

Rx

Talk directly to your sibling's guardian angels; ask the angels to intervene and help end the conflict between you.

Prescription for Aging Parents

People are living longer and longer due to advances in medicine and technology. As a result, the question of what arrangements to make for aging parents has become a major life issue that most individuals and couples must face eventually. Adult children agonize over whether to move mom or dad in with them or into a convalescent home. Doing the former may upset the adult child's spouse or partner and disrupt the couple's normal routine and personal life. Doing the latter may leave the adult child with unbearable feelings of guilt.

My client Sidney, who owns a small wine-importing business with his life partner, Antonio, found that his elderly mother's failing health was becoming a serious concern for himself and a cause of conflict with his lover. "Her eyesight's going, and I don't think she's taking very good care of herself," he told me. "She runs into the furniture and walls at home, so she's got a lot of scrapes and bruises. I'm concerned that she's going to fall and break her hip one of these days. I don't know what to do, and I go round and round in circles in my mind. I mean, should I have Mom move in with me and my partner? Antonio really doesn't relish the idea. In fact, we've been fighting over it a lot, and we almost never fight. Should I put her in a nursing home? I think that that would kill Mom. I can't get my brother to help out, so it all seems to be on my shoulders. What do the angels say?"

The angels had begun speaking before Sidney completed his question. *"You are trying to use your intellect to resolve an emotional issue. We see you wrestling with guilt and worry over this situation, and your emotional reactions are understandable to us. Anything involving your beloved mother is an emotional situation. But to resolve the situation in a way that's best for everyone involved, you cannot switch channels and attempt to find a resolution through intellectual means. You must stay on the channel of emotions from which the situation originally evolved."*

I relayed this to Sidney. "I guess I am pretty mental," he acknowledged. "I'm the one who runs the business end of our company. Antonio selects the wines. I don't know how else to approach a problem but by thinking about it. What should I do?"

"What we say to you is this: You are uncomfortable with what you see as all your current choices. If you bring your mother home to live with you, you worry about your partner's reaction. You worry that your mother may feel uncomfortable around Antonio, or that she may feel she is imposing on you. Conversely, you are concerned that if you place your mother in a retirement home, she may feel you don't love her and may whither away from depression or neglect.

"We say to you that there are other options available, and we will guide you with your permission. Allow us to help you find a suitable home for your mother to reside in. With each location, use your emotions to make your decision. Notice what your belly tells you as you 'try on' different retirement homes. It is your connection to the Divine. Pay attention to your heart, and you will know which residence will lead to peace for you, your mother, and your partner."

At the angels' suggestion, I asked Sidney to imagine his mother living at his home. He closed his eyes, grimaced, and placed his hand on his stomach. "What is your belly telling you?" I asked.

"That it won't work out," he said. "It feels like my mother and partner will be cold and distant to each other. It will drive a wedge between me and both of them and be really uncomfortable for all of us."

"Now," I counseled, "imagine your mother living in a senior retirement center. Not a convalescent hospital, but more like an apartment complex where meals and other services are provided. What does your belly tell you now?"

"That as long as I visited my mom frequently, she'd be really happy. We'd both be really happy, because she'd have freedom but would also be supervised somewhat."

Letting his emotions be his guide, Sidney and Antonio visited a number of elder-care homes in the city where they live. Eventually they found one that they both agreed had good vibes. When Sidney brought his mother there to inspect it, both were astonished to find that one of her girlhood friends was already a resident. Sidney's mother brightened immediately, and she looked forward enthusiastically to the move.

Rx

Faced with the need to make decisions about elderly parents, try to imagine all of the various possible solutions. Use the way your body and emotions react as a barometer to gauge the optimal solution for everyone.

CHAPTER SEVEN

Prescriptions for Career, Business, and Finances

Most of us spend the majority of our lives working. More time is invested in work than in family, love life, or health. Yet, careers deeply impact those areas of personal life as well. Worries about money keep us up at night and trigger arguments with loved ones. Ambitions to get ahead at work turn co-workers into feuding contestants and fuel stress-related illnesses. Business owners faced with fierce competition fear losing the source of their livelihood and self-esteem.

For many, our job is our personal identity. After all, the first question when meeting a new acquaintance usually is "What do you do for a living?" The answer often stimulates or disqualifies a potential friendship. We invest ourselves in our job, whether we enjoy that job or not. If we start up our own business, we invest our hopes, dreams, future, spare time, and personal savings account.

The angels don't just want to provide prescriptions for our personal and love lives. They also want to help us with solutions for business, career, and financial dilemmas. Heaven has guidance for how we can earn a meaningful living in meaningful ways. God also can advise us on how to turn a failing venture into a resounding success. Any of our deceased loved ones who had areas of business or financial expertise stand by ready to lend advice and counsel.

Prescription for Finding the Right Career

Surveys show that picking the right job and making the right career choice plays a major role in determining whether or not you view your life as truly satisfying. The wrong choice can imprison you in a painful situation that is bad for your body, mind, spirit, family, and even your personal finances. The wrong job can destroy your health and marriage, whereas the right job can be the keystone of a satisfying, enjoyable life.

Sadly, far too many people slave away at what feel like unrewarding, dead-end jobs that have no connection to their real interests and seem to hold no potential for fulfillment. They go home every night from a job of drudgery, feeling they have spent another empty and meaningless day just to earn another dollar. They long for something better but don't know if it exists or if they can find it, or if they would be worthy if they could find it.

Some people reject this approach as unrealistic. They don't think it's wise to put personal fulfillment first when seeking work. They feel other considerations must come first, such as family responsibilities, debts, and earning a living. "Oh yes, it's great when someone is lucky enough to get work they enjoy," these scoffers say. "But we can't all count on being that lucky. I have three kids to feed and a roof to put over their heads."

But, God and our guardian angels say not only that you deserve spiritually satisfying work that pays an adequate wage, but also that they will help you get it. All human beings have been given special gifts and passions, things they do well and enjoy so much that they would do them all the time whether they got paid for it or not. It might be a knack for figures, a gift for playing the violin, the ability to calm and reassure others, the sensitive fingers of a surgeon, unusual physical endurance and dexterity, a yen for public service, or an unusually stable personality.

God gave you these gifts to be used, and He will do whatever is necessary to ensure you get to use them, one baby step at a time. What you need is faith in yourself and God to set out on the path without a map, trusting that because this is what God also desires, the angels will ensure that you ultimately arrive at your destination. Divine guidance may take the form of an unexpected phone call, an article you read in a magazine, a chance remark overheard at lunch, a fascinating class you learned about, or bumping into an old friend at a supermarket. Eventually, without you or your family ending up on the street, you will be guided to the career and job you were meant for.

Gillian, a business school graduate, had reached a crisis over the direction of her career. She was sick of her position in middle management at a large data-processing firm and was considering a change. Gillian had felt the same kind of restlessness before and had switched jobs within the middle levels of the business community several times. She had worked for a recording company, a tennis racket manufacturer, and a health maintenance organization, as well as in the company headquarters of a national chain of appliance stores. Each time she believed a new work environment and co-workers would give her the boost she was looking for. But somehow Gillian always seemed to end up feeling dissatisfied, frustrated, and bored once again.

"Obviously I'm doing something wrong," Gillian lamented. "I'm always certain every new job is the one that will make me happy, but I'm always miserable within a couple of months after I start. Can the angels find me a career I can live with? I just can't keep going on the way I am."

"You have chosen your professions based upon the income you could derive and not upon the conditions that truly lend to your happiness and peace," the angels counseled.

She wrinkled her brow. "Oh sure, I get tired of being a manager, and I've thought about making a clean break and doing something completely different. But I invested a lot of time in my MBA, and I need the money to pay off my student loans. I just signed a three-year lease on a new apartment, and I am chipping in on my mother's hospital bills. Nothing else I could do would pay as good. I just can't afford to quit."

"Stay in the here-and-now," the angels strongly urged. *"Don't worry about 'How am I going to pay for this?' or 'How can I be qualified for this?' Your only duty is to nurture your heart and soul by seeking more fulfilling work. You will have more energy and enthusiasm to give to everything in your life. Leave the 'how' up to God. He will guide you step by step, and all the doors will open for you at the right moment. Have trust.*

"Don't procrastinate until you get absolute assurance that guarantees your success. Until you take step A, God won't tell you what step B is. If you seek a fulfilling future, be assured that whatever roadblocks lie along the way, you will be guided to that future with God's help."

"I'm willing to try anything," Gillian responded, "but I really haven't got a clue what kind of job I would like. I have tried to imagine my future before, but I just can't see it clearly. Can the angels help me here?"

Gillian's angels showed me a mental image of Gillian feeling exuberant whenever she was amid trees, plants, and flowers. *"We urge you to try again in your job search, and keep in mind that you are happiest among the outdoors and the nature angels. Nature holds a very special place in your heart. Conversely, you are unhappy when you are cooped up indoors for extended periods of time. Do not believe that you must suffer for your money, dearest one. For you are perfectly capable of a delightful career working amid the trees, plants, and flowers that you love so dearly."*

For the first time Gillian's face lit up. "That's a wonderful idea. I'm going on-line tonight to start researching some possibilities."

Several weeks later Gillian phoned me. "This is embarrassing. I've discovered several wonderful job possibilities, but I don't know how to decide which one to take. Do you or the angels have any suggestions?"

The angels gave her a quick reading, *"Request that we assist you in knowing which career would best suit your interests and needs. You can voice this request aloud, mentally, or by writing it. Ask for the guidance to be very loud, clear, and specific in our answers to you. Or, before you go to sleep, ask us to enter your dreams and give you a vivid picture of your life's purpose."*

"How will I know the answers when they come?" Gillian asked. "I'm not a psychic."

I told her what I have repeated to clients so many times before. Angels' guidance toward the right career would come in the form of strong, unexplained feelings, vivid dreams, a sudden picture, or a phrase or name she might hear as if spoken in her head. If she wasn't certain she understood the message clearly, she could ask her angels for a sign to validate her interpretation. If you ask, the angels will always find ways to give you palpable, indisputable reassurance that you are receiving their suggestions clearly and correctly.

Further, I explained to Gillian that if she had several good career possibilities and couldn't get a clear answer as to which one to take, she should not get caught up in the illusion that there was only one perfect job. She would drive herself crazy attempting to puzzle it out. Just as each person has not one, but many potential soulmates, each person also has many possible career paths, each of which could bring them great fulfillment. I added that as long as the work the person chooses gives them ample scope to use their God-given interests and skills to the fullest, they will experience profound satisfaction and success in every area of life. Gillian promised to bear all this in mind as she continued her job search.

When next I saw Gillian, she rushed up and gave me a big hug. "The angels were so right. I'm working for the National Park Service. I manage the maintenance division and spend all day driving through nature. I've never been happier in my life."

Always, the angels want you to seek work in fields that are aligned with your natural interests and passions. For someone like Gillian who loves to be outdoors, an office job would be akin to a prison sentence. For someone who is creative, drudgery would be just as terrible a fate. For someone who loves the visual, working with numbers all day long would be torture. For someone who likes helping people, being stuck in a cubicle at a computer terminal would be bleak and meaningless. Once Gillian found a job that kept her outdoors, she experienced a level of satisfaction and happiness in her work she had never imagined possible.

Rx

Seek fulfilling work in line with your talents and interests. Trust that the path to your ideal position will be opened one step at a time.

Prescription for Career Timing

When you are anxious to get a better job or leave your current position and seek a whole new vocation, you may pray for guidance and not receive an instant response. No one you contact is hiring, and no mysterious coincidence occurs to steer you in the right direction. Clear guidance as to what you should do next is not forthcoming. When this happens, you may begin to doubt the angels. If the angels are real, you wonder, and they are supposed to leap instantly to fulfill my needs when I ask for help, then why haven't I gotten the contact that leads me to that new job by now?

In regard to career transitions and other matters, the angels caution you to exercise patience. The angels know all about your deep desire to work in your chosen field. Yet, the angels also know that you might suffer enormous setbacks if you enter a profession or make a major change prematurely. Thus, when that dream job hasn't materialized yet, the angels say it's not because it isn't waiting in the wings. It's because you haven't allowed sufficient time for the angels to arrange matters so that it can fall directly into your lap. The angels also say that sometimes you may not be quite ready for the changes, that you may need to learn a specific lesson first, or that you should heal relationships with co-workers through forgiveness, or it could be as simple as enrolling in a class you need to take.

If you're praying for help with your career, remember that the universe sometimes keeps the doors closed until it is time for you to walk through them. This is called Divine timing, and it is the way God and the angels arrange things synchronistically so that a multitude of events and people work harmoniously to bring something about naturally and effortlessly.

This is the lesson the angels taught Carla. As Carla, a thirtyish woman about whom I knew little except that she was a CPA, took her seat in my office, her angels began showing me vivid movies. I saw an image of Carla as a giraffe, her neck stretched high up into the trees to eat foliage, symbolizing that she was reaching toward something new. In this way, the angels made clear their point that she was currently in a growth period.

"The angels show me you're in a time of tremendous growth right now," I said. "You're extending and stretching yourself."

Carla acknowledged that this was true. I saw Carla's guardian angels clapping their hands to express their approval at the serious effort she was making to grow as a person. I shared this vision with Carla and relayed what her angels were saying *"You're going to see things from other perspectives and vantage points this way. You do have the courage to do this. Some people are afraid to look at things a different way. Your angels bless you for your willingness to see things in a new light."*

"That's all very well," Carla said, "but where are the angels when I really need them? I'm very unhappy in my current work. My life is in chaos. My husband and I have just separated and are divorcing. I've moved back in with my parents. I have been reassessing my entire life, especially the question of what kind of job I want to be doing for the next twenty or thirty years. I am seeking a new direction in life, and the kind of fulfilling work you talk about. I've done just like you say and asked the angels to send me guidance, to direct me to a new job, a new career, to something that would allow me to use all my talents and help make the world a better place. But the angels don't seem to be responding. It's been a couple of months now, and nothing has happened. I'm beginning to wonder if there really are angels. Or am I just doing something wrong?"

"No, dear one, you are doing nothing wrong," the angels replied. *"However, you are naturally impatient to complete this transition and move on to your future life. There is a Divine timing to events, directed by God's hand. It has not quite arrived, as far as leaving your present job is concerned. We ask you to have patience with yourself, with us, with outside circumstances, and with heaven. When you ask for a life change in your career or other area, we immediately ascertain what conditions are necessary. Just as the reconstruction of a building proceeds step-by-step in a certain sequence, or the structure will be flimsy, unstable, and prone to collapse, so too does the reconstruction of a new life and a new career.*

"For you, the construction of your new life has not quite been completed. Nor have you yet had sufficient time to fully understand all the changes you are undergoing from the ending of your old life. This would not be the opportune moment for you to make a significant change in career and work. You could in fairness do justice to neither, and it would hinder rather than further your progress and growth.

"Trust that we know your true heart's desire, and we are working to prepare you and your new circumstances in the best possible way. In a few months, you will have a better grasp of your new self and what you need to do next in life. Until that time, though, you must keep an open mind and continue reading and learning about the topics that interest you the most. What you study doesn't have to be applicable to

your current life, as long as it interests you strongly. In the meantime, your joy of learning these things is your road map to your new career."

Reassured that the angels were indeed listening and that all she needed to do was to have a little patience, Carla went home with a lighter heart. She told me that what the angels said had inspired her to wait the present period out less anxiously and to continue reassessing her life and the lessons to be learned from her divorce and unhappy career choice.

> Rx
>
> When that new job or career change you want so badly doesn't come through right away, don't despair. The right combination of circumstances can take time to culminate. There is a Divine timing behind things.

Prescription for Disliking One's Work

Some of you never even think about leaving a job you detest. You may believe it is childish to worry about whether one's work is fulfilling, satisfying, or joyous. Something, perhaps from our Puritan heritage, has given the erroneous impression that earning a livelihood should be difficult and painful, or even that it is the way God meant it to be. "Why do you think they call it work?" sums up this attitude.

But the angels say God does not intend you to suffer in any way. Work as a pain-filled burden is not a part of God's plan for human kind. The angels want you to find satisfying work that makes you happy, where you can follow your true talents and interests to be of service in the world. God and the angels will support you in every way necessary as long as you aim toward this goal.

The angels and I tried to explain this to a single social worker named Clarence. Never before had I sensed such a low ebb of life energy in one of my clients. His voice sounded drained, as if his soul itself was exhausted. It didn't take a psychic to know that Clarence was suffering from extreme burnout. His profession was clue enough—after all, social workers are faced with heavy case loads that involve them in many intensely emotional and volatile family situations. Yet, Clarence sounded as though he had pushed himself beyond burnout to the point of being a walking zombie. Everything his angels showed me only reinforced this theme.

I commented on how tired he looked. Clarence responded defensively, "Well, what do you expect? I'm a social worker and it goes with the territory."

I asked Clarence if he had ever considered changing jobs. He quickly put the brakes on. "Quit my job. Get in some other line of work. Sure, I've thought about it. Who hasn't? It's nice to dream and everything. But let's get real. No one likes their job. That's not what working is about. It's about drawing a paycheck, and getting three squares a day, and medical insurance, and having some kind of retirement fund for when you're old. Sure, I can't stand my job. Most people feel that way, don't they? I'm not alone in that. I've got to bring in enough money to pay the bills, don't I? I have an ailing mom I have to help support."

Clarence's negativity upset me at first, and I wondered whether he was determined to stay miserable and would resist the angels' help. Then I decided to follow what I always think is the best advice and asked the angels for guidance on how I could get through to this unhappy man. Immediately I felt their energy calm me.

"Actually, Clarence," I said, "many people enjoy their jobs. They wake up feeling excited about their day and can't wait to get to work. I'm not necessarily talking about workaholics, but rather people who have found work they love so much that simply the doing of it fills them with energy."

"You expect your job to be painful," the angels confronted Clarence lovingly. *"But this is not what God intends for His children.*

You watched both your parents suffer in their jobs, and you've held this negative belief about work ever since. But those were choices they made as part of their spiritual path in order to make a better life for you. To them, those were rewarding, fulfilling jobs. Didn't you feel the fullness of their love for you? How could they be so full of love if their jobs were so empty?"

Clarence puzzled over the question. "I don't know. I don't know," he repeated. I could see that he was still resisting what the angels were telling him.

"Reflect on the friends you have who do work at jobs that make them excited and happy, that they are proud of and would say give them some kind of contentment. This is what we want for you, too. Try to find the courage to believe that joy, love, and fulfillment are what work is intended to be about. Then let us help guide you to it."

Clarence still looked unconvinced, and I felt with a sinking heart that he was going to disregard the angels' prescription. Alas, I was right. I heard from a friend that he had left our session saying it was all a lot of angel bunk. He stayed at his job and didn't change in any way. A few years later he died of a stroke.

If Clarence had been able to see work as the angels do instead of something that was meant to be a burden, and if he accepted the notion of vocation as a source of fulfillment, he would have been free to seek the job that might have saved him and kept him alive for many satisfying, meaningful years.

Rx

Look around you at the people you know who enjoy what they do. Learn that work doesn't have to be joyless or painful. Follow your friends' examples and seek the kind of fulfilling vocation you deserve.

Prescription for Job Stress

Stress, particularly job-related stress, is one of the top killers today. It is the cause of strokes, heart attacks, digestive disorders, and pulmonary complications that kill millions every year. Job stress often is a factor in divorce, child abuse, alcoholism and drug abuse, suicide, and mental illness. Socially and personally, the costs of work-related stress are incalculable.

Job stress is especially rampant today as companies downsize and employees are expected to assume the work of two or three people. No wonder so many in the workforce feel they are stuck on a treadmill, running from activity to activity from the time they awaken until the time they go to sleep. Contributing factors adding to their stress load include boredom, abusive employers, noisy work environments, time-consuming commutes, tension between co-workers, juggling family and work schedules, and financial strain.

The angels know the negative consequences of stress better than we do and want to help us lower our stress levels. When your guardian angels notice you are feeling pressure, they will whisper stress management suggestions in your ear. This manifests when you suddenly get the urge to spend time outdoors in nature, to go to a museum or ballgame, to rent a new comedy on video and spend the evening laughing before the television, to take a brisk lunchtime walk through the park, or to spend time engaged in some other relaxing, tension-releasing activity.

If you're not aware that these messages come from heaven, you may discount them as lazy or wishful thinking. Yet, when you have the courage to follow these inner angelic voices and heed their advice, you not only free yourself at least temporarily from the pressure you normally live and labor under, but you also significantly increase your productivity and creativity at work.

Sophia, a forty-seven-year-old executive assistant for a local department store chain, phoned me for an session, saying she didn't have time to meet with me in person. "I need help," she stated. "I feel like I'm going crazy. My job is killing me."

Sophia explained that she had originally loved her job organizing and doing data input for the district manager.

"Then our company was bought out by another corporation. That's when a third of our staff was laid off, and the rest of us had to take on the extra work."

She was assigned two additional bosses whose work she also was required to keep up with. With three bosses, her workload tripled. "Not only that, but each of my bosses wants me to drop everything and pay attention to his needs, even if I'm in the middle of something urgent for one of my other bosses. Almost every day, I bring work home."

To make matters worse, Sophia's husband was upset that she didn't have time for him anymore. He wanted her to quit. Sophia was afraid she could never get another job that paid as well. "We fight about it constantly. But what else am I going to do? The stress of trying to get everything done, and do it well, is beginning to really get to me. I'm much more short with people, I feel tired and grouchy all the time, and I often say things I wish I hadn't. I find myself getting depressed a lot, too. I'm beginning to feel I'm incompetent and it just isn't worth trying anymore. Sometimes I just want to lie down and die. I haven't felt well since the merger."

The angels told her, *"Fun is a necessity, not a luxury. We applaud your desire to be all things to everyone. It comes from your loving nature. However, by pushing yourself to the limit, you are not being loving to yourself and your family. We ask you to simply do this: Fulfill your responsibilities while you are at work, ask for and accept help from your co-workers whenever possible, and then leave your work at work at the end of the day."*

"But I can't keep up with the workload unless I take it home with me at night," Sophia argued.

"By doing so, you are supporting a policy of overwork and contributing to the undercurrent of frustration at your job," the angels continued. *"They cannot see that you need help when you shield them from the unreal nature of your current schedule. We say that you must do your job diligently during the day, and then go home and rest and enjoy yourself at night. Let the chips fall where they*

may. Your original boss will aid and support you in getting assistance for your many tasks. He welcomes the opportunity to have you as his personal aide, believe us."

I added, "Your angels say that you need to take a break and rest, that the constant stress is the issue. Can you take one or two days off and rest, truly rest? This is the answer, the angels say."

Sophia said she and her husband had been talking about taking a seaside vacation. I urged her to consider taking it in the very near future. I've heard the angels frequently prescribe time-outs like this to those under stress. Sometimes they advise vacations; other times they suggest a simple getaway or a weekly date at a nice restaurant or concert away from the kids. Most often the angels recommend people take these respites outdoors, next to the ocean, or a lake, or in the mountains or the forest. They know that reconnecting with nature puts humans back in touch with God and provides a balm for tired souls.

In Sophia's case, her angels also prescribed exercise. The angels suddenly showed me a movie of Sophia jogging and told her, through me, that it was time for her to begin exercising regularly. "Your angels say that your father died of a heart attack when he was forty-eight," I told Sophia, who nodded in confirmation.

"As you near that age yourself, it's even more important for you to care for your heart and cardiovascular system. That is because of the amount of job stress you carry, plus the fact that you worry about your heart's health. By exercising, you will reduce your worry about health, and by worrying less, you will in fact cut down on your health risks."

Other proactive remedies for job stress the angels have given my clients include changing jobs; returning to school to facilitate a major career change; carpooling or moving closer to work to cut commute time; avoiding or reducing the consumption of caffeine, alcohol, or nicotine; restructuring schedules with children, baby-sitters, and spouse to eliminate panicky rushes to and from work; and delegating responsibilities.

> Rx
>
> Rest is a necessity, not a luxury. Let go of stress by taking a time-out. Get out into nature or relax with an enjoyable activity.

Prescription for Making Bad Jobs Better

Of course, you don't need to leave every unsatisfactory job in search of greener fields. Because of family and financial obligations, sometimes you can't leave. The angels say it may be in your best interests to see what you can do to transform the situation and mold it closer to your heart's desire. It makes no difference whether the problem is an exploitative boss, a spiteful co-worker, unbearable noise, a dead-end job, business politics, a pressure-cooker environment, boring work, or even corporate practices that run counter to your morals. The angels advise that if you stick it out and put forth a positive effort to make things better, you can turn the situation around and create those greener pastures right in your own backyards.

With so many people seeking career changes these days, I frequently consult with clients whose first thought is to seek employment elsewhere without ever pausing to wonder if there is anything they themselves could do to heal their situation at work. One such was Trina, a twentysomething facilities manager. Trina was employed by a paint manufacturing company that found it more profitable to pollute and simply pay whatever fine was levied rather than follow the law and help protect the environment. Trina felt guilty about many of their corporate practices and was embarrassed to tell people what company she worked for. The company had recruited her while she was in college, and at the time she hadn't realized what she was getting into. Now, after several years, she truly detested her job for a long time and had dreamed of nothing but quitting.

Trina wanted advice on how to go about seeking a less repugnant situation. "I don't want to earn my paycheck from anything that is hurting our environment," she began. "I want to switch to something more in line with my own inner beliefs so that I can feel good about what I do. But I have to care for my husband, who is now in a wheelchair after an auto accident. I can't afford to quit until I have that job in my hand."

For almost a year Trina had been job-searching without any success. She'd tried placement services, networking groups, and Internet chat rooms, and had sent out mass mailings of her résumé. "Nothing panned out," she lamented. "I'm stuck at a job I can't stand, that makes me feel worse about myself every day. I have even tried praying, but that hasn't gotten me anywhere either. Do you have any suggestions?"

Trina's angels immediately began communicating with me. They were going so fast that even after years of practice, it was hard for me to keep up. I advised Trina that the angels had a prescription for her, but that she should brace herself, because it wasn't the remedy she probably was expecting.

"Nothing has come to replace your present job, because you are not supposed to leave it. You were brought to this job for a reason, and you still have important work to perform and an important contribution you can make. You cannot expect to leave a spiritual and moral wrong like environmental pollution behind without trying something to help correct it and at the same time expect to be guided to spiritual and moral work that will give you peace and contentment. You must become involved in resolving this situation before your work there is completed."

The angels said they wanted Trina to use her position as facilities manager to show her bosses that safer environmental practices were more cost effective in the long run. At first Trina balked at the thought, protesting that her job wasn't that important, that she was helpless to change her company's ways, that no one would pay any attention to her because she wasn't an expert.

Naturally, the angels had an answer. *"You will show them the financial benefits of upgrading their waste control systems, which will save them money over their present system of paying fines. We will guide you to the right information so that your report will bring you great favor at work. All you need to do is commit to completing this project. We will do the rest."*

"Actually," Trina admitted, "I've been thinking, and it does seem wrong to quit the paint factory without trying to do anything to make things better. If you and the angels will show me what to do, I'll give it a try." She laughed. "I guess I haven't got anything to lose, anyway."

The angels reiterated that they would guide Trina every step of the way, and that if she took the first steps, they would ensure that she would have everything she needed to make her case successfully before the company's top brass.

I could see Trina was still dubious, but she resolved she would start that night by logging onto the Internet and researching all the fines the company had paid over the last ten years. "As long as I can call on you for advice now and then," she told me. I nodded

Puzzlingly, Trina never contacted me again. I wondered what had become of her and whether she'd stuck with the task the angels had assigned her. Many months later I ran into her one night when I was snowed in at an airport, and all flights had been canceled. I stopped to purchase something to drink, and as I turned around to find a table, there was Trina right behind me in line. She beamed and began chattering enthusiastically.

"It was amazing what happened after my session. I was going to call you about where to start and what to do. But that night on the Internet I posted a single question onto a mailing list, and I started getting flooded with information. People would send me Website addresses or photocopies of magazine articles. I got what was like a graduate course in environmental protection law and successful strategies for persuading companies and corporations that it is in their best interests to bring their practices in line with their environmental responsibilities. Whenever I'd start to lose steam or get stuck as to where to go or what to do next, here would come an e-mail with just the right facts and figures or note of encouragement to spur me on. It was like I had invisible researchers and coaches helping me all the way. And I guess I did at that. It was the angels, of course.

"Soon I had everything I needed to present an unarguable set of facts, figures, and conclusions proving step-by-step how much money we were spending each year on fines, and how much less it would cost us to stay within environmental guidelines using the new waste disposal technologies. My knees were shaking as I walked into the meeting where I was to describe my proposals. When I saw the company president and comptroller sitting there, they looked so serious and businesslike I wanted to run out. Just then, something the angels had said at our session came back to me. I had forgotten it until then. They said that if I would just present their proposals, they would do the rest. I felt calmer right away. I guess I realized it really was in their hands, or in someone's hands anyway. It sure was out of mine now. What the heck, I didn't like the job anyway.

"I handed out copies of my report to everyone and began my presentation. I ended by pointing out that not only would we save several million dollars each year, but we'd also generate millions of dollars more in goodwill and free publicity. Afterward, when I looked around the table, I expected blank expressions or disapproval or contempt. But the president and comptroller actually were looking at each other and nodding. Maybe the angels whispered in their ears, because they're actually going to implement most of what I suggested."

Trina was put in charge of the new program and received an increase in salary. She is now happy in her job and has no plans to leave.

> Rx
>
> God helps those who have attempted to help themselves first by trying to make a bad job better. Before writing off a job you aren't happy with, take a closer look and see if it could be turned around with a little effort.

Prescription for Conflict with Co-workers

Nothing can turn a joyous job into a living nightmare faster than a co-worker or boss you can't get along with or who can't get along with you. The workplace is challenging enough without having the constant expectation of conflict and strife. It may be a situation where two of you somehow strike sparks off each other, no matter how hard you try not to, or a situation where someone has taken an instant dislike to you. Having someone in your face all day long is a one-way ticket to stress, strain, and severe job dissatisfaction. If the situation is bad enough, it can even carry over into your home life, adding to the stresses and strains of your marriage, too.

Fortunately, there are angelic remedies for healing these workplace conflicts, as my client Lars found out. Lars had come for an angel therapy session because he was unhappy at work. A fourth-grade teacher, Lars complained that his school's new principal, Anita, was making his life miserable.

"I don't know what it is, but Anita seems to have it in for me. She constantly takes issue with everything I say. At faculty meetings the woman never misses the opportunity to put me down in front of everyone. When I try to avoid her, I swear she seeks me out. She's even called me at home to chew me out about something she thinks I've done wrong at work. I can't take it anymore. I know I'm going to crack soon. I'm afraid to say anything to her since I don't have tenure yet at the school."

Lars said that he'd never been in a situation like this before. He had gotten along exceptionally well with the previous principal, as had the rest of the teachers and most of the students. His conflict with the present principal was inexplicable. "The woman just seems to have taken an instant dislike to me from the moment we met," Lars said, appealing to the angels for guidance.

I repeated the name Anita over and over to contact the principal's angels. I saw a picture of an intense woman arguing with Lars. Beyond Anita was a figure I instantly knew was her departed father, who was acting as one of her guardian angels. I also saw an elderly woman, Anita's maternal grandmother, who told me she was serving as additional support during her granddaughter's trying first months as principal.

Both angels spoke to Lars: *"Anita is enduring a bitter divorce involving a child custody dispute. Her heart is broken because her husband left her for another woman. Your very presence causes her pain because you remind her so much of her husband in appearance and manners. What we have here is a case of pure projection, with Anita unleashing onto you the anguish that she feels toward her husband."*

Lars was clearly surprised and a bit doubtful. This was not what he had expected. He had never heard a whisper about the new principal's private life and didn't know anything about the divorce. Later Lars would confirm everything the angels had described that day.

"This kind of projection is often the cause of so-called natural antipathies that sometimes spring up between two strangers when they meet for the first time. We see it occurring among humans quite frequently," the angels continued. *"And the answer as to why this occurs is clear: You attract to you the people who will help you forgive. Anita has been attracted into your particular orbit because through you she can learn to forgive her husband and the situation. You must look upon this not as a trial, but with patience, as an opportunity to extend a great healing opportunity. When you think of Anita, when you see Anita, it is vital that you set your intentions to help this woman. Instead of feeling fear or resentment, which exacerbates the illness within the situation, do this: Send her thoughts of love. Literally*

think, I love you, Anita, and I forgive you, *and you will see the situation heal in ways beyond the scope of your imagination."*

"So I should love the hell out of her?" Lars asked wryly. He was still doubtful, but he was willing to try anything that might potentially offer hope. He promised to keep me posted on how things turned out.

"I literally had to force myself to think loving thoughts about Anita in the beginning," he told me two months after our session. "I guess I'm stubborn, because I kept at it even though I couldn't see any results initially. I have to admit that I felt a little better, even though Anita was still treating me badly.

"Then something like a miracle occurred. Anita and I were sitting in her office and we had a long talk. It didn't begin well, but I concentrated on listening and thinking good thoughts. And you know what? Suddenly she really opened up to me and began talking about her divorce, her husband, and her kids. She showed me a picture of her family, and I was shocked at how similar her husband's looks are to my own. After a while, I genuinely started feeling love for this woman—not romantic love, of course, but compassionate love. After school we went out for coffee together. I'm almost starting to think of Anita as a friend."

Lars said he was grateful for the way the angels' prescription had healed the problem with his boss. He was glad he had learned to face such conflicts with love, because he was now determined to apply the same principle to other situations. He is already trying it on some of his most difficult and challenging pupils.

Rx

Keep in mind that one of you has been brought into the other's life as a learning experience. Continue to project loving thoughts onto the other person. Sooner or later, whoever the lesson is for and what the lesson is will manifest.

Prescription for Financial Shortfalls

Many of you scrimp and scrape and save throughout your lives, fearful that you will not have enough money to take care of yourself and your family, or that you will not have enough money during a future crisis. Money ranks close to sex as a top instigator of marital disharmony. Arguments and hurtful words over how to spend money, who earns the money or who earns the most money, and how to save or invest money are common.

Worrying about money can drag you down physically and mentally. More important, it can make you lose sight of what's important—friends, family, leisure time, children, or your own inner fulfillment. Everyone has seen normally cheerful friends turn haggard and depressed by sudden financial woe. It's difficult to enjoy life if you don't know where your next meal is coming from, or the next month's rent, or how you will afford that new set of tires, or how you will pay for little Johnny's braces.

Cheer up. The angels say everyone has a spiritual ATM inside. ATM stands for Automatic Thought Manifester, meaning that your thoughts, in combination with God's, are powerful forces that can literally bring the money you need into your orbit. It's only your belief that you won't have enough, or that you don't deserve to have more, that determines whether you experience financial abundance or poverty.

One of my spiritual-counseling students, Charmaine, was lamenting about her financial situation. She and her husband, Floyd, owned a small juice bar. Although business was steady, the income was small and their cash flow was barely adequate to keep them afloat. "We never seem to have enough money," Charmaine said. "All of our income goes into paying off the licensing fees, our employees, the property taxes, and utility bills."

The couple had dreams of opening up a second juice bar across town in a new mall, where they estimated their business would triple while expenses would go up by only about 50 percent. What they didn't have was the capital to rent a space at the mall. "If we could do that, we would be on our way to easy street," Charmaine remarked.

Charmaine asked her angels what to do. They were prompt with an answer. *"You and Floyd don't completely feel you deserve abundance. As a result, you haven't pursued attracting more customers to the franchise you have now, which would help give you some of the money you need to realize your dreams. Another symptom is the haphazard way you deal with your billing and paperwork. You are overlooking opportunities to save money and to make money."*

I asked Charmaine if there was any truth in all this. She looked at me, amazed. "I think there is. You know, I lie awake at night sometimes, planning how we could get rich. I keep thinking, *This can't happen to you, Charmaine. You are just a little girl from the 'hood.* It doesn't matter that I have a degree. I think people like me don't get rich. It's other people who get rich. I wouldn't be surprised if Floyd feels the same way."

The angels offered their prescription for financial abundance: *"If you and Floyd can come to absolutely believe that you deserve abundance and will experience abundance, you will find that your cash flow will begin to grow. But as long as you accept your current financial want, it is impossible for you to earn more. You must put your foot down with yourselves and life, as it were, and commit to having a different, a better, relationship to money.*

"Commit to knowing that you deserve compensation for your hard work. Commit to knowing that you deserve to be organized in your accounting system. Commit to knowing that you deserve to attract more customers. And it shall be so nearly immediately."

"That all sounds good," Charmaine said, "but just how do I go about feeling more deserving when I'm having trouble doing it right now?"

I passed on two angelic suggestions. *"Remember, you aren't asking for money simply for the sake of having money. You are desiring money to support your basic needs. You desire money to help and support those whom you love. Why wouldn't God want this for you? Don't be afraid to pray for and accept financial help that will enable you to better help your loved ones and others. This would include money for formal or personal education, travel, experiences, sustenance, shelter, business expenses, transportation, and other basic needs.*

"Second, Charmaine, you're not holding a selfish, earthbound focus on money. You are seeing it as simply a tool that will help you to assist your loved ones and others in your world."

Charmaine lowered her eyes in embarrassment. "Might the reason we aren't doing better be because it's wrong for us to want to be well off? Doesn't the Bible say money corrupts and it's easier for the rich man and all that? Isn't it a sin to want money too badly?"

Laughing gently, I said she was probably thinking of Jesus' pronouncement that it is easier for a camel to go through the eye of a needle than it is for a rich man to enter the kingdom of heaven. The angels tell me that Jesus' words and similar biblical passages were meant only to warn against allowing money to become an obsession. His words were to help people see God, not Mammon, as the true source of abundance and wealth.

The angels told Charmaine, *"There is nothing inherently wrong or right with money. It is simply a tool that can be used in service of love and light, or darkness and fear. If you choose the former, you will feel rewarded as if you were millionaire for the rest of your days. Use it in the latter, and you will never feel that you have enough."*

Feeling reassured, Charmaine said she would give the angels' advice a try. I didn't run into her again for nearly a year and a half. We encountered each other at the mall. She was behind the counter of the juice bar she and Floyd now owned. They were opening up a third near a busy office park and across the street from a junior college, Charmaine told me. She said that she and her husband had done as the angels prescribed.

They made a firm commitment not to live hand-to-mouth any longer. Together they decided they could not expect to deserve financial abundance unless they ran an organized and financially sound business. When she hired a professional bookkeeper, Charmaine found several places where they were wasting money and through more efficient management was able to boost their bottom line. She and Floyd also began to advertise their establishment, emphasizing the health benefits of fresh fruit and vegetable juices, and they began to give away discount coupons at the local college. Within six months they were seeing their bank balance grow every month. At the end of a year, between bank loans and their savings, they were able to open up the stand at the mall.

Rx

Believe you deserve and will experience abundance. Be as organized now as you would be if you already had the money.

CHAPTER EIGHT

How to Receive Divine Prescriptions

If you are fascinated by the idea of Divine prescriptions and want to know how you can receive advice directly from God and the angels, take heart. I have some wonderful news for you.

God wants to pass along Divine guidance to you every bit as much as you want to receive it, so He has made it easy. You don't have to come for an angel reading in order to get Divine prescriptions. You can get them directly for yourself via the innate sixth sense God has given everyone for receiving His heavely counsel (see the preface for a more complete discussion of the sixth sense). God has made it so easy, in fact, that it often takes only a single practice session to learn how to how use your sixth sense to begin receiving angelic prescriptions for your personal concerns.

If you are someone who thinks everything in life must somehow be difficult, you may find all this hard to believe. As I've stated in this and my other books, God and the angels always surround you and constantly shower messages, remedies, and guidance on you.

You may be rejecting these angelic messages without realizing so for several reasons: One, you simply aren't listening to them and don't know how to go about tuning in to them. Two, your own emotional pain or turbulence may be drowning out heavenly messages. Three, you may dislike being told what to do and being controlled by God, so you ignore advice even if it is an answer to your prayers.

Through diligent practice in asking questions and staying alert for heaven's replies, however, *anyone* can develop a clearer, stronger rapport with his or her angels. God and His helpers will assist you along the way, and they want you to know that you do have the ability, right now, to accurately receive their messages.

In this chapter, you will learn how to recognize some of the ways your angelic messengers deliver their remedies. You also will learn how to clear away emotional disturbances that can distort or block heavenly guidance. You then will be led through a proven two-step process that enables *anyone* to ask for and receive guidance for life dilemmas, whenever and wherever it is needed.

Emotional Clearing: Freeing the Way

The initial step in receiving angelic counsel is to clear yourself of any turbulent or negative emotions. These kinds of emotions cut off access to the four modes of Divine communication (see chapter 1): Clairaudience (words and sounds), Clairvoyance (images and pictures), Clairsentience (emotions and sensations), and Claircognizance (a sudden knowingness). The heavenly prescriptions being beamed down at you strike all the dark, chaotic energy and bounce back up. They have difficulty penetrating the barrier that negativity erects in front of you.

The angels urge you to take the time to release any unhappiness or discord you may be feeling before seeking Divine prescriptions. (In an emergency, of course, you should immediately ask for whatever advice you need.) You should do this even if you don't feel you are experiencing any negative emotions. People often have these feelings at work deep within them but aren't aware of them unless they pause for introspection or the feelings suddenly surge up from where they are buried.

Unlike psychotherapy, which involves lengthy analysis of the causes of negative feelings, emotional clearing is an angelic meditation I've found empowers individuals to release any anger, unforgiveness, resentment, jealousy, hurt, and harmful emotional baggage in their life quickly and completely on their own. This meditation will free your heart so that the positive energy beaming down from heaven, which emanates from a place of Divine love, can enter with the angelic prescriptions you have been seeking.

Plan to devote at least one half-hour of uninterrupted time alone for emotional clearing. Turn off your phone, fax machine, cell phone, and pager to avoid distractions. Put a Do Not Disturb sign on your door if you're not alone.

Sitting or lying down in a comfortable position, take three very slow, deep, and deliberate breaths. Inhale and exhale as deeply and slowly as possible.

If you have a preference for a devotional figure—Jesus, Quan Yin, Mohammed, Moses, Saint Christopher, Mary the Great Mother, Holy Spirit, Father Wind—mentally call on him or her to surround you. For my own emotional clearing, I usually call on Jesus, the Archangels Raphael and Michael, and the other healing and clearing angels.

Say to them either mentally or aloud: "I now give you permission to enter into my heart. I ask you to please enter into my heart right now and clear me emotionally. I ask you to clear my heart of any anger that I may be hanging on to." Spend a few moments in silence, feeling the angels work within your heart. It will feel similar to waves of energy, and your body may spasm as you let go of old anger. When your mind, body, and heart feel still, you'll know that it's time to move to the next step.

"I ask you to clear my heart of any pain that I may be harboring from this life or past." Again, spend a few moments while the angels clear you. Be sure to breathe during this process, as holding your breath can slow the clearing.

"I ask you to clear my heart of any resentment that I'm holding toward myself, my life, other people, agencies, or the world." Rest for a moment while the angels release you from all forms of resentment.

"I ask that you clear my heart of any feelings that I've been betrayed by myself or others." Breathe deeply to allow the angels full access to your heart and emotions.

"I ask that you clear my heart of any fears I may have about losing control or about having control." Sit for a moment while the angels clear away these fears.

"I ask that you clear my heart of any unforgiveness I may be holding toward myself." Take a few moments to allow the angels to clear you.

"I ask that you clear my heart of any unforgiveness I may be holding toward family members, friends, lovers, employers and co-workers, strangers, agencies, and the world." Repeat this sentence until your body feels calm as you say it. This is a sign that the angels have cleared you of the emotional charge of unforgiveness. Remember that you do not necessarily have to forgive someone's actions, just the person involved. Forgiveness is a healing remedy for you, as well as a way to clear the way for heavenly communication.

Receiving Divine Prescriptions: A Two-Step Technique

When you have completed the emotional clearing meditation, you are ready to consciously access Divine counsel. Although you may feel a bit intimidated at first, just follow these two steps:

1. State the problem (or situation) you need guidance about.

2. Receive a Divine prescription.

Doesn't that sound simple enough? Here's an angelic tip for making the process even easier. My own readings are more detailed, clear, and accurate when I precede the session with a prayer. You may want to preface your requests for a Divine remedy with a prayer, too. My prayer, which I've come to rely on because of its miraculous results, is: "God, Holy Spirit, Jesus, and the angels, I ask Your help in this reading. Please give me detailed information that will help this person and give them many blessings. Thank You so much for Your love and help, God, Holy Spirit, Jesus, and the angels. Amen."

It also can be helpful to meditate for a few moments before an angel reading. Studies show people are more open to inspiration and inner signals when they are in a meditative state. This makes it easier to tune in to your own angels and those of the other person if you are reading for someone. (If you're unfamiliar with meditation, consult the many fine books on the subject, along with any church, temple, or private meditation groups in your neighborhood. My own favorite book on meditation is the Workbook for Students section of *A Course in Miracles*, which gives daily meditations to help you focus your thoughts. Two other excellent books are *The Best Guide to Meditation* by Victor N. Davich or *The Joy of Meditating* by Salle Merrill Redfield.

STATING THE PROBLEM

I emphasize to all my clients the importance of consciously asking God and the angels for a Divine prescription for your problems and difficulties. Every time you ask a question, you automatically trigger a Divine response. It can be a specific question about a specific problem, such as "What can I do about my domineering mother?" or "Should I look for a new job?" Or, it could be a general question, such as "How can I be happier?" or "What should I do with my life?"

Make your request for a Divine prescription in whatever way you feel the most comfortable:

1. *Verbalize* your question by asking it aloud.

2. *Mentally* ask the question in your head. (The angels hear your thoughts as clearly as they do your spoken words. Don't worry; they won't judge your thoughts.)

3. *Write* the question down in a diary or journal, or in a letter that you seal and destroy later, for example.

4. *Visualize* the question by mentally picturing the situation you seek guidance on. (You may see yourself being calm and serene rather than angry with your hyperactive three-year-old, or you may visualize a blank check made out to a local college with a question mark on it if you are considering going back to school for a degree.)

Receiving the Prescription

Because the angels can hear the question being posed in your mind, you may receive your remedy before you finish asking for it. The answers can come to you as a vision, a thought, a physical or emotional feeling, or audible words. To enhance your likelihood of receiving the message the first time, you must settle your mind in a state of *relaxed concentration. Relaxed* because any tension blocks awareness of the answer. *Concentration* because if your mind is wandering, you'll be thinking of something else when the answer appears. You can rapidly achieve both states by taking a couple of deep breaths or pausing for a moment of silent prayer immediately after you request angelic guidance.

Be aware of any impressions that come to you right after you ask the question. These will be in one of the following modes of Divine communication:

1. *Clairaudience.* Words, songs, a musical theme you hear inside or outside your head. Ask your angels, "How do these words or this song relate to the circumstances I just asked about?"

2. *Clairvoyance.* A dreamlike mental movie, a fleeting mental picture, even a symbolic image. Ask your angels, "How do these visions relate to my problem?"

3. *Clairsentience.* Joy, warmth, dread, anticipation, and other emotions. Your stomach tightens or feels fluttery; the air pressure changes; you experience certain smells or other physical sensations. Ask your angels, "How do these feelings relate to my question? Are they a road map of how I would feel in the future if I make certain changes?"

4. *Claircognizance.* You may suddenly know what to do without the solution even passing into your mind as thoughts. It will be a conviction that seems to unfold from the very depths of your soul.

Interpreting and Validating Divine Prescriptions

When you ask for a Divine prescription, the reply typically is clear and straightforward. For instance, in response to a question about how to rekindle the warmth in your relationship, you see an image of the two of you walking on a beach followed by a candlelit dinner at a restaurant. You can be confident that the intent is for you to spend more time doing fun things with your partner. Or, after asking about ways to improve your health, you get a gut feeling to take a different route home. On the way, you discover a new gym being built. You are probably safe in concluding that you are being told to get on an exercise regime immediately.

Occasionally, an answer will be less straightforward and may leave you somewhat confused and uncertain how to interpret it. Say you ask the angels what you should do about your stress level, and you receive a mental image of a children's slide at a park. You wonder, "Does this mean I'm sliding downhill, or that I'm supposed to have childlike fun? Or maybe it's just a coincidence and it means nothing at all."

Again, there is nothing to worry about. Since the angels truly want you to understand the remedy you receive, they will do everything they can to ensure you get it, moving heaven and earth or even hitting you over the head with it, literally, if that's what it takes. If you ever feel stuck, flustered, or confused over how to interpret a Divine prescription, the angels guarantee the following four strategies will help make the meaning crystal clear:

1. *Ask for clarification.* Request that your angels provide additional clarification when you get a message that you don't understand or that doesn't seem to make sense. If you cannot hear an auditory answer, say, "A little louder, please." If you cannot understand their visual message, say to your angels, "Could you please show me something else to help me grasp your meaning?" If you cannot comprehend an idea or revelation that suddenly pops into your mind, ask your angels, "How is this relevant to the question that I asked?" If you don't know how to interpret your feelings, ask, "Could you help me to know what I'm feeling and how these emotions and sensations relate to the answer I'm seeking?"

   Don't be shy or worry that the angels will think you are stupid. The angels are on your side. They will never judge you negatively. Speak up and ask for the clarification you need. They will be happy to fulfill their purpose by supplying it. When I asked my angels many years ago about how I could increase my clairvoyance, I received visual images of food. This made no sense to me at first; I couldn't imagine how the two were related. I asked my angels to explain. In response, I heard a voice tell me that the vibrational energy of food affected my ability both to receive answers and to think clearly. I followed the angels' prescriptions to stop consuming certain foods, particularly meat, fatty substances and sugar- or chocolate-based products, and beverages like coffee, carbonated drinks, and alcohol. My clairvoyance increased dramatically as a result.

Keep asking questions until you feel satisfied that you understand the answer. Pretend that you are interviewing your angels and that you must obtain crystal-clear answers for your audience members. With practice, you and your angels will develop a simpatico style that will result in quicker and clearer heavenly messages.

2. *Request signs to validate your answer.* If you think an angelic communication may be just your imagination, or if you are in doubt about whether you have made a correct interpretation, request your angels to validate it for you. Mentally say, "Please give me a clear sign to show me that I've heard [or interpreted] you correctly."

   In the coming hours, watch for words you see, hear, or think. Notice patterns—for instance repeatedly hearing a song, seeing a bumper sticker, or having a friend unknowingly repeat the very same message word for word as you first received it.

3. *Stay alert to repetition.* One of the key characteristics of true angelic help is that their advice is given repeatedly. I've learned you can ask the angels a question several times, and you'll keep getting the same answer. That's one of the ways you truly know it's the angels speaking, since the imagination tends to give different answers each time.

4. *Pay attention to how you feel about the answer.* Does the answer you received ring true? Often, the guidance

will be similar to what the angels have already given you, which you have ignored. Does it have an "I knew that" sense to it? Does the answer coincide with feelings or thoughts you previously had? Does it make you feel warm and safe? If your answer is yes, you can be fairly certain that your remedy is truly from the Divine spiritual realm.

Acting on the Prescriptions You Receive

Many fledgling angel readers lack confidence in their ability to receive heavenly messages. They are terrified of getting a message wrong or seriously misleading themselves or someone they are reading for. As a result, they don't follow through and act on the counsel they are given. As with the prescriptions medical doctors give you, if you don't follow directions, you don't get the healing you seek. What good is heavenly advice if you don't make use of the guidance God bestows? For that matter, what do you have to lose from acting on it? The alternative is to remain stuck with the same problems you asked for heavenly assistance with in the first place.

That's why trust in the message you receive is essential. It's also important because disbelief can prevent a message from coming through fully or cause you to ignore parts that seem outrageous or meaningless.

Remember, God never makes mistakes, and He is the one delivering the messages. God knows how to send clear, understandable Divine prescriptions. After all, He's been doing it for millions of years! As with everything in life, however, if you don't understand, keep on asking questions until you do. The angels will keep replying until you do. You needn't fear wearing out God's patience—it's infinite, and you could never exhaust it if you lived to the year 3000. Remember, there are no stupid questions.

If you find, however, that a message you have received is so off the wall it makes even your confidence in God's abilities waver, ask the angels to help fortify your faith. Before you go to bed, request the Archangel Raphael (the healing angel) to enter your dreams. Say to him, "I am willing to release any beliefs, thoughts, or emotions that are blocking me from enjoying full faith. Please clear me now of anything that obscures my faith."

Once you've given him permission, Raphael will do the rest of the work for you. When you wake up, you'll feel less afraid, less alone, and less worried than the previous day.

As with any skill, time, practice, and experience will build trust in your ability to receive and understand heavenly messages. Once you feel confident you are receiving Divine prescriptions clearly, you aren't limited to using your sixth sense to seeking guidance solely for yourself. You also can ask a question on behalf of another person and receive an answer for them. (You will find specific guidance in giving readings for others in the following chapter.)

CHAPTER NINE

How to Deliver Divine Prescriptions

If you're like some of my workshop participants, you may be interested, even enthusiastic, over the idea of conducting angel readings. You may want to become a vehicle for delivering Divine prescriptions to others. When you take on this role, you become an earth angel—in effect, a member of God's heavenly messenger service. The messages and remedies the angels pass on through you can help transform, save, and illuminate lives.

I've taught thousands of typical men, women, and young people how to use their sixth sense to receive and deliver angel prescriptions. These successes have convinced me that *anyone* can learn to open the channels of Divine communication and develop this ability. You don't need to be specially gifted or have any formal training to receive remedies from God and the angels. I don't have a unique talent that allows me to talk with the heavenly hosts. The angels surround us, attempting to communicate with us at all times, and you're already receiving their messages unconsciously. You're simply bringing the awareness of this process to the surface.

In this chapter, you'll find everything you need to know to use your own innate sixth sense to successfully receive angel messages for others. Delivering a Divine prescription to another person is an excellent way to strengthen your own ability to receive them for yourself. With the other person's feedback, you can learn to refine your methods of asking questions of heaven, understand the symbols they sometimes use when answering your questions, and gain confidence in your abilities to receive accurate messages.

To become a conscious courier for God's Divine prescriptions, all you need to do is open your ears and eyes, ask to hear what the angels have to say, and see what they have to show you. The only requirement is a *willingness* to be used as a Divine communication instrument.

When you read for someone else, you may wonder whose angels you are talking to. Are they yours or the other person's? The answer is both. Your own angels will guide you as you give readings, but you'll also receive a lot of advice, information, and input from the other person's angels. If the person has asked a specific question about an important area of life—money, love, health—the angels that specialize in these issues will answer.

A final word of encouragement: Don't get discouraged if your first angel reading isn't a huge success. It will take a little practice. Also, the problem might not be you at all. It could be a matter of incompatible chemistry with the other person or their angels. Some people are easier to give angel readings for than others. Their guardian angels are noisy and extroverted and want to tell you everything about your subject, which makes their messages come in loud and clear and in detail. Other people have quiet, reserved angels who will answer your questions but won't volunteer information. You may have to request additional clarification and detail from them several times before you and the person you are reading for fully understand the remedy. A few departed loved ones send out weak signals that are difficult to hear.

I recommend giving at least ten angel readings before making a decision as to how well you are doing and whether to continue giving them. By then you probably will have worked out all the kinks and should be encountering smooth sailing as a reader from then on.

Requesting Divine Prescriptions for Others

The following is a foolproof, step-by-step blueprint for conducting successful angel readings for others. Thousands of my workshop participants have reported that by using it, they were able to receive heavenly remedies for other people in just one or two tries.

1. *Sit face-to-face.* Sit facing the other person, holding his hands. Both of you close your eyes and begin taking slow, deep breaths.

2. *Synchronize your energies.* Together, mentally affirm "One Love, One Love, One Love," slowly and repeatedly. This phrase opens up the heart and mind to Divine communication and synchronizes the two of you to each other's rhythms. The other person can continue mentally affirming this phrase throughout the reading to create a deep connection with the angels.

3. *Psychically scan the other person's angels.* With both eyes still shut, scan the area of the other person's left shoulder. Mentally imagine what it would look like if you could see his guardian angels. Then mentally scan around his head and right shoulder. Give yourself permission to see the angels. If you could see his angels above his right shoulder, what would the angels look like?

4. *Select an angel.* Continue breathing slowly and smoothly. Choose one of the angels that you have seen or felt an essence of, and focus on that one particular angel.

5. *Ask the angel.* With eyes still closed, have the other person ask his question of the angels aloud. Or, if he has come for a general reading, mentally ask the angels something like, "What message would you like me to convey to this person?"

6. *Mentally repeat the question.* Repeat the question to your angels and his angels silently in your mind several times. As you repeat the question, you'll begin to receive impressions in mental, visual, audible, or emotional form.

7. *Relay what you receive.* As soon as you begin receiving impressions, begin repeating them out loud to the other person. By expressing them in words, you begin the flow of additional angelic impressions.

8. *Ask the other person and the angels for clarification.* If you don't understand what a particular message means, ask the individual you are reading for. You might say, "The angels are showing me a little boy with brown hair next to you. Is this your son?" or "Why do the angels keep showing me a red truck? Is this a vehicle you've owned?"

   If the other person can't understand the meaning of the impression you've received, it could relate to a future event or one he has forgotten. Ask the angels mentally or aloud for further clarification. This is usually more beneficial than trying to interpret a confusing message yourself, which wastes time and energy that is better spent on the reading.

   You will soon discover that your role in giving an angel reading is to help validate the other person's internal guidance. He already knows, deep down, what the angels' prescription will be. The angels only want you to confirm that their heavenly guidance has been received accurately.

Delivering Divine Prescriptions

The single most important guideline to keep in mind when relaying remedies from the angels to another person is to deliver the guidance verbatim as it comes to you. Just as a physician does with her prescriptions, the angels give specific details and instructions with theirs. As a member of God's heavenly messenger corps, an important part of your duties is to convey the *details* of the prescription you received, accurately and in full. These details help the person you are reading for establish the authenticity of the guidance you deliver, as well as the specific steps she needs to follow to benefit from it.

There is another reason you need to pass on all the impressions you receive during a reading. Though an image, phrase, or a song might seem insignificant to you, it will likely make perfect sense to the recipient. The angels transmit their prescriptions specifically for their intended recipient.

Resist the temptation to edit or censor messages before delivering them, or a critical part could be lost forever. Let's say a client has just told you that her husband is the one who starts all their fights. However, the picture the angels show you is quite the opposite. If you relay this news, you know the woman may become upset with you. If you withhold it, you might be depriving her of the insight she needs to stop blaming her husband and turn her marital life around. Or say an image shows an individual engaged in office flirting, although you know the person is married. Censoring the image might prevent the person from realizing that his behavior is having an adverse effect on his relationship. The only way to ensure that your personal feelings don't impact your reading is to relay the message exactly as you received it.

According to *A Course in Miracles,* faith is essential when you receive a message that makes no sense to you. In the Manual for Teachers, the *Course* says:

> The teacher of God [meaning someone who desires to help others in a spiritual way] accepts the words which are offered him, and gives as he receives. He does not control the direction of his speaking. He listens and hears and speaks. A major hindrance in this aspect of his learning is the teacher of God's fear about the validity of what he hears. And what he hears may indeed be quite startling. It may also seem to be quite irrelevant to the presented problem as he perceives it, and may, in fact, confront the teacher with a situation that appears to be very embarrassing to him. All these are judgments that have no value. They are his own, coming from a shabby self-perception which he would leave behind. Judge not the words that come to you, but offer them in confidence. They are far wiser than your own. God's teachers have God's Word behind their symbols. And He Himself gives to the words they use the power of His Spirit, raising them from meaningless symbols to the Call of Heaven itself.

At one of my workshops, LeAnn, a participant, was giving an angel reading to a man named Kim, who had asked whether he should return to college. During the reading, LeAnn saw a departed female loved one appear over Kim's left shoulder. The woman kept repeating a solitary word to LeAnn, but it wasn't in English. LeAnn didn't feel qualified to relay this word to Kim because she was worried she'd make a mistake in pronouncing it. Only at my urging did LeAnn finally, stumblingly tell Kim the word.

It turned out LeAnn was talking with Kim's departed maternal grandmother (LeAnn's description of her hair, clothing, and body size was confirmed by Kim). The grandmother had spoken only Cambodian and was saying a word in her native language that meant "college." Kim knew this was his confirmation to return to school, a sign he almost missed due to LeAnn's reluctance to relay a word that made no sense to her.

Another workshop participant, Sally, was giving her very first angel reading for a woman named Bethany. Sally heard Bethany's angels say, *"Tell her that she's going to be OK on her left temple, in her chest, and on her lower left side of her tail bone."* Sally was reluctant to tell a stranger such a personal message, for fear she might be incorrect and suffer ridicule. I urged her to openly share whatever message they'd received.

Sally took a deep breath and forged ahead. She said to Bethany, "The angels say that you're going to be OK here, here, and here," pointing to the areas that she'd received during her reading. Bethany began crying, and Sally feared that she'd offended the woman.

Then Bethany explained to Sally, "I was at the doctor's office yesterday, getting tested for physical pain that I've been having in all three areas you just pointed to. The test results won't be in until Monday, and I've been so worried. Thank you for helping me to have faith that everything is going to be OK."

Sometimes, when I'm giving a reading, I feel it might clarify what the angels have said if I interject my own opinion. I always preface these remarks by clearly stating, "This is me speaking as a psychotherapist; this isn't the angels. What I think they mean is . . ." or "What I would do in this situation is . . ." or "One way to follow their advice about dieting might be . . ." That way, my client knows I'm not delivering a Divine remedy, but my own fallible human opinion, which they can accept or reject as they will.

Whenever you give an angel reading, it's vital that you pray for guidance. You need to be processing your own feelings at the same time. If you have any fears or doubts, bring them to the surface and mentally ask God and the angels to lift these feelings away. Self-honesty is the foundation of being a healed healer, a term that refers to someone who doesn't let her own issues interfere with the message being delivered.

THE MIRRORING METHOD

Many of you may feel that no one really "hears" you. That is, you feel other people really aren't listening to you. Consequently, you feel discounted, ignored, misunderstood, and just plain alone. After all, how often does someone really listen? Aren't conversations often filled with interruptions, one-upmanship, and the other person thinking more about replying than what you are saying?

During angel readings, you have a perfect opportunity to help another person feel that she truly is understood and heard. One of the best ways to do this is with a basic counseling technique called mirroring that draws the other person out. Popularized by the late great psychologist Carl Rogers, mirroring is a communication device that lets the other person know you are listening to her and understanding what she means.

Mirroring involves rewording what the person has said and saying it back to them. For example, the person who has come for a reading says, "I'm really worried about my job because my boss has been so hostile to me lately." You would rephrase her statement and say it back for the express purpose of letting her know that you heard her. You might say, "You are wondering whether your boss is angry with you, and that you might lose your job as a result."

Although this rewording and rephrasing may feel contrived when you first begin using it, you'll be amazed at the results. The other person will excitedly say yes or nod vigorously. She will genuinely feel like a million bucks knowing that another human connected with her feelings. By mirroring, you offer a refreshing oasis of attention to the person in crisis. This method also encourages the person to talk more, which often can help reveal new solutions to her dilemmas.

Delivering Prescriptions to Skeptics

Inevitably you will be asked to read for someone who is a skeptic at heart, someone who doesn't believe in God, the angels, or angelic messages, and whose main interest is in proving to himself that you are a quack. When this happens, you are likely to have some concerns. Let's address these individually.

The first concern is that the person's skepticism will drive the angels away. The truth is that *nothing* can keep the angels away, not skepticism, not negative emotions and actions. Nothing! The angels are always with you, and they are with skeptics, scoffers, and atheists as well. Don't worry that they might somehow desert you in your hour of greatest need.

The second concern is that the skepticism will interfere with the reading, like psychic static. It is indeed difficult to read for a doubting Thomas (or Thomasina), but only because it's normal to feel tense around a person who seems to be testing you. Your tension—not the presence of a scoffer—is the only thing that can interfere with a message from the angels. Simply maintain unwavering faith in the validity of the prescriptions you receive. If you falter and let fear influence your presentation of the message, you may omit a crucial detail that would have made the difference in convincing the other person of the validity of the message.

A good example of this solution happened to me when I was on a promotional tour for one of my books. Because I appear on the radio frequently, I am often called on to deliver angel messages for the audiences of skeptical radio talk show hosts. Typical is the man who interviewed me one night for his Phoenix, Arizona, program. At the start of his show, he confessed to me on the air that he absolutely didn't believe I talked to angels. The only reason he'd booked me, he announced, was because he thought angels were big with his listeners and my appearance would be good for ratings.

I make it a practice never to tell someone about the psychic impressions I receive about his life, unless the person specifically asks me to. I'm not a voyeur, and I also believe in the golden rule. In addition, I'm likely to be as diplomatic as possible when I am asked to give readings publicly or on the air, respectful of the person's dignity and reputation. So when this radio show host asked me to give him a reading, live on the air, the angels began showing me some of the reasons why he came across as an angry skeptic. I was in a dilemma as to how to proceed. Normally, my first instinct in such a case is to put the person off and talk to him in private later. But the host kept insisting. "Tell me something about my life nobody else could know," he pressed.

With thousands listening in, I felt on the spot. "The angels show me that you and your wife just had a baby," I said. "Your wife is going through some strong postpartum blues right now. She's depressed, and this is very upsetting to you."

The host immediately began screaming at his staff. "All right, who told her this? Which of you guys told her that?" He was quite upset that I was privy to such sensitive, personal information. And, since he didn't believe I could talk to angels, he was certain the information had been leaked by a staff member. When his staff repeatedly swore that they'd told me nothing, the man finally conceded that there was no other possible explanation, that I really must be talking to his angels. After that, his attitude underwent a complete reversal.

The third concern is whether you should try to remove the skeptic's doubts in some way. The answer is an emphatic NO! Remember, you are there for a reading, not a debate. Philosophical debates can be a worthwhile way to pass the time, but that's not what an angel reading is about. I'm a person who is won over by experiences more than by arguments, and most scoffers are the same way. I've had more luck changing their attitudes by giving them valid readings than by arguing with them.

In fact, most scoffers are afraid you are going to try to convert them from their skepticism. Attempting to convert them only raises their hackles and makes them defensive. They dig in their heels and cling to their skepticism all the more tightly.

Deep down, we all want to believe that angels surround and protect us. Skeptics are simply afraid of being wrong, tricked, or manipulated. Many feel God has betrayed them at some time in the past by not answering an important prayer for help or healing. Thus they defend themselves against possible future disappointment by becoming cynical about God, the angels, and most spiritual issues. But beneath this armor of skepticism, they cling to a hope that God really exists, that God loves them, that there is life after death, that God sends angels to watch over us. They are afraid you might make them believe and set them up for having their hearts broken again.

When you are faced with reading for skeptical subjects, keep this in mind: Although you are not there to win them over, they are more afraid than you are. Set them at ease right from the first by anticipating this fear and reassuring the skeptic, "I'm not a crusader, and I am not going to try to win you over to my way of thinking."

Although it is satisfying to gain a new supporter and friend, I always remind myself that I'm not giving angel readings in an attempt to gain converts to my way of believing. The point of giving and receiving angel messages is to help convey God's great wisdom. If an angel reading strikes a resonant chord in the person you are reading for, she will instantly gravitate toward believing. Your only role is to be alert to the guidance you receive, and to have faith in delivering it verbatim to the skeptic.

I learned this lesson when I was interviewed on a Midwestern network affiliate news program. The anchor, yet another self-proclaimed, hardheaded skeptic, asked me to give him a reading while the cameras were rolling. Folding his arms, he said, "OK, Dr. Virtue, prove to me that you really can talk to angels."

A part of me gulped with nervousness, and I hoped I didn't visibly flinch at the anchor's blunt challenge. I asked his angels, "What would you like me to know about this person?" Immediately an elderly man appeared behind the anchor's head, and I got the message that this was his grandfather. As I looked at the grandfather, I also realized that my eyes were bombarded by the clutter in the anchor's office, where we were filming. Particularly distracting was a large antique-style globe of the world directly behind the anchor's head. I was looking at his angels against a very busy background of color, shapes, and words. To top it all off, the grandfather, in answer to my question, was himself holding an antique globe of the world. He slowly circled the globe with his index finger to let me know that his grandson had just returned from an around-the-world trip.

For a split second I was worried. Was I really seeing an antique globe, or was it a mirage inspired by seeing the globe behind the anchor's head? Was my mind extrapolating my physical vision into an illusion of a spiritual vision? I knew the grandfather was real, as he was quite detailed and animated. But what about the globe?

With pressure mounting, cameras rolling, and the anchor awaiting my reply, I opted for faith in the validity of my clairvoyance. "Your grandfather is standing right behind you," I said. The anchor's jaw dropped, and he demanded a physical description of the man.

As I gave his grandfather's height, approximate age at death, hair, and mode of dress, the anchor nodded vigorously. "Yes, that's what he looked like. Yes, that's how Grandpa dressed."

I took a deep breath and said, "Your grandfather is showing me that you've just returned from an around-the-world trip."

"Yes. That's true. I just got back last week," the anchor said excitedly. The rest of the reading went swimmingly, with the grandfather providing other details that boosted my credibility in the anchor's eyes. The anchor had been a scoffer, but his grandfather was not.

When receiving and giving messages for a person who has doubts, focus on the validity of the impressions you receive. As long as I concentrated on having a conversation with the grandfather, instead of worrying about convincing the anchor, everything went fine.

Delivering Unpleasant Prescriptions

The medicine physicians prescribe for our ills often has an unpleasant taste, but its results can be miraculous. As adults, we know what we didn't know as children: that it's worth putting up with the unpleasant taste to reap the results of health.

In the same way, when you are giving an angel reading, you may be asked to deliver a prescription you know the other person won't like, at least not initially. For instance, she may ask you about the biopsy she is having on Monday, and you hear the angels say that the condition is serious. Or, he wants to know how to patch up a broken relationship, and the angels convey to you that such a reunion is highly unlikely. Our human belief system calls this type of message bad news, even though in the long run great blessings may result from heeding the remedy.

What should you do when someone consults you about a problem and the angels convey an unpleasant answer? If she asks you, "Is my business going to survive?" or "Is my marriage going to end?" she is hoping for positive reassurance that her worst fears are not going to be realized. Instead, the reply you receive from the angels confirms that no, her business isn't going to survive, and no, her marriage can't be healed. Should you stay mum or deliver the bad news?

Before you do anything else, ask the angels to give you additional guidance about whether to deliver the message and how you could best phrase it so as to cause the other person as little upset as possible. Also, ask additional angels to surround the person, to help place her in the best possible frame of mind to hear the prescription.

If you are still in doubt, my own personal answer is simple. When the angels give me any kind of message for someone else, I trust that the person really needs to hear it. I try to think of myself simply as the Internet connection through which the e-mail passes on its way to its designated mailbox. This principle has guided me in conveying critical prescriptions from the angels to my counseling clients that later turned out to save lives, careers, and romances. I have told lifelong couch potatoes that they had to begin a proper nutritional program immediately or risk serious health consequences. I have had to tell women they were at risk of AIDS because their husbands were having multiple affairs. I have had to tell men they could never find the woman of their dreams if they didn't first work on their anger, quick tempers, and need to be in control (and I have told the same thing to other men about finding the *man* of their dreams).

At one of my workshops, a beginning angel reader, Lilly, a dark-haired, thirtysomething businesswoman, was asked for an angel reading by Dwayne, a businessman many years her senior. Lilly heard Dwayne's angels say that he was about to develop a serious cardiovascular condition if he didn't alter his current lifestyle and reduce the fat in his diet. Lilly felt reluctant to relate this to Dwayne, but she remembered me advising the workshop participants that they should trust that the person needs to hear the message or the angels wouldn't have given them the prescription for delivery. Lilly passed on Dwayne's prescription exactly as she had received it.

As she feared, Dwayne didn't take the news very well. He became annoyed, arguing that he felt fine, that he had had a medical examination only the year before and had been in perfect condition, and that no doctor had ever suggested he might be at risk for a stroke or heart attack. "You must have gotten your signals from the angels crossed somehow," he replied.

I had been watching Lilly during her reading and had seen the angels clustered around her. I knew that she truly received her message from them. Since it was one of her first readings, Lilly had let Dwayne knock down her confidence in her abilities to hear heaven speaking. "Well, I guess I'm not very good at receiving angel messages," she responded. I took her aside afterward and reassured her that this was not true.

A year later Lilly would be proven right. She had indeed heard the angels correctly about Dwayne's condition. It happened at an annual reunion for my workshop participants, at which both Lilly and Dwayne were present. We discussed how the angel readings we had received a year earlier had turned out.

Dwayne spoke up first and said he wanted to apologize to Lilly. Her angel reading had proven to be chillingly accurate. "I suffered a stroke five months ago," Dwayne began, his voice still slurred . "The doctor has me on a completely low fat, nearly vegetarian diet. Plus, I'm exercising regularly now. I sure wish I'd listened to your angel reading, Lilly. Although maybe in the long run, the stroke was the wake-up call I needed to make profound changes in my life. Right now I feel better than I have in a long time, plus I've dropped twenty-five pounds."

A request to make major lifestyle changes, or to prepare for difficult, challenging times ahead, initially may feel unpleasant to the person who receives it. But just like the bitter medicine doctors prescribe, swallowing the pill now can prevent or minimize fatal complications in the future.

Delivering Prescriptions to Friends, Family, and Other Loved Ones

After word gets out that you do angel readings, close friends and family are going to ask you for one. As with a doctor operating on her own child, or a therapist trying to psychoanalyze his own spouse, these situations pose unique pitfalls for both parties. A friend or loved one may dismiss an important Divine prescription because it's coming from a familiar person instead of from a stranger who, being an unknown, seems more mysterious and wise. Or, the friend may react negatively and become angry with you, putting a strain on your relationship. However, the angels have their own prescription for how you should proceed when you are relaying heavenly messages for people with whom you work or live closely.

Let's say your sister asks you for a reading about her marriage. How could you set aside your dislike of her husband so it doesn't tinge your reading? What if your nephew, who owes you money, asked you for a reading about his financial future? Wouldn't your personal interests in recovering your money color the way you interpret his reading? What do you say to your best friend when the angels show you that her husband is cheating on her? How could you tell your brother-in-law tactfully that the angels say he should quit smoking, change his diet, and begin exercising?

This is the reason fledgling psychologists are cautioned by their professors not to accept loved ones and close friends as clients. "No one is objective enough to help someone they're personally involved with," one of my professors warned. "If a family member or friend ever needs counseling, you'd be wise to refer them to someone outside your family or social circle."

In a formal reading, emotional closeness clouds your ability to receive and interpret the angels' remedies clearly. This is different from the *spontaneous* Divine messages everyone receives about close loved ones. Many people report instances where they suddenly *knew* their child or sibling needed their help. In the case of a formal angel reading for someone else, however, I think you would do better with strangers than loved ones.

A close friend once asked me for a reading about her finances. During our session, the angels showed me exactly how much money she had in her checking account. They also showed me that my friend needed to cut up her credit cards to eliminate the temptation to incur additional debt. I passed on the prescription, but afterward our relationship felt strained and we drifted apart. I felt uncomfortable about being privy to my friend's personal bank balance, and she was embarrassed that I knew so much about her personal finances. I have since adopted a policy of not giving readings to family and friends. When a loved one asks for an angel reading or for advice, I immediately pray for guidance for us both. Then I refer them to an objective outsider I trust and know well, typically another angel reader, or if the issue is serious enough, a psychotherapist or counselor. I've never had anyone object. After all, I explain, it is love that underlies my reasoning.

If they are seeking a remedy for a personal difficulty, I pray for God to send extra angels to intervene and heal the situation. You can do the same thing. Such prayers are the greatest contribution you can make, and they will help your loved ones in immeasurable ways.

Delivering Prescriptions on Sensitive Subjects

The angels answer any question asked, and in explicit detail, when necessary. When conducting a reading for another, you may find yourself the recipient of much extremely personal information about finances, sex life, or other sensitive subjects. You may feel embarrassed to say out loud what the angels have prescribed, or find yourself wondering how you can tactfully deliver it in such a manner that avoids hurting, dismaying or embarrassing the person you are reading for.

If a reading makes you the recipient of information that feels too hot to handle and you aren't sure how to proceed, the angels share two rules for delivering their prescriptions without scorching your fingers.

1. *Preserve confidentiality.* Giving an angel reading is a privilege conferred on you from above, and you should maintain the same kind of confidentiality about what

you learn during these sessions as you would if you were a minister or therapist. A wrong slip of the tongue could destroy the life of someone who put his trust in you, and with whose prescription the angels have trusted you. I make it a rule never to discuss details about my clients' readings with anyone, except with the clients' permission, and I urge you not to as well. (Even when I do discuss them, as in this book, I alter many of the details to protect my clients' privacy.)

2. *Be tactful.* The angels may not be diplomatic, but as a reader and a communication channel for heaven, you must be. Although you should relay the messages you receive verbatim, that doesn't mean you have to share everything that is potentially embarrassing or hurtful to you or the other person. If you are given information that makes you feel awkward, pray for guidance about whether and how to convey it. The angels will walk you through every aspect of communicating sensitive material, if you only request their help.

   I once gave an angel reading to a couple who had lost their daughter in an auto accident. The daughter showed me that her parents, in their grief, were arguing constantly. She showed me that her mother was seriously considering leaving her father but hadn't spoken of it openly. I didn't bring this fact to the surface because the daughter told me that as things stood, this information would create needless pain for both her parents and likely precipitate the divorce. She said that given time, they would work out their differences and remain together.

   I asked my own angels for guidance in how to proceed. They helped me carefully allude to the fact that the wife was considering divorce, but I did so in a way that only she would understand. The angels suggested I focus on the message their daughter had for them from heaven:

"I'm happy and adjusting very well. Please don't blame yourselves or one another for what happened. Grandma is here with me, and I visit you all the time. In fact, Robby [their dog] barks when he sees me. I know this is so hard for all of you, and I'm so sorry about the pain that the accident has caused. But I can see into the future, and I know that everything is going to heal for our family."

Delivering Prescriptions to Someone in Crisis

A troubled person often has difficulty hearing the voices of his own angels. The intensity of his emotional distress blocks his Divine communication channels. This is one reason why people in crisis hear their angels' voice as a shout outside their head. The angels have to turn up the volume to be heard through the mental and emotional noise inside.

During a crisis, many people turn to God and the angels for help. As soldiers say, there are no atheists in foxholes. If others know you can provide Divine prescriptions, you will be faced with doing readings for people who are in crisis, pain, depression, and extreme emotional turmoil. On occasion they may even be desperate, suicidal, or out of control. When you are asked to perform a reading for someone who appears to be experiencing a profound personal crisis, you can be certain you are responding in a way that is healing for both of you if you keep the following four guidelines in mind. They will keep you from making a serious mistake.

1. *Don't worry about your focus and concentration.* During a reading with a person in a serious emotional crisis, you may find your conscious awareness split. You may feel you are in two places at once, or the room you are in

might appear to alter. This is because one part of your mind is attending to the troubled person, while the other is simultaneously having a mental two-way conversation with her angels. Don't let this worry you; it's no different than having a conversation with a friend while simultaneously watching your favorite television show. If you experience any difficulty, ask heaven to send co-counselors to help you.

2. *Don't focus on the person's problems; focus on the person's strengths.* Do your best to see the other person as their true self: someone who is a perfect and holy child of God. Do not succumb to human illusions that tell you this person is needy, broken, or impaired. If you see weakness, you will augment weakness. If you see strength in the other person, you will engender further strength.

3. *Don't play doctor.* You can do a great deal of good in the world by being a conduit for Divine remedies. However, you may at times need to defer to other earth angels, like therapists, who are specially trained in crisis intervention. Unless you have mental health training, don't try to be the other person's psychologist. Don't try to analyze his situation unless God and the angels give you clear messages of their own on the subject.

   If a person is exhibiting any signs or symptoms of severe physical or emotional trauma, refer him to a licensed health professional. If he talks about taking his life or harming another, call for emergency help immediately. This way you will never get in over your head in crisis counseling.

4. *Don't talk about yourself.* Some beginning angel readers, in a well-intentioned attempt to say "You're not alone in your problems," begin describing their past

troubles and how they overcame them. Rarely is this sort of homespun counseling technique helpful. Most people in crisis find it distracting. How would you feel if you went to a physician for severe body pain, and she said, "You think you're in pain? Let me tell you about the problem I had last week."

The angel reading session is not about you, your past difficulties, or how you've surmounted adversity. It's about helping the other person. The best way for you to do that is to pray for clear Divine prescriptions and guidance in conveying them to the other person.

Dealing with Those Who Become Dependent on Angelic Prescriptions

One of the greatest traps facing those who conduct angel readings is becoming overentangled with people of low self-esteem, who quickly become dependent on you. Instead of an occasional reading, they seek you out for advice on an almost daily basis. Unless you are careful, one or two chronically problem-ridden people can end up monopolizing all your free time to the exclusion of the rest of your life.

You might say, "That's what I'm here for, isn't it? To help people? I've got to help Linda overcome her problems before I can begin helping the rest of the world." Trouble is, Linda has no immediate intention of overcoming her chronically dramatic life. She's too hooked on the adrenaline rushes associated with a roller-coaster lifestyle. All she is interested in is finding people who will sit patiently, listen to her, and make her the center of their attention for hours, and then tell her what to do so she doesn't have to take responsibility for her own life. You are the newest in a long line of recruits.

In addition, this person's constant litany of "You're the only one who can help me" makes you vulnerable to a major ego trap. You can begin to think you are gifted or special just because you can deliver angelic messages for other people. The moment you begin to see yourself as different, you lose awareness of your Divine oneness with God and all of life. Thoughts of separation block your ability to clearly hear Divine messages because the ego has no access to heaven's messages, whereas the true self is completely connected to the Divine.

When a person confronts you with the contention that "only you can help me," remind him and yourself that he possesses access to the same source of information that you do, and offer to teach him how to receive angel readings for himself.

People who monopolize your time by asking for readings can lead you into still another trap. You begin unconsciously using the time you spend counseling them as an excuse for not getting on with your own life and goals. If you suspect this to be the case, ask your angels to release you from any fears you may have about moving forward toward your own goals, such as the fear of success, failure, rejection, or ridicule. Then, start cutting back on the time you invest in rescuing others. Send extra angels their way, instead, or offer to show them how to do a reading for themselves.

Hint: If you are devoting more than one hour-long session a week to reading for a "drama queen" or "drama king"—people who are constantly embroiled in self-inflicted crises—consider that *you* may be using this relationship as a way of avoiding working on your own life's purpose. This is especially true if the other person rarely acts upon the advice that you give them.

Following are signs that a person may have become dependent on you for angel readings:

- This person asks you for the opinion of the angels two or more times a week.
- The person consults you for an angel reading before making a decision about mundane life events.

- The person asks you for angel readings frequently instead of consulting her own feelings and angels.
- The person ignores the angelic remedies you deliver during readings and wants advice more akin to fortune telling and psychic readings about the future.
- You find yourself avoiding a person's visits or phone calls because he chronically asks you for angel readings.

If you encounter any of these situations, you probably have lost the ability to provide effective readings for that particular person. It's best for both of you to discontinue angel reading sessions with each other. Tell the person, "My angels say it's best that I not give you readings for the time being while I adjust to some changing circumstances I'm undergoing." Again, offer to teach him how to give an angel reading for himself.

AFTERWORD

God and the angels are happy to be involved in our lives and deliver all the Divine prescriptions we need. Yet, they are not here to take responsibility for us, weaken us, or take away our free will. Ultimately, we learn and grow from making our own choices. The heavenly realm merely stands by in the role of adviser, ready to give us advice if we solicit it. Still, it is wiser to follow their healing counsel rather than our egos, compulsions, or lower natures.

Time and again, the angels stress to me that we always have several alternative futures before us, depending on what choices we make in life. They liken it to going to a multiplex movie theater, where we can choose from several films, each with a different scenario. The angels say our expectations and intentions determine which of our life "scenarios" we will follow. If we hold angry, fearful expectations, we experience a violent or attack-theme scenario, creating a tragic drama or a comedy of errors. When we focus our minds on positive, loving thoughts (through processes such as regular meditation, affirmations, and avoiding mind-altering substances), we experience a scenario of harmony, peace, and fulfillment.

A workshop participant once said to me, "Dr. Virtue, I've attended two of your lectures now. I love what you have to say, but I need to tell you that when you talk about living free of fear, that is a frightening thought to me."

The man explained that he believed his fear kept him safe because it was a product of hard-won experiences. He didn't want to be naive or gullible and fall into traps that had hurt him in the past. Instead, he wanted to stay guarded against future pitfalls.

"Hanging on to the past doesn't ensure your future safety," I advised him gently. "In fact, when we feel afraid, we actually attract to us the situations we fear the most." The angels have taught me that when we are attached to past pain, we are like a plow horse dragging a tremendous plow behind us. This huge weight lowers our energy and robs us of peace of mind. Peacefulness is the reason why we are here, our purpose in living. When we are at peace, everything works out: Our relationships flourish, our health remains optimum, we experience joy and prosperity, and we serve as role models of peacefulness for friends, family, and strangers.

Yet, I find many myths and misnomers about peace. Let's talk about what peace of mind *isn't*. Peacefulness isn't the equivalent of being passive or having low energy. It isn't boring to feel peaceful, and it doesn't mean being without goals, direction, or financial success.

Let me next share with you an example I think perfectly illustrates what peace *is* and what it *does* for others. I was walking on the beach soon after the storms of *El Niño* had ravaged Southern California. My walk was not a leisurely stroll by any means. The storms had washed much of the sand off the beach, and the violent waves had deposited layers of small stones where the smooth sand once existed.

I was gingerly walking barefooted across the tiny rocks, experiencing pain with each step. "Ouch! Eeek! Ouch! Eeek!" I mentally moaned each time the ball of my foot connected with a sharp rock. "What's the point of this walk?," I thought. "All I'm doing is watching out for my physical safety and comfort. I'm supposed to let go of thoughts about my body and self and just enjoy the expansiveness of nature."

I was just about to give up my attempt at a tranquil nature walk when I heard a pounding sound above my head. I turned and saw a man and his dog jog by on a trail that I'd never known existed, high against the cliff next to the beach. This man never saw me and has no idea what impact he had on me. But right at that moment, this man became my savior because *he let me know, through his example, that a higher and smoother path existed.*

When I realized that a better way existed, I quickly located the path. Soon I too was enjoying the smooth trail that allowed me to finish my nature walk in complete peace.

The angels ask us all to be like the man who was jogging on the trail. Our purpose and responsibility is to locate a peaceful path and then live in peace. Other people will notice. They'll see our radiant expression, our youthful vigor, and the inner light that is visible to even the most unspiritually minded person. When we focus on living in peace, we do more good for the world than a thousand peace marches, a million lectures, or a zillion self-help books. We become billboards for the light by exhibiting those qualities in ourselves.

In this world, peace can seem like a pie-in-the-sky goal. Yet every day, in every city I visit, I meet extremely happy people who have learned to see the world through the eyes of an angel. They look past the surface of every situation and every person they view. They look past surface personalities, gender, race, and religion. They focus only on the Divine love and light that is visible and palpable to those who hold the intention to see and feel the truth.

The angels' prayer, along with mine, is that we will all discover the beautiful world that parallels our own. Right alongside the strife, chaos, and problems, we swim in an aquarium of angels who want to help us. The healed world is already manifest and waiting to be revealed, if only we ask for its unveiling.

The angels say that the word *angel* begins with *A* which stands for "Ask." It ends with *L,* which stands for "Listen." "If you'll remember to Ask and then Listen," the angels say, "everything in between will begin to gel." Let's all ask together:

Dear God and the angels,

Please help us to keep our thoughts centered on peace and love. Please remind us when our minds wander from the path. Help us to know that we truly create our reality each moment, and guide us in making the best choices in our thoughts and deeds. We ask for and accept additional angels in our lives. Please help us to know and feel Your love, so that we may experience and teach the peace that is Your will for us.

Amen.

APPENDIX A

Who's Who in the Angelic World

People receive Divine prescriptions from God through three types of spiritual beings. I mention all three frequently throughout this book. If you seek heavenly guidance, you are likely to encounter them, too. The three beings are:

- Angels (including specialist angels, guardian angels, and archangels).
- Departed loved ones.
- Ascended masters.

About the Angels

The beings I call angels are entirely angelic, being formed directly in heaven by God, and they have never walked as a human on the earth. However, they can appear as incarnated angels who look like humans. The sight of the angels exceeds the beauty of anything I've ever seen upon earth. They are opalescent and transparent, without flesh or race, possessing wings and a glowing radiance. Very often they look like something out of a Renaissance painting. Angels exude a feeling of great love and deep peace. Each angel has a name, distinct personality, and purpose, just like human beings do. The angels speak to each person continuously, and everyone has the equal potential to receive and understand their words.

There are several different types of angels, among them:

- guardian angels
- archangels
- specialist angels

GUARDIAN ANGELS

Everyone has two or more guardian angels that are assigned to him or her at birth. The duty of these angels is to watch over you personally and always know what is best for you. They know you better than you know yourself, for they have watched you grow and evolve throughout your life. Your guardian angels' mission is to use their special knowledge of you to provide the basic support and guidance you need to lead a healthy, successful life.

When I tell my audiences about guardian angels, someone always asks, "What about evil people? Do they have guardian angels, too?" The question implies that you must somehow earn the right to have guardian angels. This is not true. God assigns guardian angels to all of us at birth, and they never leave our side no matter how many mistakes we make. People who are considered evil simply block out their guardian angels' guidance, but the angels are still there.

When you are faced with serious crises and feel in need of more than a normal measure of heavenly assistance, you also can call specialist angels to your side for additional help (detailed later in this section).

ARCHANGELS

The archangels are the "managers" assigned to oversee the work of the other angels. You can easily recognize them on sight, as they are taller and bigger than other angels and appear more opaque with a bit of coloring. Whereas the typical angel exudes a white glow, the archangels have halos that shine in jeweled colors.

There are many archangels, but the most famous are described below.

Michael. Michael is the protector angel who helps eradicate fear and infuses people with courage. His halo is cobalt blue mixed with royal purple. If you ever feel afraid, mentally say, "Archangel Michael, please guard and comfort me now." In fact, you can ask Michael to be stationed permanently by your side so you will always feel safe under his powerful protection. Because Michael, like all of the angels and ascended masters, has no time or space limitations, he can manifest his presence with everyone who calls to him simultaneously. Call on the archangel Michael whenever fear, sudden life reversals, or negativity threatens your peace of mind. Michael will help bring a peaceful end to quarrels with loved ones, neighbors, agencies, or strangers.

Michael also is given charge over mechanical and electrical devices of all sorts, including computers, cars, radios, and plumbing. Call on him for assistance and guidance anytime any of these devices go on the blink. However, it's important to remember that the angels sometimes orchestrate cern glitches to teach an important lesson or to protect you from harm. For instance, the angels might arrange for your fax to break down, giving you time to notice a serious mistake in the letter you were faxing that could have created an enormous misunderstanding. Pray for help, guidance, and understanding whenever you have trouble with anything mechanical or electrical. Either Michael will fix the problem, or he will guide you to understand why it has broken.

Gabriel. The only female archangel I know of (her face graces the hardcover of my book Divine Guidance), Gabriel's halo is copper colored, like the trumpet she carries. Gabriel and the legions of angels she leads help people whose life purpose involves communication. These people include writers, teachers, speakers, actors, photographers, and others.

Call on Gabriel for assistance with a career or problem that involves putting forth your ideas and impressions to others. Mentally summon her by saying, "Beloved Gabriel, please help my inner truth find perfect creative expression. Thank you." Gabriel will answer with inspiration, motivation, information, and unforeseen opportunities.

I am aware that many books contend that Gabriel is male, and that many others imply that all angels are genderless. I have *seen* and talked with Gabriel many times, however, and she is definitely a *she*. Many early paintings of the Annunciation depict Gabriel as feminine. I believe Gabriel's gender was changed when everything in the Bible was patriarchalized. Even God, referred to as both "mother" and "father" in early versions of the Bible, was turned into a male.

Raphael. The archangel of healers and healing, Raphael surrounds and nurtures people with the emerald green light of his halo. He coaches and motivates would-be healers and whispers instructions into the ears of surgeons, psychologists, and other caregivers. Call on Raphael to aid you when you are in pain of any type—physical, emotional, romantic, intellectual, or spiritual. Raphael can intervene to promote healing in rocky marriages, addiction, grief and loss, family relationships, and stress-ridden lifestyles. All these situations respond positively to Raphael's healing touch. Simply say his name or make a specific request: "Archangel Raphael, please come to my side and help me to feel better about breaking up with Tom. Please envelop me in your healing energy and guide my actions and thoughts so that I am healed."

Raphael is a busy archangel who also is given responsibility as chief protector angel of tourists and travelers. Raphael helps you have safe and comfortable trips, with luggage arriving in tow. As you check in at the airport, ask Raphael to watch over your suitcases and travels. Working with the travel angels, he can quell airplane turbulence, give you directions when you're lost, keep a leaky tire inflated, and prevent your car from running out of gas.

Uriel. The archangel, Uriel, whose halo is pale yellow, is the master of bringing harmony to chaotic situations. He helps to center you in the place of inner serenity that exists within each of us. Uriel also is credited with helping to prevent and minimize damage in natural disasters such as earthquakes, tornadoes, and floods.

Ask Uriel to assist you whenever your life seems so chaotic you feel overwhelmed. Say, "Uriel, please help me to experience harmony and peace in this situation. I ask that you help to undo the effects of any mistakes that have been made."

Uriel will soothe your mind and emotions and bring greater harmony to chaotic situations. For instance, if your finances or relationships feel as though they are falling apart, Uriel can help you to think straight. This will enable you to set about finding a solution to your problems with a calm, clear, collected mind. Ask Uriel to help smooth the path whenever you undergo any turbulent life change.

SPECIALIST ANGELS

Like human beings, most angels specialize in performing specific kinds of jobs so that they can better help people achieve their goals in key areas of life. These angelic specialists include romance angels, job angels, dream angels, money angels, music angels, health angels, home-finder angels, mechanical angels, travel angels, safety angels, friendship angels, angels whose task is to aid you in achieving your dearest goals, and hundreds of others—a group to assist you with every aspect of and endeavor in life.

I often can tell what's going on with a person just by looking at the specialties of the angels around them. A person accompanied by several romance angels usually is actively engaged in the search for a soulmate relationship. Someone surrounded by money angels might be working his way through a financial crisis, or making a million dollars in the stock market!

Among these angelic specialists are the following:

Romance angels. Those who yearn for love and intimacy are attended by romance angels. Are you looking for a soulmate? Ask the romance angels to come to your side. They will steer you to the person best matched to your needs. Want to revive the waning passion in a long-term relationship? Mentally ask the romance angels to work with both you and your partner to help warm up the relationship.

Money angels. The money angels will help find solutions to financial challenges and desires. Are you experiencing a financial crisis? Do you yearn for an increased income and fewer liabilities? Is your business facing a crisislike competition or a sudden slowdown? The money angels will guide you toward saving more money, spending less, learning about marketing, or paying off debt. However, they also will help you manifest and attract a windfall in emergency situations. When a little voice at the back of your mind whispers "Save your money," "Don't spend foolishly," or "Start a new business," this is their way of angelically helping you.

Home-finder angels. These angels will guide you to the home you need at the price you can afford, whether it's an apartment or a mansion. Looking for a new place to live? Jot down a list of the features you desire, and ask the angels to find you a home to match. Be open to their guidance. To bring you and your home together, they may nudge you to go somewhere unexpected, take a shortcut, or call an old friend.

Parking-space angels. When driving, call these angels to guide you to an easy parking space close to your destination. Do you have only a few minutes on your lunch hour to buy that wedding gift for your niece? Call on these angels as soon as you know you will be making the journey to give them advance warning so they will have sufficient time to orchestrate your request. Be careful how you ask for their help: These angels take requests literally. I once asked for a parking space in front of the store I was traveling to. When I arrived, a front-row space was waiting for me. Alas, it was clearly marked 10 Minute Parking Only.

Travel angels. Guiding you safely and speedily through any journey is the job of the travel angels. Traveling during peak vacation season? Must you absolutely arrive on time? Your flight, drive, taxi rides, and other means of transportation will go more smoothly when you ask the travel angels to accompany and watch over you. Call them when your airplane encounters turbulence; they'll support the plane so that the rough air doesn't shake it too much. Call them when your luggage is lost and you need your tuxedo for the award banquet that night. Call on them when your car is stuck in traffic and your daughter is about to have her baby in a hospital across town.

Healing angels. Led by the Archangel Raphael, healing angels appear whenever someone is in pain, emotionally or physically. Are you or a loved one dealing with a physical challenge? Do you feel emotionally hurt, afraid, or confused? Are you suffering from an addiction? Call the healing angels. They will immediately surround you and your loved ones with God's healing love. They also may guide you in taking the steps necessary to help heal yourself further.

Nature angels. These tiny, fairylike angels, who resemble Disney's Tinkerbell, are assigned to help plants grow and thrive. Do your plants wilt and die as soon as you bring them home from the nursery? Do you long to get outdoors more often? Do you want the bees to leave you alone? Is it your desire to glimpse a rare bird in its native habitat? Do you want to spend a peaceful day in the park? Call on the nature angels for help.

Animal angels. Animal angels watch over animals the way nature angels watch over plants. Your pet has its own animal angels, and they interact with you whenever you play with your beloved animal friend. Is your dog misbehaving? Are you grieving over the loss of a beloved pet? Call on the animal angels and ask them to help you with your pet's health or behavior.

Locator angels. These angels work with God's omnipotent Mind and sleuthlike ability to know where everything you can't find is located. Can't find your checkbook or car keys? Upset because your heirloom ring is missing? Wondering where to buy a replacement part for the old car you're restoring? Whenever you can't find a missing or desired object, call on the locator angels. They will guide you to the lost item through audible words that you'll clearly hear, an idea that pops into your mind, a vision, or a gut feeling. Locator angels also will guide you to the store that sells any item you're searching for.

Creative angels. When you need a creative idea or are stumped for a way to solve an urgent problem, the creative angels help inspire you. Do you dream of being a concert pianist or professional writer? Are you longing for a flash of inspiration? Are you trying to find the right software program to lend form to your screenwriting genius? Call on the creativity angels. Robert Louis Stevenson, author of the classics *Treasure Island* and *The Strange Case of Dr. Jekyll and Mr. Hyde,* claimed to get all his ideas from "brownies" (a Scottish fairy-creature that resembles an elf crossed with a pixie), which came to him in his sleep. The famous composer Wolfgang Amadeus Mozart often heard his melodies floating in the air.

Athletic angels. These angels look over you when you are engaged in some sport, or athletic or recreational pastime. Do you want to lose that wicked golf slice? Do you yearn to pitch a perfect no-hitter? Is the Olympic decathlon your goal? Are you dreaming of a pro quarterback career? Or do you simply want to avoid looking like a dork in the company softball game? Call on the athletic angels.

About Departed Loved Ones

During readings, as I describe the heavenly beings I see around clients, my clients are frequently surprised to learn that departed loved ones (DLOs) like Grandpa Amos or Great Aunt Agatha are with them. It's easy to understand why they return to aid us. Just as your interest in your children and grandchildren, cousins and aunts would continue if you departed this life tomorrow, so your parents' and grandparents' interest continues after they depart.

Usually, DLOs are great-grandparents or grandparents who died before you were born and have agreed to serve as your guardian spirits for the family. They also could be a parent, cousin, aunt, significant other, child, or even a close friend who has preceded you into the heavenly realm. Typically, more recently deceased loved ones don't stay with you continuously. It takes a while to adjust to the spirit world, and they have "schooling" to attend and other duties to perform. However, most recently deceased loved ones are within earshot. If you call their name mentally or aloud, they will hear you and immediately come to your side.

DLOs devote their time on earth to gently supporting and guiding family members through life. As you learn and grow through this guidance, they learn and grow as they aid and watch you make decisions and live by the consequences. Sometimes, if a DLO who, say, wanted to be a violinist didn't fulfill her life mission before departing, she may be assigned to a relative with a similar life purpose, such as becoming a musician. By helping the relative overcome whatever fears and obstacles lie between him and that goal, the DLO's own purpose also is fulfilled. I often find that while deceased people watch over all their children, they will devote extra time to any child who is experiencing a major crisis.

When I tell some clients that their deceased loved ones are with them, they worry about how the DLO will judge their current lifestyle. They wail, "Is my grandma watching me *all the time*?" They feel uncomfortable at the thought of having DLOs with them during personal times such as lovemaking, bathing, and the like.

I always reassure them that the DLOs aren't voyeurs! They withdraw discreetly when they think you would consider their presence an intrusion. I also point out that DLOs are on a heavenly plane and see things from a heavenly perspective, and so they understand and sympathize with your physical needs and desires. They become concerned only if you are harming yourself or other loved ones in any way.

Because DLOs were once human beings, they still retain personal traits and limitations from their physical incarnations, and as a result their advice is sometimes warped or not in your best interests. Your departed mother might be too tolerant of your drinking, or your deceased grandfather might push you too hard toward a business career. I recommend taking a DLO'S advice with a grain of salt in the same way you would if the person were still living. If you are in doubt about anything said, ask the angels to send you a sign confirming or denying what your DLO has told you.

Most of the counsel you receive from DLOs will lead you toward a happy, healthy life. However, your deceased loved one may have issues of his or her own. In this case, exercise caution in following any prescription offered without angelic confirmation. Look for the following warning signs:

- Giving you advice that doesn't ring true or makes you uncomfortable.
- Asking you to make an immediate lifestyle change you don't feel ready for.
- Offering you a prescription for getting rich quickly.
- Fostering a "you against the rest of the world" mentality.
- Counseling you to do anything that could hurt you, your family, or your friends.
- Using abusive, foul, or critical language. (Angels and loving people never do this; instead, they treat everyone with respect.)

If you become involved with a DLO who displays any of the above behaviors, firmly ask her or him to stop. Then call on God and the Archangel Michael to heal the situation or escort this being out of your life.

About the Ascended Masters

Ascended masters are those who walked on the earth in human form but who have achieved such an extraordinary level of spiritual growth that after their death, they returned to earth in soul form to continue contributing their wisdom and healing power for the benefit of the humans still struggling on the earthly plane. The ascended masters include such teachers and healers as Jesus, Buddha, Moses, Mother Mary, Krishna, Mohammed, Saint Germaine, Quan Yin, John the Baptist, Lao-tzu, Paramahansa Yogananda, Saint Helena, and most of those considered saints and prophets by the world's various religions.

Like DLOs, the ascended masters become nondenominational once they are inducted into the heavenly ways. They work with people of all faiths, although of course they have a special mission to come to the aid of their followers, or those born to the same religious faith. Rarely do they talk about church, mosque, or temple, and do so only to encourage a person to go where he or she will find loving energy and fellowship, not because one particular religion is favored over another.

A Word About Fallen Angels

People often fear that instead of a true angel, they might unknowingly come into contact with a fallen angel. They fear being tricked into following dangerous, destructive guidance rather than the healing prescriptions written by God's Divine hand. They ask me, "How can you be sure that you're really talking to God's angels and not a fallen angel?"

I consider the term *fallen angel* an oxymoron. The beings that cleave to the darkness, whom people mistakenly call fallen angels, were never angels at all. They are actually negative thought-forms that have the appearance of medieval gargoyles. These two-foot-tall creatures with batlike wings and squashed facial expressions are created by man's fearful thoughts, not by the hand of God. They have a grotesque, distorted form, with large talons that painfully grip people's shoulders (causing a great deal of pain), and sometimes take the form of dark dragons that hover over people's heads and exert a black-cloud effect on their moods and lives.

None of the so-called fallen angels can masquerade successfully for even one minute as a true angel. It's not difficult to tell the difference between a gnat and a beautiful butterfly, and it's not difficult to tell the difference between a gargoyle and a radiant angel. Gargoyles have no light within them with which they can imitate that radiance.

Gargoyles are believed by some to be protectors. Statues of gargoyles have again become quite popular in recent years. As a precaution, I would never allow a gargoyle statue or picture in my home or office. These images may beckon true gargoyles to your environment, and you don't want their company, believe me.

In general, though, gargoyles and dark dragons are attracted primarily to people who are ego-centered, dishonest, or substance abusers—*not* to people who give angel readings. In fact, they steer clear of angels. You will never have to worry about allowing one of these fallen angels to your side if you hold love in your heart, ask God to personally send all your angels, and hold honest intentions toward others. You also can ask for the Archangel Michael to ensure that only beings of the highest integrity work with you. Like a nightclub bouncer, he'll guard you, ensuring that only invited guests are allowed in.

You'll know it's truly an angel of light speaking to you if its conversation is infused with love, warmth, and prescriptions for resolving your problems in win-win ways. The fear-based messages of gargoyles always make you feel cold and prickly, and their advice always implies other people are better or worse than you. True angels know that each one of us is equally special and worthy of love.

We are all surrounded by heavenly helpers of many varieties. It is their pleasure to offer us prescriptions for becoming stronger, happier, and more centered individuals. Free will empowers us to accept or reject heavenly advice. It is my hope that one day we will all learn to recognize and benefit from the angels' Divine prescriptions for a healthier, more successful life.

APPENDIX B

How Foods and Beverages Can Increase Your Awareness of Divine Prescriptions

Just as our spiritual growth affects our relationships with people, so does it affect our diet. The spiritual path creates a more positive outlook on ourselves and life. This uplifted attitude makes us feel lighter and freer emotionally and physically. Yet, no matter how much we work on ourselves spiritually, our diet plays a significant role in how we feel. A heavy, chemical-laden diet can make the lightest spirit feel heavy, whereas certain other types of foods can rapidly boost a person's spirit, mind, and heart. Many spiritually minded people receive intuitive messages to delete certain foods or beverages from their diet. Other people on the spiritual path lose their tolerance for low-frequency substances such as coffee or sugar. They develop sudden adverse reactions to ingesting these substances.

The angels explain that each food and beverage has a "frequency" according to how much "life force" is in it. Life force comes from the sunshine and air that the plant has grown from. A food's life force also varies according to how it is processed before being eaten. High life-force foods compliment and uplift a person's spiritual growth. These foods help us to feel lighter, more energetic, and more aware of our Divine guidance.

The highest life-force foods are those grown above ground in areas with lots of sunlight, such as the tropics. Fresh pineapple, guava, mango, and papaya contain a lot of life force. If you eat these foods frequently, you'll find that your sensitivity to spiritual intuitive abilities will increase.

Foods grown in lower sunlight conditions have slightly lower amounts of life force, as do vegetables grown underground. Organic foods have higher life force frequencies than non-organic foods as pesticides carry the energy of killing, which lowers the vibration of foods. Cooking, canning, freezing, and other processing methods also lower or eliminate the life force in foods. Life cannot survive in a freezer, and neither can the life force in food. The angels guide us to eat foods that are as close to their natural state as possible, such as fresh or lightly steamed organic vegetables.

Bread products made from sprouted grains (available in most grocery and health-food stores) have a higher life force than those made from ground flour. Grinding kills the life force of grains, as does bleaching the flour.

Sugar, caffeine, and chocolate have no life force and actually block your abilities to clearly receive Divine guidance. Meat, fowl, and other animal products (including dairy) also have no life force, as they are dead or inert. If the animal was cruelly treated during its life or its slaughter, the energy of the animal's pain is carried in its flesh and its by-products (such as dairy products). The energy of pain lowers our body's frequency. For this reason, if you choose to eat meat, fowl, or dairy products, say grace or blessings to transmute the energy of pain. Or choose only free range fowl and eggs or kosher meat products to ensure that the animals were humanely treated and slaughtered with the least amount of pain possible.

The angels say that fish is a higher frequency source of protein than fowl or meat. The water in which fish swim creates electrochemical reactions that transmute any energy of pain the fish feels upon its death. Those on the spiritual path who are concerned about the energetic repercussions of diet may choose to become semivegetarians. Their meals may consist of fresh or lightly cooked vegetables, fruits, whole grains, and fish.

Life Force in Beverages

The angels say that we should drink water in "as natural a state as possible." They wish we could all drink water freshly drawn from a river or a well. In the absence of this option, bottled water labeled "spring water" or "artesian water" has a much higher life force than processed "drinking water" or "reverse osmosis water." The angels also ask us to avoid artificially carbonated beverages.

Juice has a high life force *provided* it is consumed within twenty minutes of being squeezed from fresh fruits or vegetables. After twenty minutes, the spirit of the fruit or vegetable leaves. Organic fruits and vegetables create a higher life-force juice than nonorganic ones, and frozen or concentrated juice has no life force.

Alcohol, coffee, and beverages that are sugared, chocolate-based, or carbonated have no life force at all. They also rob the body of life force that has been consumed via other foods.

Let Heaven Help You with Cravings

If you crave high-fat, processed, or low life-force foods and beverages, mentally ask Archangel Raphael and the healing angels to help you. Before you go to bed tonight, ask Raphael to enter your dreams and release you from unhealthy cravings. Each time you feel controlled by a food or drink craving, mentally ask for heaven to help you.

Through my use of this method, God and the angels have healed all of my cravings for junk food. I don't feel deprived by my diet at all, thanks to heaven's help. Instead, I joyfully choose to eat healthful, light foods. As a result, my body is well-tuned to receive Divine prescriptions, and many of my students report similar successes.

APPENDIX C

Two Angelic Oracles for Tuning In to Divine Prescriptions

If you are having difficulty receiving prescriptions or receiving them clearly, you might find it easier to tune in to them through angel cards or through dreams. Both are age-old oracles famed for getting the angels' Divine prescriptions flowing toward you. The cards are especially useful in clarifying a reading you are doing for someone else.

I have taught both of these step-by-step methods successfully to audiences across North America. I recommend you try each one; you may find one works better for you than the other.

Angel Cards

Cards are an ancient channel for connecting with Divine prescriptions. These can be angel, I Ching, Tarot, or other oracle cards. Although I don't use cards for all of my readings (mostly because my clairvoyance gives me enough details to suit me and my clients), I find cards tremendously helpful when I do use them.

Angel cards help me validate the many sensations, messages, gut feelings, and interpretations that I experience during readings. Over the years I have found that when I am too drained to understand what the angels are telling me, or the message is confusing or unclear, I can rely on my angel cards to supply information about my clients. For me, they are a diagnostic tool that I use to obtain confirmatory evidence, much the way a doctor uses ultrasound, a blood-pressure reading, or a heart monitor.

If you believe in angels but the idea of reading cards smacks of occultism and black magic to you, you may find the following story about angel cards reassuring. When I discovered oracle cards, I experimented with several types, including angel cards, Tarot cards, and oracle cards. I found them all tremendously accurate in giving useful information to me, my friends, and my clients. However, I also noticed that the decks with angels on them left me feeling uplifted, while some (not all) other decks left me with mixed and even negative feelings. I soon realized that I personally preferred to work only with angel cards. I gave away all my other decks.

If you don't already have your own deck and you want to make doubly certain the angels guide your reading, I recommend cards that have pictures of angels on them. Today there are many wonderful angel decks to choose from. They are sold on the Internet, at most bookstores, and in spiritually oriented or metaphysical shops. I particularly like the Angel Blessings and Angel Oracle decks. (In addition, I have published my own set of Healing with the Angels oracle cards.)

How can a deck of cards help the angels contact you more easily? Each oracle card has a picture, number, or word printed on one side (in the case of angel cards, usually an image of an angel and a word or two describing the card's meaning). When you draw a card, the angels act through you and the deck, so that the card you draw contains the message they want you to receive.

I've found that angel cards are consistently accurate, provided you follow these steps:

1. *Ask a question.* The more specific you can make the question, the more specific your answer will be. If there is no

specific question or problem, simply ask heaven for a general reading and give them carte blanche to send whatever messages they consider of greatest importance. Mentally repeat the question to yourself two or three times before you shuffle the cards.

2. *Connect with your angels while you shuffle the cards.* Hold the mental intention of asking heaven to guide your reading. I especially recommend asking for the Holy Spirit (or your own religion's nearest equivalent) to guide you. In addition to the angels, I find that the Holy Spirit's assistance is awesomely powerful. You can make this request in the form of a prayer, or during meditation, or simply say it out loud (or silently within your own mind) as you shuffle the cards. It doesn't have to be stated in a formal manner. Continue shuffling until a feeling tells you to stop.

3. *Follow your guidance as to how many cards to lay out.* The angels have taught me to follow their inner guidance about how many cards I should use in each reading. Traditional methods of reading cards dictate putting down a set number of cards. To make their message as clear as possible, your angels may want you to lay out more or fewer cards than the instruction books recommend. (Most readings will consist of between one and twelve cards.) Ask your angels to give you loud and clear input in this respect. You will feel, hear, see, or know this information.

4. *Lay out the cards.* Place the number of cards that you are guided to lay out in a straight line, side by side, in front of you.

5. *Interpreting the meaning of each card.* Refer to the faces of the cards, and the book that came with it, to interpret the meaning of the individual cards that

have ended up before you. Don't discount your own intuitions and interpretations, however. These are often more accurate than a one-size-fits-all definition found in a booklet.

6. *Interpret the position of the card.* The card at the far left refers to the immediate past of the person being read for (whether it is you or another person). The second card (to the right of the first card) depicts the present. The third card describes the immediate future. The fourth card shows the person's life three months from today. The fifth card discusses life six months from today, and so on, in three-month increments. Correlate the meaning of each card with its location: A sorrow card second from the left would mean sorrow in the present. A success card in the fourth position would mean prosperity is just around the corner if you were doing a reading that involved business or finance.

7. *Interpret the patterns.* As you proceed through the reading, you will begin to notice common threads or patterns. Ask your angels for help in seeing these common denominators and in understanding how they relate to the original question.

Here's another tip from the angels: Notice which cards are right side up (in relation to you, the reader) and which are upside down. The cards that are right side up indicate areas where there are few obstacles in the life of the person being read for, while those that are upside down indicate areas where the person and her energies are blocked. An upside-down forgiveness card suggests the person is holding on to resentment or anger toward someone. Part of the meaning of this card would be that for the person to unblock herself, she would need to release these negative feelings and learn to forgive.

Dreams

Your angels find it especially easy to work with you while you're sleeping. This is because your heart and mind are completely open to receiving heavenly messages. When you are awake, your conscious mind can be so crowded with thoughts and doubts that it blocks out the angelic voices. Here is a simple prescription for receiving Divine instruction through your dreams:

1. *Invite the angels to speak through your dreams.* Request your angels to enter your dreams with the information you need to answer your question. Ask them to help you to remember the dream and their answer in the morning.

2. *Ask your question.* Write your question on a piece of paper. Place the paper under your pillow. After you get into bed, mentally repeat the question several times before you go to sleep. This will program the question into your unconscious, and you will carry it with you into your sleep.

3. *Record your dream when you awake.* Immediately upon awakening in the morning, write down whatever you remember from your dreams. Even if you don't recall much at first, start with whatever you do remember—an image, something you were doing, the way you felt, a color, a sound, a person. Once you write down one small memory, it will trigger another memory, and so on until you find yourself remembering a much bigger chunk of the dream than you initially thought you could recall.

4. *Ask for help in your dream interpretation.* Ask your angels to assist you in understanding how your dream is related to the question you asked. Dreams are symbolic by nature, and their meanings are unique to each individual dreamer. Aside from a few universal symbols, the images that appear in your dreams are custom tailored by your angels just for you. You should not have too much difficulty interpreting them. The angels will be happy to help you with anything you can't understand.

About the Author

Doreen Virtue (yes, that *is* her real name) holds B.A., M.A., and Ph.D. degrees in Counseling Psychology. The daughter of a Christian spiritual healer, Doreen is a fourth-generation metaphysician who grew up with miracles and angels. She blends psychology, spiritual communication, and the principles of *A Course in Miracles* in her private practice, where she conducts angel therapy and spiritual healing. Doreen gives Divine Guidance workshops and lectures across the country. She is the author of *Divine Guidance*, *Angel Therapy,* and *The Lightworker's Way*.

For information about Doreen Virtue's "Divine Guidance" weekend courses, to correspond with Doreen, or to receive her complete lecture schedule, please write to Renaissance Books at 5858 Wilshire Blvd., Suite 200, Los Angeles, CA 90036 or visit her Web site at www.angeltherapy.com.

Also by Doreen Virtue

Books

Divine Guidance

Angel Therapy: Healing Messages for Every Area of Your Life

The Lightworker's Way: Awakening Your Spiritual Power to Know and Heal

"I'd Change My Life If I Had More Time": A Practical Guide to Making Dreams Come True

The Yo-Yo Diet Syndrome: How to Heal and Stabilize Your Appetite and Weight

Constant Craving: What Your Food Cravings Mean and How to Overcome Them

Losing Your Pounds of Pain: Breaking the Link Between Abuse, Stress, and Overeating

Audiotapes

Chakra Clearing: A Morning and Evening Meditation to Awaken Your Spiritual Power

Losing Your Pounds of Pain (abridged)